D1881201

BUDDHA

BUDDHA:

HIS LIFE, HIS TEACHINGS, HIS ORDER

[TOGETHER WITH THE HISTORY OF THE BUDDHISM]

MANMATHA NATH SHASTRI, M. A., M. R. A. S.

GYAN

Published by

GYAN

Gyan Publishing House
5, Ansari Road
Daryaganj, New Delhi-110002
Phone: 011-47034999, 9811692060
E-mail: books@gyanbooks.com

Distribution Network
gyanbooks.com
India, USA, Canada, UK, Australia, France

© Publisher

All rights reserved. No part of this work may be reproduced, stored, adapted, or transmitted in any form or by any means, electronic, mechanical, photocopying, micro-filming, recording or otherwise, or translated in any language, without the prior written permission of the copyright owner and the publisher.

ISBN: 978-81-212-8688-6 (PB)
First Published, 1901

2nd Impression 2023

Printed at: Gyan Press, Delhi.

The book is sold subject to the condition that it shall not, by way of trade or otherwise, be lent, resold, hired out, or otherwise circulated without the prior publisher's written consent.

BUDDHA
Author: Manmatha Nath Shastri

BUDDHA:

HIS LIFE, HIS TEACHINGS, HIS ORDER

[TOGETHER WITH THE HISTORY OF THE BUDDHISM.]

BUDDHA:

HIS LIFE, HIS TEACHINGS, HIS ORDER

[TOGETHER WITH THE HISTORY OF THE BUDDHISM.]

BY

MANMATHA NATH SHASTRI, M.A., M.R.A.S.

PUBLISHED BY

THE SOCIETY FOR THE RESUSCITATION OF
INDIAN LITERATURE,

CALCUTTA:

1901.

WITH

HIS HIGHNESS' KIND PERMISSION

THIS WORK

IS MOST RESPECTFULLY DEDICATED

TO

H. H. FARZAND-I-KHAS-I-DOULAT INGLISHIA
MAHARAJA SAYAJI RAO GAEKWAR SENA KHAS
KHEL SHAMSER BAHADUR G. C. S. I.

AS A TOKEN OF

HIGHEST ESTEEM AND ADMIRATION

FOR

HIS HIGHNESS' MANY VIRTUES, ACCOMPLISHMENTS

AND

SCHOLARLY ATTAINMENTS

BY

THE AUTHOR.

PREFACE.

In this work I have attempted to place before my readers all the researches relating to the life, teachings and Order of the Lord Goutama, in a condensed form so that they may form an idea of what the scholars have said and written on the great life and work of the Buddha. In presenting this sketch of the life and teachings of this Great Teacher I have consulted almost all the works extant either in Sanskrit or Pāli. And in this respect I may assure my readers that the informations they will meet with in this volume are all culled from original sources and supported by the researches of the erudite scholars of both the East and West.

In compiling this handy volume I had three objects in view: Firstly, to present before the English-knowing public a short but continuous history of Buddhism describing the age in which the Lord Buddha was born, his family, his life, his teachings and his Order: Secondly, to place before my readers a complete summary of what the Eastern and Western savants have said and written on Buddha and Buddhism and thus save them the trouble of rambling over numberless volumes written on this subject: thirdly, to prove that Buddha's religion is in no way antagonistic to the pure faith of the Rishis, it being a mighty protest against the prevailing corruptions and superstitions with which the Hinduism of his age was steeped.

How far I have succeeded in my objects is to be judged by the perusal of the following pages. But one thing I may say that like many I have not started with an opinion of my own. I have always attempted to keep *self* in the back ground and pourtray the life and teachings of the Great Tathagata in the light of the contemporaneous accounts that we still find in many eminent Sanskrit works as well as in that of many Pāli works written by his disciples under his immediate inspiration. In interpreting these sacred records I have not distorted their sense to support my own theory pre-conceived and formed before but have simply arranged them to present the Great Teacher and his religion in their true colours before the English-knowing world.

The Buddha's religion still claims a greater number of followers than any—it has given salvation to thousands and inspiration to many faiths of the civilized world—it is the glory of India and the Indians. It is indeed a pity if any misconception is formed against such a grand system of religion and philosophy. If any for that we are to blame and not the Great Teacher who has left for us a path to emancipation—a road open to the king and peasant to the learned and illiterate alike, if only we wish to avail of it.

I cannot conclude my prefatory remarks without offering grateful thanks on behalf of myself and my countrymen to the eminent scholars of the West who have devoted their leisure and talent to the propagation of Buddhism. I am personally more grateful to them for the valuable help that their learned volumes have afforded me in the execution of this work, more specially to Dr. Hoey, the translator of Oldenberg's "Buddha" and Professor Rhys Davids from whose works I have taken the liberty of making quotations with a view to popularize their erudition and scholarship in the East. We owe them a debt of endless gratitude for what they have done for India, her literature and religion.

ELYSIUM BOWER
Barnagore, Calcutta,
June 1901.

M. N. D.

CONTENTS.

INTRODUCTION.

CHAPTER III. Page.

CHAPTER IV.

CHAPTER V.

CHAPTER VI.

CHAPTER VII.

CHAPTER VIII.

CHAPTER IX.

CHAPTER IX.

PART III.

SANGHA.

CHAPTER I.

CHAPTER II.

CHAPTER III.

CHAPTER IV.

CHAPTER V.

CHAPTER VI.

INTRODUCTION.

CHAPTER I.

IS BUDDHA A MYTH?

THAT great French student of Indian antiquity, Emile Senart, asks, "Has Buddha ever lived? There are innumerable legendary narratives which the Buddhist Scriptures relate concerning the Great Founder of their faith, but has that Buddha ever lived whom these narratives seem to present to us, though in a superhuman form and in miraculous surroundings?"* And Emile Senart answers this question with an absolute No. Like many other great oriental scholars of Europe, who seem to take a peculiar pleasure in seeing allegories and myths in everything found in the Scriptures of the Hindus, M. Senart, after laborious study, stupendous researches and ingenious methods, seeks to trace step by step in the history of Buddha's life the history of the Sun-Hero. Dividing the legend into twelve divisions, M. Senart thus sums up the history of the Sun-Buddha.†

1. Resolution to quit heaven :—The Buddha, before his birth, is a hero, the chief of the gods;—to speak correctly, he is not born; he incarnates himself among men for their good and for their salvation.

---

* See Senart's Essai Sur le legende on Buddha, p. 504.

† Ibid, pp. 504—507.

2. *Conception* :—His conception is altogether miraculous. He has no mortal father; his descent from heaven takes place under the symbol of a god of light, veiled in the cloud-womb of his mother. His presence reveals itself there by his first rays which call all the gods to prayer and awaken them to life.

3. *Birth* :—He is born, as the hero of light and fire, from the fire-producing tree by the aid of Maṟva. That virgin mother, representative of the Sovereign-Creative-Power and at the same time the half-obscure Goddess of the Vapours of the morning, dies away from the first hour in the dazzling radiance of her son. In reality, she survives under the name of the Creatress, the nurse of the universe and of its God. Her son, powerful, irresistible from his birth, advances in space, illuminating the world and proclaiming his supremacy, to which all the gods form a retinue and render homage.

4. *Trials* :—Growing up amidst the "young daughters" of the air, among whom his power and splendour are hidden and unknown or only reveal themselves at rare intervals, the day comes when he makes himself known, tries himself in his first battles against his gloomy foes and shines without a rival.

5. *Marriage and pleasures* :—With him the young nymphs have grown up; the companions of his games become now his wives and sweet-hearts. The god delays and forgets himself in his heavenly palaces amidst the delights of his cloudy harem.

6. *Departure* :—But his hour has come. He tears himself violently,—miraculously,—away from his splendid prison; the heavenly charger leaps over the walls of the demon fortresses and traverses the river of the air.

7. *Austerities:* :—From that moment begins the struggle. The hero first appears tired and enfeebled, wandering as he is in the forest of space. Soon does he regain his strength in

the heavenly pastures, where he drinks ambrosia and bathes in the water of immortality.

8. *Defeat of Mara* :—He is ripe for his destined mission, —the conquest of ambrosia and of the wheel, fertilising rain and light. He takes possession of the divine tree. The demon of the storm runs to dispute it with him in the duel of the storm; in his struggles against darkness the benificent hero remains the conqueror. The gloomy army of Mara, broken and rent, is scattered. The Apsaras, the daughters of the Demon, the last light vapours which float in heaven, try in vain to clasp and retain the vanquisher. He disengages himself from their embrace,—repulses them. They writhe, lose their form, and vanish.

9. *Buddhahood* :—He appears then in all his glory and in his sovereign splendour. The god has attained the summit of his course. It is the moment of triumph.

10. *The Wheel* :—Free from every obstacle and from every adversary, he sets in motion across space his disc with a thousand rays having avenged the attempts of his eternal foe.

11. *Nirvana* :—A little later he reaches the end of his career, he is on the point of extinction,—victim in his turn of the demon, the glowing wild boar; but first he sees all his race, his retinue of light disappear in the sanguinary melee of the clouds of evening.

The famous Buddhistic scholar, Rhys Davids, remarks, "At M. Senart's hand the myth has marvellous grace and beauty, but the reader would do wrong to conclude from the above poetical language that M. Senart regards the whole story of Goutama's life as a Sun-myth debased into prose, or the whole of Buddhism,—though its adherents know it not,— as a worship of the sun. He propounds no theory of the rise of Buddhism and only strives to show that much of the old Sun-myth has been incorporated into the legend of the Buddha, and has almost driven out the historical basis in which it rests."* In M. Senart's opinion a real Buddha did exist, but the fancy of his followers has attached to his person the great allegorical ballad of the life of the Sun-God in human guise—the life of the man Buddha is thus completely forgotten.

Is then the life of the great Buddha, who is even now adored by the three fourths of the human race,† really fallen

* See Rhys Davids' Buddhism, p. 193.

† We give below the number of Buddhists now living in various countries, as well as a Comparative Table showing the number of the followers of other religions.

Ceylon	1520,575
Burmah	5447,831
Siam	10,000,000
Anam	12,000,000
China	414,686,994
Japan	32,794,897
Tibet	6,000,000
Mongolia	2,000,000
Manchuria	3,000,000
Nepal	500,000
Kashmir	200,000
Bhutan and Sikim	1,000,000
Koria	8,000,000
Lieu Khen Isles	1,000,000
British Possessions	5,000,000
Russia "	600,000
Dutch "	50,000
Total	500,000,000

Comparative Table.

Parsees	150,000
Jews	1,200,000
Hindus	160,000,000
Muhammidans	155,000,000
Christians	327,000,000
Buddhists	500,000,000

See Rhys Davids' Buddhism, pp. 4—6.

into oblivion without the least chance of its ever coming again before the world? Fortunately for the cause of history and truth, another great scholar, Dr. Oldenberg of Germany, took the trouble of refuting the formidable array of arguments and researches put forward by M. Senart. Dr. Oldenberg has proved beyond all doubt that the life of the great Buddha still exists in the legends and fables now extant amongst the Buddhists, both of the Southern as well as of the Northern Schools;*—specially in those traditions which are now preserved,—and were evidently written only a few years atfer the death of the Great Master,—in the Gatha and Pali languages. We would rather quote our author's own words which he has used to prove the historical basis on which the story of the Buddha stands. He writes:—† "One cannot read the ingenious efforts of M. Senart without admiring the energy with which the French scholar constrains the Veda as well as the Indian Epic,—the literature of the Greeks as well as that of the Northern races,—no small constraint was necessary here—to bear witness to his Solar Buddha. But one is astonished that this so extensive reading has not availed itself, when dealing with the legends of Buddha, of one field, which would have presented not less important sources of information than the Homeric hymns and the Edda, the oldest available literature of Buddhism itself, the oldest declaration of the body of the Buddha's disciples regarding the personality of their Master. Senart bases his criticism almost wholly on

* From the very early days of Buddhism, it is found that it branched off into two distinct branches—now known as the Northern School and the Southern School of Buddhism; the former followed by the northern people, *i.e.*, of Tibet, Tartary, China, Japan, &c., the latter by the Singhalese, Burmese, Siamese, &c. The story of the Buddha's life and his teachings are found in the Pali language amongst the Southern Buddhists and that in the Gatha dialect and Sanskrit language amongst the Northern Buddhists.

† See Oldenberg's Buddha, His Life, His Doctrine, his Order, pp. 74—75.

the legendary biography, *Lalita Vistara*, current amongst the Northern Buddhists in Tibet, China and Nepal. But would it be allowable for any one who undertook to write a criticism on the life of Christ, to set aside the New Testament and follow solely the apocryphal gospels or any legendary works whatsoever of the Middle ages? Or does the law of criticism which requires us to trace back tradition to its oldest form before forming an opinion on it, not deserve to be so closely observed in the case of Buddhism as in that of Christianity?"

"The most ancient traditions of Buddhism are those preserved in Ceylon and studied by the monks of that island up to the present day. While in India itself the Buddhist texts experienced new fortunes from century to century, while the ceremonies of the original Church were vanishing continually more and more behind the poetry and fiction of later generations, the Church of Ceylon remained true to the simple, homely *Theraveda*,—the word of the Ancients.* It is to the Pali traditions we must go in preference to all other sources, if we desire to know whether any information is obtainable regarding the Buddha and his life."

After completely refuting the arguments of M. Sanart, Dr. Oldenberg remarks:—"If we now abstract from the traditions those of the catagories indicated, which are wholly unhistorical, or are at least suspected to be of unhistorical character, we then have left us the very pitch of these stories regarding the Buddha, a thread of facts which we may claim to

* Immediately after the Buddha's death, a Council of the Buddhist Monks, numbering 500, was held near Rajgriha. Kasyapa, the most revered of Goutama's disciples, presided. There did they all recite their great Scriptures, *Thera Veda*, following Upali, when the subject was the Rules of the Order,—following Ananda when the subject was the general rules for the Buddhists. In this Council Buddhistic Philosophy was also propounded by Anurudha. See Venaya Texts, Vol, III, Book XI.

be a perfectly reliable, though it may be a very meagre, historical acquisition."

Further more to refute the arguments of these learned *savants*, who do not unfortunately see any thing historical in the story of Buddha, we have now found some writings written in the very language which is now dead, but which was the vernacular of the people amongst whom Buddha lived and preached. In this language has been left written some works relating to the Great Master's life and teachings. If they were not written when he was actually living, they must have been written immediately after his death; for we know this language, which is called Gatha, became dead and changed into a new language, which is now known by the name of Pali,* soon after the Buddha's death.

Burnouf describes the Gatha language "to be a barbarous Sanskrit, in which the forms of ages, of Sanskrit, Pali and Prakrit, appear to be confounded." He attributes it to the ignorance of the Sanskrit language of the writers of these ballads.†

Dr. Rajendra Lala Mitra remarks:—"The more reasonable conjecture appears to be that the Gatha is the production of bards, who were contemporaries or immediate successors of Sakya and who recounted to the devout congregations of the Prophet of Magadha the sayings and doings of their great Teacher in popular and easy flowing verses, which in

---

* This new dialect which is called *Gatha* is found in the Sanskrit Buddhist Literature of Nepal, the discovery of which is due to Mr. B. H. Hodgson. He collected three sets of the manuscripts of this literature, one of which he presented to the Asiatic Society of Bengal, another to the Royal Asiatic Society of Great Britain, and the third to the Asiatic Society of Paris. The first of these remains intombed, the second has been catalogued, but the third fell into the hands of Burnouf, who drew from it the materials for his invaluable work named Histoire du Buddisme Indien. We shall describe some of these works in the next chapter.

† See Histoire du Buddisme Indien, p. 105.

course of time came to be regarded as the most authentic source of all informations connected with the founder of Buddhism."*

Proiessor Max Muller† and Dr. Weber‡ has adopted this theory of the Gatha dialect. Professor Lassen thinks otherwise.§ He has supported Burnouf's hypothesis. Dr. Muir remarks:—"The peculiarities of the Gatha dialect are so anamolous that it is very difficult to explain them. In any case it is clear that, if not a spoken language, it was at least a written language, in a remote age."‖ Professor Benfey supports Dr. Rajendra Lala.¶ But all the oriental scholars however have agreed in saying that it is an intermediate dialect between the Pali and the pure Sanskrit. Now as the Pali was the vernacular language of India within three hundred years after the death of Buddha, i.e. when great Asoka was holding his sovereign sway all over India,**—it would not be unreasonable to say that the Gatha,

---

* See Indo-Aryan Vol. II. p. 290.

† See MaxMuller's Chips, Vol. II. p. 290.

‡ See Indesche Studien Vol. III. pp. 139—140.

§ See Indischi Alt II. p. 9.

‖ See Muir's Sanskrit Texts II. p. 126.

¶ See Gottengen Geleherte Auziegen for 1861, p. 134.

** We get the vernacular of Asoka's time from his inscriptions found in various places of India. Regarding Asoka's inscriptions, which were written in the vernacular language of his time, Professor H. H. Wilson says:—"The language itself is a kind of Pali, offering for the greater portion of the words forms, analogous to those which are modelled by the rules of the Pali Grammer still in use. There are, however, many differences, some of which arise from a closer adherence to Sanskrit, others from possible local peculiarities, indicating a yet unsettled state of the language." (See Journal of the Royal Asiatic Society XII. pp. 236—238.) Mr. Prinsep remarks,—"The language differs from every written idiom and is, as it were, intermediate between Sanskrit and Pali." We shall quote below a few specimens of these different languages, so that our readers may compare one with the other.

which preceded it, was the dialect of the people at the time of the Great Prophet's advent. From what has been stated above, it must be obvious that the Gathas are the earliest works on the life of the Founder of Buddhism, and they were compiled immediately after his death, if not during his life-time.

Dr. Oldenberg asks :—"Who would admit it possible for the memory of Joseph and Mary, of Peter and John, of Judas and Pilate, of Nazareth and Golgotha to be forgotten or supplanted by inventions in the early Christian Churches of the first Century?"* If so, we ask, who will not admit that what is written about the great Buddha in the Gatha and Pali dialects,—languages one of which he himself spoke and the

---

Sanskrit :—

ब्राह्मणीं क्षत्रियां कन्यां वैश्यां शूद्रां तथैव च ।
यस्या एते गुणाः सन्ति तां मे कन्यां प्रवेदय ॥
न कुलेन न गोत्रेण कुमारो मम विस्मितः ।
गुणे सत्ये च धर्मे च तत्रास्य रमते मनः ॥

Gatha :—

किं सारथे पुरुष दुर्ब्बल अल्पस्थाम उच्छुष्कमांसरुधिरत्वच स्नायुनद्धः
श्वेतशिरो विरलदन्त कृशाङ्गरूप आलम्बदण्ड, व्रजतेऽसुखं स्खलन्तु ॥

Asoka's Inscription :—

देवानाम्प्रिय पियदशि लाजा हेभस् आहा आतिकामताम आन्तालाम
नो हुता पुलुभ सभम् कलम आता काम्मे भा

Pali :—

थिरो मग्गालि पुत्तो सो जिन शासनयो तकनिश्रो
पेख्वान् सञ्जितिन पेच्चया मानो अनागतान ।
शासनास्स, पतित्थानात् पच्चान्तेषु अपेच्छिय नेसेसि
कार्त्तिके मासिते रेथिरे ताह्हिन ताह्हिन ॥

Readers will mark how gradually Sanskrit turns into the vernacular.

* See Oldenberg's Buddha, p. 92.

other of which his countrymen spoke within three hundred years after his death ;—is much historically based ?"

It is natural that every word that fell from the lips of the Great Master was, as it were, devoured by his disciples. They got it by heart and repeated it by day and by night, in their begging excursions, in their public preachings, and in their private discourses. It is natural that the beloved disciples of the great Buddha would put into colloqual verse the chief events of his life and every word of his lips, and sing them from house to house. Such things do even now take place in India,—it must have taken place at the time of the Great Prophet.

We have then the chief events of the great Buddha's life and every word that fell from his lips in these original Gathas and Pali Sutras. We can, therefore, write the story of his life on a sure basis and give his teachings as they were really delivered by him. But what are these original Gathas and Pali Sutras? We shall discuss them in the next Chapter.

—:o:—

CHAPTER II.

AUTHORITIES ON THE LIFE OF BUDDHA.

What are then the authorities on the life of Goutama? We do not possess now the *Theraveda* which was recited by the monks in the First Council immediately after the death of their great Master.* We have now two sets of the

* Rhys Davids in his Buddhism, p 214 says:—"The Southern Buddhists believe that the Theraveda is identical with the Three Pitakas as now exist in Ceylon. This cannot, however, be the case. Some parts of the Pitakas however much of the Theraveda may contain, other parts bear evident marks of later composition.

Buddhist Sacred Books,—one belonging to the Northern School and the other belonging to the Southern School. The Southerners have their *Tri-Pitakas* and the Northerners have their *Maha Vaipulya** and both claim that the *Theraveda* remains in their respective Sacred Books. The Dipavansa, the celebrated Pali work, gives the following divisions of the *Theraveda*.†

1. Sutta (discourses).
2. Geyya (mixed prose and verse).
3. Veyyakarana (exposition).
4. Gatha (verse).
5. Udana (songs of exultation).
6. Itivathaka (words of the Blessed One).
7. Jataka (stories).
8. Abhuta (mysteries).
9. Vedalla (long treatises).

We now give a complete list of the three Pitakas which are considered to be sacred by all the Southern Buddhists of Ceylon, Burma, Siam, Assam etc. Readers will find they are quite different from the above.

Pitakas are three in number and therefore they are called *Tri-Pitakas*,—namely (1) Sutta, (2) Vinaya, and (3) Abhidharma. They are all in Pali.‡

---

* They are also called *Nava Dharma*. See *Aitihasika Rahasya* by Ramdas Sen.

† Dipavansa, Canto IV. Sloka 17. See also Hardy's Manual of Bhuddhism, p. 175. Childer's Dictionary, Alma's Pali Grammar pp. 60-61., Barnouf pp. 51-63.

‡ Professor MaxMuller in his Introduction to the translation of the Dhammapada thus speaks of the *Tri-Pitakas*. "The Pitaka consists of five Nikayas,—the Digha-Nikaya, the Majjhima-Nikaya, the Samyutta Nikaya, the Anguttara Nikaya and the Khuddaka Nikaya. The fifth or the Khuddaka Nikaya comprehends the following works :—(1) Kuddakapatha (2) Dhammapada (3) Udana (4) Itivattaka (5) Sutta Nipata (6) Vimanvattu (7) Petavattu (8) Theragatha, (9) Therigatha. (10) Jataka (11) Niddesa (12) Patisambhida (13) Apadana (14) Buddhavansa (15) Chariya Pitaka."

A. SUTTA :—GENERAL DISCOURSES.

1. Digha Nikāya contains a collection of 34 long treatises, one of which is Mahā Parinibbana Sutta. It gives a detailed description of the events of the last three months before Buddha's death.*

2. Majjhima Nikāya—contains 152 treatises.

3, Samyutta Nikāya—contains some connected Sutras.

4. Amguttara Nikaya—is the largest book in the three Pitakas, dealing on miscellaneous subjects.

5, Khuddaka Nikaya contains—

(*a*) Khuddakapatha, containing short passages,†

(*b*) Dhammapada, containing scripture verses.‡

(*c*) Udana contains songs of Exultation, sung by Buddha.

(*d*) Itivathuka contains one hundred ten sayings of the great Master.

(*e*) Sutta Nipata contains 70 religious poems.§

(*f*) Viman Vattu describes the celestial mansions.

(*g*) Petavattu describes the Spirits.

(*h*) Thera-Gatha contains poems composed by the monks.

(*i*) Theri-Gatha contains poems composed by the Nuns.

(*j*) Jatāka contains 550 stories of Buddha.‖

(*k*) Nidesa is a commentary on Sutta Nipata.

"According to another division, however, the whole Buddhist Canon consists of five Nikayas,—the Digha Nikaya, the Majjhima Nikaya, the Samyutta Nikaya, the Auguttara Nikaya and the fifth Khuddaka Nikaya, which Khuddaka Nikaya is then made to comprehend whole of the Vinaya and Abhidhamma together with the fifteen books beginning with the Khuddaka patha."

* M. Burnouf, M. Gogerly and Made Grimblot have translated in French these Suttas.

† This has been translated into English by Mr. Childers.

‡ This has been translated into English by Professor Max Muller as Vol. XI of the Sacred Books of the East.

§ This has been translated into German by Professor Fousboll.

‖ This has been translated into English by Rhys Davids as "The Buddhist Birth Stories."

(*l*) Patisambhida describes the intuitive sights possessed by the Buddhist monks.

(*m*) Apadana contains stories about the Buddhist monks.

(*n*) Buddha-Vansa contains short Life of the 24 previous Buddhas along with that of the Goutama Buddha.

(o) Cariya Pitaka contains poetical versions of some of the Jataka stories.

B. VINAYA—DISCIPLINE FOR THE ORDER.

1. Sutta Vibhangya contains Patimokha with commentary; it narrates all the hard rules and regulations fixed for the monks of the Buddhist Order.

2. The Khandakas.*

3. The Parivarsapatha.

C. ABHIDHAMMA—PSYCHOLOGY OF BUDDHISM.

1. Dhamma-Sangani describes the conditions in different worlds.

2. Vibhanga contains eighteeen treatises on different subjects.

3. Kathavattu contains arguments on one thousand controverted points.

4. Paggala-Pannati contains explanations of personal qualities.

5. Dhatu-Khatha contains discourses on elements.

6. Jamaka deals on apparent contradictions found in the world.

7. Patthana deals on the course of existence.†

It is needless to say this stupendous mass of literature cannot possibly be the *Theraveda* which was recited in the Buddhist Council just after Buddha's death, though no doubt the subjects, dealt in the *Theraveda* as they existed, now lie

---

* Many of these Pali Texts have now been published by the Pali Text Society.

† See Bhanavara V.

buried in them. Besides these there are two most notable Books in the Pali language,—namely Divavansa and Mahavansa, which may be termed the Histories of Buddhism. From them we know that the Sacred Books of the Buddhists went through many additions and alterations in course of time. Even one hundred years did not pass after the death of the Great Master before his followers fell out amongst themselves. We find that just one hundred years after the great Buddha's death two Councils were successively held by the monks at Vaisali, and the result was that two distinct branches were created of the Buddhists then living,—the branches which later on took the name of the Northern and Southern Buddhists. The author of Dipavansa thus remarks*:—

"The monks of the Great Council* overturned religion.

They broke up the old Scriptures and made a new Recension. A Discourse put in one place they put in another.

They distorted the sense and the doctrine of the five Nikayas. These monks knew not what had been spoken at length,

And what had been spoken concisely,

What is the obvious and what is the higher meaning.

They attached new meanings to new words as if spoken by the Buddha.

They destroyed much of the law by holding to the shadow of the letter.

They partly rejected Sutta and Vinaya and Text,

The Parivara† and the Commentary and the six books of the Abhidamma,

---

* When the Orthodox Party held a Council (who later on became the Southern Buddhists), the others in number larger than they held another Council which became known by the name of the *Maha Sangiti*, (Great Council).

† The last book of the Vinaya text.

The Patisambhida, the Nidesa and the portion of the Jataka.*

So much they put aside and made others in their place."

The Mahavansa says :—

"Heretics assumed the yellow robe in order to share in its advantages; whenever they had opinions of their own, they gave them forth as the doctrines of the Buddha; they acted according to their own will and not according to what was right."

All this evidently shows that the Buddhist Sacred Books passed through many additions and alterations, but at the same time it is certain the followers of the Buddha never lost sight of their Master, His Life, his Preachings and his invaluables Discourses. Whatever changes might have come over the Buddhists, they always fondly cherished their Great Master's words. Thus his two great followers, through long after, have given us two elaborate Histories of Buddhism in the two famous books, Dipvansa and Mahavansa. We get a complete history of the last three months of the Buddha's life in *Mahaparinibbana Sutta.* We get many stories about him in the *Jatakas*; we know much of him from the *Dhammapada.* The opening chapters of the *Mahavagga* in *Vinaya Sutta* give us a connected recital of the events following Goutama's attainment of Nirvana down to the inauguration of his great Order. We also get his complete first sermon in the Dhamma Chakka Pabbitana Sutta.†

* These are the three well-known books of Khuddaka Niyaka, the number fifth of the Sutta Pitaka.

† The Revd. Spence Hardy has written his "Manual of Buddhism" based on various Singhalese works, which took their inspiration from these Pali Buddhistic Records. These original Pali Records, however, contain but incidental references relating to the period before the day on which Goutama attained Nirvana. These fragments of the Buddha's life have also been collected together in Dr. Oldenberg's "Buddha, His Life, His Doctrine, His Order."

Let us now see what we can get of the history of the great Goutama from the Sacred Books of the Northern Buddhists. The Northern Buddhism may be divided into three distinct periods of development. The earliest includes the period during which the teachings of Buddha are brought northwards and there dessiminated. This is called the "Little Vehicle" (*Hinayana*). The seemed period is that during which the expanded form of belief denoted as the "Great Vehicle," (*Mahayana*) was accepted. Thirdly was the infinitely expanded form (Vaipulya) which finally triumphed over the others. These books were all originally written in the Sanskrit and the Gatha languages from which they were translated into Tibetan, Chinese and Japanese.

Amongst the Sacred Books of the Northern Buddhists originally written in the Sanskrit and the Gatha languages, from which in course of time they were translated into Tibetian, Chinese and Japanese, there is a complete Biography of Buddha named the *Lalita Vistara.* This is what Rhys Davids says of *Lalita Vistara.*

"The *Lalita Vistara* is the standard Sanskrit work of the Northern Buddhists which carries the life of Goutama down to the time when he came openly forward as a Teacher. It is partly in prose and partly in verse, the poetical passages being older than the others. M. Foucaux has published a translation into French of a translation of this work into Tibetan. He holds the Tibetan version to have existed in the 6th century A.D. How much older, the present form of the Sanskrit work may be is quite uncertain.* The Sanskrit text and part of a English translation by Rajendra Lala Mittra has been published at Calcutta and Professor Lefmaun of Hedelberg has published a translation into German."†

There is another complete Biography of Goutama Buddha

---

* See Senart, page 497 and Journal Asiatique, 1866, p. 275.

† See Rhys Davids' Buddhism, p. 11.

called *Buddha Charita* written in poetry by Ashwaghosha Bodhisatta who flourished about one thousand years after the great Nirvana. It was originally written in Sanskrit, but was afterwards translated into Tibetian, Chinese and Japanese as well as in Pali, Shinghalese, Burmese &c. The Chinese translation was done by Dharmaraksha in about 400 A. D. It has now been translated into Engiish by Samuel Beal in the Sacred Books of the East.* Mr. Beal says :—"The most reliable of the lives of this Buddha known in China is that translated in the present volume, the *Buddha Charita.* It was no doubt written by the Bodhisatta Ashwaghosha who was the twelfth Buddhist Patriarch and a contemporary of Kaniska. Translators in China attribute both this book and the work which I have called the "Sermons of Ashwaghosha" (Chinese :—Fa-Chwang-yan-king-leen) to him, and there is no reason to question it. Kumaragiva who translated the latter work was too familiar with Indian subjects to be mistaken in this particular, and Dharmaraksha was also a native of India and deeply versed in Buddhist literature. Both these translators lived in about 400 A.D."†

Besides these two complete biographies of Buddha in the Sanskrit language, there are many other works in the Sanskrit—thence translated into Tibetian, Chinese and Japanese, —which are considered as their Scriptures by the Northern

---

* Besides this work which is called in the Chinese "Fo-Sho-Hing-Tsan-king," there are no less than 14 other biographies of Buddha in the Chinese. But they are all either translations or adaptations of the original *Lalita Vistara* or *Buddha Charita.* We give below the Chinese names of these 14 works. (1) Fo-pen-hing-king, (2) Sin-hing-pen-ki-king, (3) Sian-pen-ke-king, (4) Ta-Tsen-sni-ying-pen-ku-king, (5) Kung-pen-ki-king, (6) Phee-yan-king, (7) Kwo-hu-yin-ko-king, (8) Kwo-hu-hien-tsai-yin-ko-king, (9) Fo-pen-hing-king, (10) Fang-kwang-tai-Kwang-yan-king, (11) Sang-kia-lo-cha-sho-tsih-fo-hing-king, (12) Fo-pen-hing-tsih-king, (13) Fo-shwo-chang-hu-mo-ho-ti-king and (14) Shin-lung-yaon-hi-king.

† See Sacred Books of the East, Vol. XIX, pp. XXX—XXXI.

Buddhists. We can find many incidents of great Goutama's life scattered through all these works. We mention below some of their names.

(1) Asta Sahasrika, (2) Ganda Buha, (3) Dashavumishwara, (4) Samadhiraja, (5) Lankavatara, (6) Sadharma Pundarika, (7) Tathagatha-Gujhaka, (8) Suvarna Pravasha, (9) Prajna-paramita, (10) Abhidharma, (11) Sariputra Sutra, (12) Karan-dabuha, (13) Dharmaskandapada, (14) Dharmabodha, (15) Dharma Sangraha, (16) Venoya Sutra, (17) Mahanya Sutra, (18) Mahanya Sutralankara, (19) Jatakamala, (20) Anuman-khanda, (21) Chaitya Mahatma, (22) Buddha-Sikkhasamuchaya, (23) Buddhapala Tantra, (24) Sankirna Tantra, etc.

We need not say,—so far as it is possible,—we have taken the help of all these works to write this biography of Goutama Buddha. We have consulted each and every one of them and accepted those portions which stand on undisputed historical basis.

—:o:—

CHAPTER III.

THE AGE OF BUDDHA.

RHYS DAVIDS writes:—"The first question that arises in giving a sketch of the history of Buddhism is that of the date of Goutama's death,—a question so intricate and uncertain that I have decided not to enter upon it at any length. There is not sufficient space at our disposal to make the question of the Buddhist era clear. I can only refer, therefore, to the full statement of the argument which will be found in my "Ancient coins and measures of Ceylon" and merely state here the final conclusion,—that the Buddha died within a few years of 412 B.C."*

* Rhys Davids' Buddhism p. p. 212-213.

Samuel Johnson remarks :—" The Tibetians have as many as fourteen accounts of the time of Goutama's death, ranging from 2422 B.C. and 546 B.C. The Chinese and Japanese insist on the tenth century and the Singhalese on the sixth century B.C. This last date 543 B.C., substantiated by an agreement among the Southern Buddhists, has been generally accepted by European scholars (Lassen, St. Hillaire, Burnouf Weber and Max Muller) as approximately correct."*

We thus find ourselves in a great difficulty to fix the date of the Buddha's birth and death. We further find there are altogether six different means to come,—at least approximately,—to the date of the great Prophet's death, namely :—

(1) The Pali accounts,—to be found in Ceylon, Burma, Siam, &c.

(2) The Sanskrit accounts,—translations of which to be found in Tibet, China, Japan, &c.

(3) The Pouranick accounts,—as mentioned in the various Hindu Puranas.

(4) The Jain accounts,—as found in their Sacred Books.

(5) The Greek accounts,—as mentioned in their ancient histories.

(6) The Inscriptions,—as found in many parts of India.

The Pali accounts, unanimously fix 544 or 43 B.C., as the year in which the great Buddha entered Nirvana. Ceylon was converted to Buddhism during Asoka's reign, and Asoka was reigning in Magadha in the third century B.C.† The Singhalese must have learnt the date of the

---

* Samuel Johnson's Oriental Religion p. p. 683-684.

† According to the Greek accounts 264 B.C., and those of the Singhalese 330 B. C.

According to *Mahavansa,* Mahendra was ordained a missionary in the 6th year of Asoka's reign and in the 18th year of that king's reign. Just 236 years after the great Master's Nirvana, he went to Ceylon. According to "Mahavansa" Asoka ascended the throne 218 years after the Nirvana.

Buddha from Asoka's missionaries, one of whom was his own son Mahendra. If Mahendra told them that their great Master had acquired Nirvana in 544 B.C., *i.e.*, just 236 years ago,—one can reasonably accept his word,—for the date of such a great man's death,—the day of his entering Nirvana—the *sumnum bonum* of his religion,—could not possibly have been forgotten by his disciples within three hundred years. after his death.*

But why are then so many discrepancies to be found in the Chinese accounts? A little discrepancy in these dates is naturally expected, but the great discrepancies pointed out by the Oriental scholars of Europe are mainly due to their inclination to lower down the age of every thing Indian.

In the *Asoka Avadana* of the Northern Buddhists prediction is attributed to Buddha in which he says, " 100 years after his Nirvana, Asoka will distribute his relics."† Hiwen Thsang, the Chinese pilgrim, mentions the same.‡ But in the *Avadana Sataka*, another Northern Buddhistic work, we find Asoka's date of ascension to the throne is mentioned as 200 years after the Nirvana of Buddha. Sanag-Setsen as quoted in Fo-Kwi-ki, page 249, gives Asoka's ascension as 210 years after the Nirvana.§ According to the Southern Pali accounts it took place 218 years after Buddha's death,—a difference of only 8 years, which should not be much taken account of. As for the *Asoka Avadana's* 100 years,—we have *Kala Asoka* who held the 2nd Buddhist Council exactly one hundred years after Buddha's death.|| Thus we find there is substantially not a very great difference between the two accounts.

---

* See Rhys Davids' Buddhism, p. 227.

† Burnouf's Histoire on Buddhism p. 370.

‡ Julian's Hiwen Thsang. II. p. 170.

§ Csoma De-Koros, Asiatic Researches, XX 297.

|| In the reign of Kala Asoka, the second Council was held. Rhys Davids says :—" Under the leadership of Tasa, son of Kakandaka and of Revata, a second Council, this time of 700, was held during eight

According to the *Puranas,** Sisunga dynasty reigned for 362 years. Bimbasara, the contemporary of Buddha, comes after 6 kings of this line. Calculating 20 years for each reign of these 6 kings, we get 120 years. We shall add to it 5 years of the reign of Ajatasatru when Buddha died. Then the total for this line would be 125 years. Chandragupta ascended the throne about 321 B.C.,—one hundred years after the Susanga dynasty. Thus the date of Buddha's death would be 125+100=225 years before Chandra Gupta. Then we get Buddha's date according to the Puranas 225+321=546 B.C., almost the very dates of the Singhalese or the Chinese Books.

According to the Jains, the chief disciple of their Thirthankara, Mahavira, was called Goutama Swami† or Goutama Indrabhuti,‡ whose identity with Goutama Buddha was suggested by both Dr. Hamilton and Major Delamaine and was accepted by Colebrooke.§

---

months at Vaisali, and the rules of the Order and the Doctrines of the Faith were again settled and vindicated (see "Mahavansa" by Buddha Ghosha).

* Visnu Purana, Book IV, Sec. XXIV, Says :—"Thereupon Sisunga shall be the king. His son shall be Kakavarna, whose son shall be Khatrauj, whose son shall be Bimbasara (contemporary of Buddha), whose son shall be Ajatasatru (in whose reign Buddha died), whose son shall be Udayashwa, whose son shall be Nandivardana and whose son shall be Mahananda; these ten Sisunga kings will reign for 362 years. Mahanada's son on a Sudra woman was Nanda and his sons will reign for 100 years. Then Chandragupta Mourja would ascend the throne with the help of Koutilya. He shall have a son named Vindusara whose son shall be Asokavardhana.

† Ward's Hindus, II. p. 247 and Colebrooke's Essays Vol. II. p. 279.

‡ Stevenson's Kalpa Sutra, p. 92.

§ This is what Colebrooke says in his Essays, Vol. II. p. 276.—" In the Kalpa Sutra and in other books of the Jainas, the 1st of Mahavira's disciples is mentioned under the name of Indrabhuti, but in the inscriptions under that of Goutama Swami. The names of the other ten precisely

If we admit the identity of Goutama Swami, the chief disciple of Mahavira, with Goutama Buddha, the founder of Buddhism, the date of the Nirvana would be about the year 545 B.C. Mahavira died in 527 B.C. according to the testimony of the Jaina records in all parts of India. In about 500 B.C., Goutama was a student,—a seeker after the Nirvana,—because the last 42 or 43 years of his life he past as a preacher of Buddhism. It is therefore very probable that in 500 B.C., or thereabouts he was a disciple of Mahavira, the last Jaina Thirthankara, and 44 years after *i.e.*, in 544 B.C., he died.

From inscriptions General Cunningham calculates the date of the Nirvana 66 years less than 544 B.C. He says :—* "I was fortunate enough to discover at Gya a Sanskrit inscription dated in the year 1873 of the Nirvana of Buddha on Wednesday, the 1st of waning moon of the Kartika. Here the week days being given, we have a crucial test for determining whether the Northern Buddhists reckoned the date of the Nirvana from B.C. 547 in accordance with the Singhalese Calender or whether they had a separate and independent chronology of their own. According to the former reckoning the date of the inscription would be 1873 less 544, *i.e.*, 1269 A.D., in which year the 1st of Kartika fell on Sunday, the 27th October. But by adopting my proposed correction of 66 years, the date of the inscription will fall on the 4th of October 1335 A.D., which day was Wednesday as mentioned in the inscription." But General Cunningham

---

agree; whence it is to be concluded the Goutama, first one of the list, is the same with the Indrabhuti, first of the second list. It is certainly probable, as remarked by Dr. Hamilton and Major Delamaine, that the Goutama of the Jainas and the Goutama of the Buddhas is the same personage." Two out of eleven disciples of Mahavira survived him *viz.* Sudharma and Goutama. Sudharma's spiritual successors are the Jain priests whereas the Goutama's followers are the Buddhists.

* See General Cunningham's Corpas Iucriptionum Indicarum, Vol. I. Introduction, p. V.

See Corpus Inscriptionum Indicarum, Vol. I, p. v. Introduction.

first read in the inscription 1819 instead of 1813 which he now reads. (See Archaeological Survey of India, Vol. I. p. I.)—"So (1819) was read," says he, "by learned men of Bengal." But perhaps it did not strike him that if the figures be 1819, then the date of the Nirvana falls exactly in the 544 B.C. There is exactly 66 years between 1879+1813. The figure seven if obliterated looks very like 1. Therefore we believe the figure in the inscription is 1819 instead of 1813 or 1816. Instead of reducing the date of the Nirvana by 66 years,—making it 478 B.C., in the place of 544 B.C., which we find in the Puranas, in the Jaina sacred books, in the Singhalese and Chinese records, is it not better to consider that in an old inscription a 7 has been so obliterated as it has looked like a 1? If General Cunningham reads 7 instead of 1 in the Gya inscription, then he will find the date of the Nirvana is exactly 544 B.C.

Lastly we come to the Greek accounts, and we find the date of the Nirvana according to them also falls approximately in the year 544 B.C. Alexander came to India in B.C. 325. Alexander II ascended the throne of Eperus in 272 B.C. Many years before he came to the throne, Asoka assumed the sovereignty of Magadha. When he came across Alexander II and Antiochus, it was in the 18th year of his reign.* Therefore it would be about the year 290 B.C., that he came to be the king of Magadha. We know from various sources that just 236 years before his ascension, the great Buddha entered Nirvana. Then according to the Greek accounts the date of Nirvana falls 236+290=526 B.C.,—a difference of only 18 years from those of the Pali accounts.

Whatever accounts regarding Goutama Buddha we take into our consideration they lead us to the sixth century B.C., for his birth and death. It is long way off from our own time; it is more than two thousand five hundred years ago

---

* See Asoka's Edicts in Cunningham's Inscriptions of Asoka.

that the first seed of Buddhism was sown in India, which three hundred years later spread all over this country. Five hundred years later "every nation inhabiting lands stretching from the Pacific Ocean to the Mediteranean sea, from the North sea to the Indian Ocean, have adopted it. Very savage and very civilised people—the wild hordes in the cold tablelands of Nepal, Tartary and Tibbet, the cultured Chinese and Japanese in their varying climes, and the quiet Singhalese and Siamese under the palm groves of the South —have all adopted it,"—a phenomenon never witnessed in the history of the world.*

—:o:—

CHAPTER IV.

INDIA IN THE 6TH CENTURY B.C.

In the sixth century before Christ there must have happened in India something very important,—some very great social, moral, political and religious changes,—that brought about the birth of Buddha, the Enlightened. He himself said:—†

"I am one of a long series of Buddhas. Many were born before and many will be born in future. When the wickedness and violence rule over the earth, Buddha takes his birth to establish the kingdom of righteousness on earth."‡

* See Rhys Davids' Buddhism, p. 227.

† See *Latita Vistara* and *Mahavansa*. So said Srikrishna in Bhagavata Gita, chap. IV. 7-8.

So said Jesus in St. Mathew, chap. XXIV. 7-27.

‡ Rhys Davids in his Buddhism p. 179 says:—The historical Buddha, the Goutama, of this later work, is represented to have taught that he was only one of a long series of Buddhas who appear at intervals

What is it then? We must go more than one thousand years back from the date of the Buddha's birth to see how the Aryans first settled in India, how they lived, how they prayed, and how these Aryans passed through many social and moral, political and religious changes in the course of these fifteen centuries, how their sublime religion rose higher and higher till it developed into the grandest of all religions* that Goutama Buddha preached.

The Aryans† entered the land of the five rivers, tending their sheep and cattle and singing their sweet songs of Nature,‡—a race robust and handsome, strong and healthy, innocent and simple, pure and holy,—the real children of Nature,—the true handicrafts of God. They sang:—§

"Risen in majestic blaze,
Lo! the Universe's eye.
Vast and wonderous best of rays,
Shineth brightly in the sky.

in the world and who all teach the same system. After the death of each Buddha, his religion flourishes for a time and then decays till it is at last completely forgotten, and wickedness and violence roll over the earth. Gradually then the world improves, until at last a new Buddha appears who again preaches the lost Dharma or Truth.

* Rhys Davids in his Buddhism p. 85 says:—" Buddhism was the child,—the product of Hinduism. Goutama's whole training was Brahmanism; he probably deemed himself to be the most correct exponent of the spirit as distinct from the letter of the ancient faith: and it can only be claimed for him that he was the greatest and wisest and best of the Hindus." Dr. Oldenberg in his "Buddha" p. 18 remarks:—" We now proceed to trace step by step the process of that self-destruction of the Vedic religious thought which has produced Buddhism as its positive outcome."

† See Rig Veda. For Rig Veda our readers may consult (1) Prof. Wilson's English translation of the Rig Veda, (2) French version of M. Longlois, (3) Dr. Rosen's Latin version (4) MaxMuller's English translation.

‡ See Muir's Sanskrit Texts II. p. p. 306-332.

§ See Griffith's Specimen of Old Indian Poetry.

Soul of all that moveth not,
Soul of all that moves below,
Lighteth the earth's gloomiest spot,
And all the heavens are aglow?

Hear us, O Ye Gods, this day,
Hear us graciously we pray;
As the sun his state begins,
Free us from all hineous sins!

Mitra, Varuna, Aditi,
Hear, O hear us graciously!
Power of ocean, earth and air,
Listen, listen to our prayer!"

And again.

" We have quaffed the Soma bright,
And are immortal grown;
We have entered into light,
And all the gods have known!
What mortal can harm,
Or foeman vex us more;
Through Thee, beyond alarm,
Immortal God we soar."*

They settled down in the fertile plains of the Punjab,— no longer to struggle for existence as they had to do in the foggy cold of the North, where the sun is rare, cultivation impossible, fire is God. Here over them floated the clear blue sky like a magnificient canopy,—at their feet rolled five beautiful rivers onwards to sea scattering plenty through the land they passed. The sun shone in splendour in day, and the moon shed her silvery beam in night.

While others of their race were struggling in the cold, frost and fogs of the wilds of Europe, they settled down to

---

* Atharva Veda VIII. 48. 3, also Muir's Original Sanskrit Texts Vol. III.p. 162 and Journal, Royal Asiatic Society, New series I. p. 94.

agriculture; the wealth of Nature was at their door; they multiplied in numbers and rose in civilization.*

All this brought a great change over them. Their simple settlements gradually became big villages and they soon grew to be towns and cities. They had tasted the sweets of comfort and plenty,—they had been filled with the unconquerable desire for wealth. They began to extend their holdings and came face to face with the original inhabitants of the country,—a black race who were living in the land from time immemorial. They drove them back and pushed onward. There were bloodsheds and hard-fightings and severe struggles to retain and extend their possessions. The weaker aborigenes were hurled back into the jungles and hills,—those that fell into their hands were made slaves. The victorious Aryans daily rose in wealth and civilization. But the aborigenes,—bitten though they were at every step,—did not surrender their father's and forefather's land without a hard struggle. They harrassed the Aryans at every step, looted their settlements at every opportunity and carried away their women by stealth and stratagem whenever they could do it.†

Thus the Aryans to protect themselves as well as to extend their possessions had to set apart some of their strongest and boldest young men to fight their battles of offence and defence. The duties of these young men became fighting and their sole occupation was war. They tried to better them-

---

* See Pictet's Origines Indo-Europeenes; Spiegel's Avesta II. Einteist CX.—CXV; Weber's Indischa Studien I. p.p. 321—363; Lassen's Indische Alterthumskunde I. p. 527, MaxMuller's Science of Languages p. p. 234—236; Duncker's Gesch. d. Alterthums III. p. 9; Shoebel's Recherches sur la Religion Prem de la race Indo-Europe; Whitney's Study of Language, Sec. V; Muir's Sanskrit Texts II.

† See Muir's Sanskrit Texts Vol. III.p. p. 220—230; also Bunsen's Philosophy of History, Vol. I. p. 843. The Story of Rávana's taking away Sitá in the Ramayana speaks in support of this.

selves in every way in the Science of War. One set being occupied in fighting and another in agriculture, the spiritual affairs of the race were delegated to the few old and learned men amongst the various Aryan clans.*

Thus days went on. The Aryans daily grew powerful, wealthy and mighty. They were resourceful and intelligent and energetic,—they improved themselves in every department—in agriculture, architecture, science, literature and philosophy.† Of their civilisation European scholars and others thus speak :—‡

" The historian of the Maccedonian Emperor relates that after his victory over Porus, Alexander in his harrangue to his troops assured them 'that they were now going to enter those famous countries so abundant in riches that even what they had found and seen in Persia would appear as nothing in comparison to them.' Herodotus, Deodorus and Arrian describe the strength of the Hindu armies, the number of their war-chariots, the excellence of their arms and appointments and the strength of their fortress, showing them to have made great progress in arts and arms."

But wealth brings happiness and comfort as well as misery and dissension at their heels.§ As the Aryans grew wealthy, internal dissensions slowly and silently entered into their happy homes. The fighting-class became predominent and began to lord over the others. They protected the country,—they extended their lands by shedding their precious blood,—why should they not be the rulers ? The others demurred,—but what could they do? They dared not oppose,—nay offend the mighty warriors. Those that tilled the land,—those that brought wealth and happiness in the country, those

---

* See Muir's Sanskrit Texts Vol. I.

† See Crenzer Religious de l' Antiquite, Tom I, p. 133.

‡ See History of Hindu Medicine by Dr. Wise, p. VI—VII.

§ See Johnson's Oriental Religions.

that were the mainstay of the race, became mere servitors of the warrior-class,—they played but the second fiddle in the plutocracy of the Aryan race.*

But those, to whom the spiritual affairs of the race were delegated as a matter of not much concern, who were silently performing the simple religious ceremonies of the race for the trifling renumeration which the other two classes, —the warriors and the earners of wealth,—condescendingly paid them, did not yield to the warriors so easily,—nor did they yield at all,—as did the agriculturists and traders. They had the Vedas,—the old religious songs—the traditions of their forefathers,—the old religious ceremonies of their race,—the learning and knowledge of ages,—all solely and wholly in their hands. The others in search of wealth and power, had completely given up all thought of religion and learning, which was once every one's own daily avocation in their primitive age. Thus they had become the soul property of this priestly clan,—the others having forgotten them altogether. Religion and learning reign supreme everywhere. The warriors, though they lorded over all, could not but show some respect and reverence to the men who were the custodians of their religious affairs and who had on their side learning and knowledge which they had not,—nor had they time to acquire them. Thus gradually were formed four castes amongst the Aryans;—the first the warriors or the Kshatriyas;—second the priests or the Brahmanas,—third the agriculturists and traders or the Vyasas, and lastly the conquered black slaves, or the Sudras. They sang:—†

"The wielder of the thunder-bolt, the render of the rain-cloud, Indra, had destroyed with his bolt the mighty Susena, the wrath-born son of the Danava, the walker in darkness,

* See Dutt's Civilization in Ancient India.

† See Rig Veda, V. 32.

the protector of the showering cloud, exhilarating himself with the food of these living creatures."

"When Indra raised his powerful irresistible weapon against the mighty Danava, when he struck him with the blow of the thunder-bolt, he made him the lowest of all creatures"

"The fierce Indra seized upon him that vast moving Vritra, when slumbering after having drunk the Soma, subduing his foes and enveloping the world, and then slew him with his great weapon in battle footless, measureless, speechless."

"I hear of thee influencing creatures according to the season and giving riches to the pious, but what do thy devoted friends obtain who have entrusted their desires, Indra, to thee."*

When the Aryan races were passing through these changes,—when they had become three distinct classes, though they had not yet formed into distinct and exclusive castes,—when the warriors were becoming wealthy kings and the priests were trying to hold a position greater than those kings,—there were a few—very few indeed,—amongst all these three classes of the Aryans, who were not in search of either the sovereignty, or the priestly superiority, or wealth or position or power ;—they were the poets and the philosophers of the race. Even in those early days,—some four thousand years ago,—they were the seekers after the mysterious Nature and Nature's God.† These Aryan poets and philo-

---

* Indra worship is the latest feature of the Vedic religion. Indra was not originally the chief God of the Aryans. Varuna was the chief God. See Royal Asiatic Society's Journal, Vol. I., Part I., p. p. 85—86 and Part II, p. 389 and MaxMuller's Science of Language p. p. 208-210.

† Dr. Oldenberg in his "Buddha" p. 16 says :—" The rudiments of Indian speculation extend back to the lyric poetry of the Rig Veda. Here, in the oldest monument of Vedic Poetry, among songs at sacrifices and prayers to Agni and Indra for protection, prosperity and victory, we

sophers, seeking not kingly majesty and priestly dignity, sang :—*

" He who gives breath, He who gives strength,
Whose commands all the bright Gods revere ;
Whose shadow is immortality, whose shadow is death ;
Who is the God to whom we shall offer our sacrifice ?"

" He through whose greatness, these snowy mountains are,
And the sea they say, with the distant river,
He of whom these regions are the two arms ;
Who is the God to whom we shall offer our sacrifice ?"

" He through whom the sky is bright and the earth firm,
He through whom the heaven was established, nay the highest heaven ;
He who measured out the space in the sky ;
Who is the God to whom we shall offer our sacrifice ?"

" He who by His might looked even over the waters,
Which held power and generated the sacrificial fire,
He who alone is God above all Gods ;
Who is the God to whom we shall offer our sacrifice ?".

And again :—

" There was not death,—yet there naught immortal,
There is no confine betwixt day and night,
The only one breathed breathless by itself,
Other than It there nothing since has been."

" Darkness there was and all at first was veiled
In gloom profound—an ocean without light,
The germ that still lay covered in the husk

---

discover the first bold efforts of a reflecting mind, which turns its back in the spheres of holy words of Gods and myths and in conscious reliance on its own power, approaches the enigmas of being and resigination.'

* Rig Veda, 129.

Burst forth, one nature, from the fervent heats.
Who knew the secret? Who proclaimed it here."

And again :—*

"Nor aught nor naught existed yon bright sky
Was not, nor heaven's broad roof outstretched above.
What covered all? What sheltered? what concealed?
Was it the water's fathomless abyss?
Whence,—whence this manifold creation sprang!
The Gods themselves came later into being,
Who knows from whence this great creation sprung!
He from whom all this great creation came,
Whether His will created or was mute,
The most high Seer that is in highest heaven,
He knows it—or perchance even He knows not.

—:o:—

CHAPTER V.

BRAHMANISM *vrs*. THEISM.

By this time the Aryan possessions had extended down the fertile valley of the Ganges and the Jamuna. Two very great kingdoms had been established,—the lands of the Kuru Panchala and the Koshalas were no longer the mere settlements of sturdy Aryans,—but great centres of wealth and civilisation as well as of learning and education. Within a few centuries the simple and innocent Aryan-settlers have become a great nation,—great in wealth and power, in civilization and refinement, in education and learning.

* Rig Veda, 121.

On the one hand the Aryan warriors,—the Khatryas,—had become great kings and chiefs,—vastly wealthy and powerful; on the other hand the Aryan priests,—the Brahmanas,—had formed a complicated system of religion,—hard to master and harder to understand.* The quiet Vasyas had fallen far away from both these classes and were engaged in silently tilling the land and selling its produce. The quieter Sudras existed uncomplainingly serving their masters, the three classes of the Aryans.† The Kshatryas, Vasyas and Sudras, partly because they very little cared for it and partly because the Bramhanas did not allow them to meddle with it, had completely lost all touch with their forefathers' religion, once their daily avocation,—and had thus been thrown out of the pale of all education and learning. Ignorance, however graced with wealth and power, is bound to bow down its head before learning and knowledge. Thus had now the Brahmanas become, from mere paid priests, the spiritual masters, temporal guides and supreme lords of all the other three classes of the Aryan race. If the Kshatryas are now kings and

---

* See Dr. Haug's Translation of Aitareya Brahmana Vol I. Rhys Davids in his Buddhism p. 23-24 says:—"The simple feeling of awe and wonder at the glorious battles of the storms and the recurring victories of the sun had given way before a debasing ritualism; before the growing belief in the efficacy of carefully conducted rites and ceremonies and charms and incantations; before the growing fear of the actual power of the stars over the lives and destinies of men; before the growing dependence on dreams and omens and divinations."

† The following is the Hindu version of the origin of caste. "Brahma created a son from his mouth and named Brahmana and bade him study and teach the Veda. But fearing the attack of wild beasts, he prayed for help and a second son was created from his arms and named Kshatrya to protect him. But employed as he was in defence, he could not provide the necessaries of life, so a third son Vaisya was sent to till the soil, and finally to serve the other three classes a fourth son was created and was named Sudra." See Manu I. 31., Yagnavalka III. and Rig Veda 90. 6. 7.

princes, the Brahmanas are the chief ministers and judges,— the real men of power in the land. They had formed a religion with so many dogmas and with so many and so greatly complicated sacrifices that the other classes of the Aryans looked at them in wonder and admiration. They had been completely deprived of all spiritual affairs,—all knowledge and learning,—nay of all religion. The wealthy of the Kshatryas and Vaisyas only could venture to perform those sacrifices,—so costly had they grown. Thus had the middle and the poor classes of the people fallen completely away from all religion. The Brahmanas held the reign tightly with an iron hand and did not allow any one to enter the sacred preccints of religion where they reigned supreme. The majority,—nay except the Brahmanas—all others had became completely religion-less. They obeyed like slaves the dictates of the Brahmanas and acted as it were automatically under the guidance of their spiritual masters. To them it was moral what was termed moral by these Brahmanas, right what was called right by them, religion what was pointed out by them as religion. Living as the poorest of the poor these learned Brahmanas were the richest of the rich, the mightiest of the mighty.

But the Khastryas did not allow the Brahmanas to become all supreme without a struggle. Often Khastrya youths aspired to be great Brahmans and often did they

---

The following is the version of the origin of caste given by the Buddhists. "When outrages on society began, a ruler was elected to preserve order who received for such service a portion of the produce. He was called Khattiya or Khastrya. Then by reason of the increase of crimes the people appointed from among themselves Bahmanas or Brahmanas. Other persons who distinguished themselves as artificers were called Vessa or Vaisya, and others engaged in hunting became Suddas or Sudras." See Turner's Buddhistic Legends, Colonel Syke's Notes on Ancient India and Journal of Royal Asiatic Society, Vol VI. For Castes also See Muller's Chips II. 308. Muir's Sanskrit Texts I. 160.

succeed.* So again were sometime the Brahmana youths tempted to throw away the Vedas and to take up arms. They too often succeeded in becoming great warriors, and defeated the valiant Kshatryas.† Such struggles went on for centuries after centuries till Goutama Buddha came and established in the world the kingdom of Righteousness, of Peace, of Contentment, of Kindness towards men and beasts.

But how did this come about? When the Kshatryas were becoming mighty in arms and the Brahmanas in spiritualism,—there were working a silent class, hailing from amongst the Brahmanas, Kshatryas, Vasyas, nay Sudras,—the Aryan poets and philosophers,—the seekers after God,—who saw distinctly and felt keenly the bane of all civilization,—vice and sin,—which were daily taking a strong hold of the ever-innocent and ever-virtuous Aryan race. There grew up wealth, comfort and luxury on all sides, but these silent children of Nature were not dazzled by their tempting splendour. They saw before them poverty, disease, decrepitude and death, the four fearful monsters that devour humanity. Even in the Veda we find the cry of these poets who piteously sang:‡—

"Let me not yet, O Varuna, enter into the house of clay,
Have mercy, Almighty, have mercy!
If I go along trembling like a cloud driven by wind,
Have mercy, Almighty, have mercy.
Through want of strength, Thou strong One, have I gone
to the wrong shore;
Have mercy, Almighty, have mercy!
Thirst came on the worshipper in the midst of waters,

---

* The story of Vishwamitra illustrates this. He was originally a Kshatrya, but finally became a great Brahmana.

† Read the story of Parashurama. Though he was a Brahman, yet he faught with the Kshatryas. It is said he annihilated the Kshatryas for twenty one times.

‡ See Rig Veda.

Have mercy, Almighty, hav emercy!
Wherever we men, O Varuna, commit an offence before the heavenly host,
Whenever we break the law through thoughtlessness,
Have mercy, Almighty, have mercy."

When the Brahmanas were formulating complicated sacrifices and more complicated rituals and rites, these poets and philosophers were seeking after God, the Supreme Lord of all creatures, the God of all gods, and searching for the means by which humanity would be able to get rid of poverty, disease and decripitude and to master death.* Dr. Oldenberg thus graphically describes the Brahmanas:—"He passed his youth in hearing and learning the sacred words, for a true Brahmana is he alone "who has heard." And if he acquired the reputation "of having heard," his adult life passed in teaching in the village or out in the solitude of the forest in the consecrated circle, on which the sun shone in the East, where alone the most secret instruction could be imparted openly to the muffled scholar. Or he was to be found at the place of sacrifice, performing for himself and for others the sacred office which with its countless observances demanded the most painful minuteness and the most laborious proficiency, or he fulfilled the life-long duty of Brahmana, offering, that is, the daily prayer from the Sacred Veda. Well might riches flow into his hands by the remuneration of sacrifices which kings and nobles gave to the Brahmanas, but he passed as most worthy who lived not by offerings for others, but by the gleaning of the field which he gathered or by alms for which he had not asked, or such charity as he has begged as a favour. Still living as a beggar he looked on himself as exalted above earthly potentates and subjects made of other stuff than they. The Brahmans called themselves Gods and in treaty with the Gods of

* We find this all through the various Upanishadas.

heaven ; they were the Gods of earth, knew themselves possessed of weapons of the Gods,—weapons of spiritual power,—before which all earthly weapons snap powerless."*

He thus speaks of the origin of the monastic life amongst the Aryans :—

"These speculations which represented the phenomenal world to be unstable and worthless as compared with the world's base, the Atma, had at one blow deprived of the value all those aims of life which appear important to the natural consciousness of ordinary men. Sacrifice and external observances are unable to raise the spirit to the Atman, to disclose to the individual Ego his identity with the universal Ego. Man must separate himself from all that is earthly,—must fly from love and hate, from hope and fear; man must live as though he lived not. The Aryan Rishis said, 'the intelligent and wise desire not posperity; what are descendants to us whose home is the Atma?' They relinquish the desire for children, the struggle for wealth, the pursuit of worldly weal and go forth as mendicants."† Both these Brahmanas and poet-philosophers, the latter of whom we name Theists, have left behind them long treatises expounding their respective views. The Brahmanas of the Brahmanas deal with the awe-inspiring rites, rituals and sacrifices‡ and the Aranyakas

---

* See Oldenberg's Buddha, p.p. 13—14.

† Thus we find mendicants and monks there were in India before the birth of Goutama Buddha,—but he was the first to create an Order of Monks.

‡ Dr. Haug in his Translation of the Aitreya Brahman, Vol. I. Introduction p. 73 says :—" The sacrifice is regarded as the means for obtaining power over this and the other world, over visible as well as invisible beings, animate as well as inanimate creatures. Who knows its proper application and has it duly performed is in fact looked upon as the real master of the world ; for any desire he may entertain, if it be the most ambitious, can be gratified, any object he has in view can be obtained by means of it. The Yajna (sacrifice) taken as a whole is considered to be a kind of machinery in which every piece must tally

and the Upanishads of poet-philosophers are full of the search for God and origin of the creation. We quote a few passages below.

"Maitreyi," said Yajnavalka," I am going away from this my house into the forest. I must make a settlement between thee and my other wife Kātyāyani. "My Lord," replied Maitreyi, "if this whole world, full of wealth, belonged to me, should I be immortal by it?"

"No," said Yajnavalka, "like the happy life of the rich people will be your life. But there is no hope of immortality by wealth."

Then Maitreyi said, "What shall I do with that by which I do not become immortal? What my lord knoweth of immortality, may he tell that to me."

Yajnavalka replied, "Thou, who art truly dear to me, thou speakest dear words, sit down; I will explain it to thee and listen well to what I say." Yajnavalka thus went on, "A husband is loved, not because you love the husband, but because you will love in him the Atma, the Supreme Soul. A wife is loved, not because we love the wife, but we love in her the great Soul. Children are loved, not because we love the children, but because we love in them the Divine Spirit. This great Atma it is which we love when we love wealth, Brahmanas, Kshatriyas, this world, the gods, all beings, this universe. The divine Atma, O my wife, is to be seen, to be heard, to be perceived and to be meditated upon. If we see, hear, perceive and know him, O Maitreyi, then this whole universe is known to us."*

---

with the other or a sort of chain in which no link is allowed to be wanting, or a staircase by which one may ascend to heaven; or as a personage endowed with all the characteristics of the human body. It exists from eternity and proceeded from the Supreme Being (Brahma) along with the Trividya (Threefold Science). The creation of the world was even regarded as the fruit of a sacrifice, performed by the Supreme Being."

* Brihad Aranyaka.

And again :—*

" Think that which is manifested by speech and by which speech is manifested as Brahma."

"Know that which does not see by the eye, but by which the eyes see as Brahma."

" Know that which does not breathe by breath, but that by which the breath is breathed as Brahma."

And again—†

" The indestructible Brahma is the place where all fear disappears, the refuge of those who are desirous of crossing the ocean of this world.

Know the (human) soul as the rider, the body as the car, know intellect as the charioteer and mind as the reins.

They say the senses are the horses and their objects are the roads, the enjoyer is the (human) soul endowed with body, sense and mind.

Whoever is unwise with reins never applied, has the senses unsubdued like the wicked horses of the charioteer.

But whosoever is wise with mind always applied, has these senses subdued like the good horses of the charioteer.

Whoever is unwise, unmindful, always impure, does not gain that goal, but descends to the world again.

But whosoever is wise, mindful, always pure, gains the goal from whence he is not born again."

And lastly :—‡

" All this verily is Brahma ; for therefrom doeth it proceed therein doeth it merge and thereby it is maintained. With a quite and controlled mind should it be adored. Man is a creature of reflection ; whatever he reflects, he reflects upon in this life, he becomes the same hereafter ; therefore he should reflect upon Brahma, saying—

---

* Kena Upanishada.

† Kota Upanishada.

‡ Chhandogya Upanishada.

'That which is nothing but mind, whose body is its life, whose figure is a mere glory, whose will is truth, is the Soul within me.'

'That which performeth all things, and willeth all things, to which belongs all sweet colours and all grateful juices, which envelopes the whole of this world, which neither speaketh nor respecteth any body, is the Soul within me. It is Brahma, I shall obtain Him after my transition from this world.' He who beloveth this, and hath no hesitation, will verily obtain the fruit of his reflection.'

Thus we find there was a class of Aryan poet-philosophers side by side with the Aryan Ritualistic Brahmanas. Thus did the Aryans rise step by step from the grand Vedic Nature worship, to Nature herself and from Nature to Nature's Great God. They found out the origin of creation and some of them really reached the Great Goal.

Though the Brahmanas monopolised all religious functions, and scruplously kept others off from the preccints of learning and knowledge, yet they could not prevent the births and growths of these Aryan poet-philosophers who rose from all ranks of society,—from Kshatrya kings and heroes,—from Vaisyas traders and peasants, and even from Sudra servants. Some of these poet philosophers went away into the forests, roved as beggars and monks and searched for God. The Brahmanas formed an oligarchy and a Society whereas these poet-philosophers thought and meditated in solicitude, and formulated and expounded each his individual opinion and discovery. But like the Brahmanas they remained attached to the holy Vedas, believed in their sacredness and knew them as the words of God.

CHAPTER VI.

THEISTS, *vrs.* PHILOSOPHERS.

"SOON teachers appeared in more than one place who professed to have discovered independently of Vedic Tradition a new and the only true path of deliverence, and such teachers failed not to attract scholars who attached themselves to them in their wanderings through the land. Under the protection of most absolute liberty of conscience which ever existed, sects were added to sects."*

And who are they? The most prominent amongst them was Kapila. He was followed successively by many others. Thus did various systems of Philosophy come into existence; some of them were considered to be orthodox as consistent with the theology and metaphysics of the Vedas, and the others heretical as compatible with their doctrines. The two Minansas are emphatically orthodox. The Prior (Purva Minansa) one, which has Jaimani for its founder, teaches the art of reasoning with the express view of aiding the interpretation of the Vedas, specially their Brahman or Sacrificial and the Ritualistic portions. The latter Uttara Mimansa, which is also known by the name of Vedanta and which is supposed to be written by Vyasa, deduces from the text of the Vedas, specially their Upanishada portions, a refined Psychology which denies the existence of a material world.

The Nyaya of Goutama furnishes a philosophical arrangement with strict rules of reasonings—a sort of Logic. Next comes another course of Philosophy connected with the Nyaya called Vaisesika. Its author is Kanada and it deals with atoms.

Then comes another system of Philosophy, partly heterodox and partly orthodox, namely Sankhya of Kapila and Yoga of

* See Oldenberg's Buddha p 66.

Patanjali. Though Sankhya and Yoga, Nyaya and Vaisesika are not strictly orthodox, yet they are respected and studied by the rigid adherents of the Vedas. In fact all these six systems of Philosophy have been always considered as orthodox and a part and parcel of the Vedic Brahmanism.*

But besides these six philosophical systems, there arose at this time many other teachers and philosophers whose doctrines were emphatically hetorodox,—who completely overthrew the rites and rituals of the Vedas, denied their sanctity and divine origin, and formulated new theories quite apart from the Vedas and the Vedangas. We have no less than fourteen such hetorodox systems, of which that of Charvaka stands first; then come successively Jainas, Nigranthas, Achalakas, Nastikas, &c. &c.†

We have seen that at the time of which we are speaking as a matter of fact, two distinct religions flourished amongst the Aryan races of India,—one Brahmanism,—the religion of rites, rituals and sacrifices based on the traditional sanctity of the Vedas with Theism as their moto,—and another, religion of Psychology,—with a search for the origin of the creation and freedom from the wordly miseries. These Philosophers went a step farther. Sankhya put aside the consideration of God altogether, said nothing about the Vedas and attempted to find out by Knowledge the means of cutting the bonds of rebirths and of freedom from all miseries. The Yoga did exactly the same, but by means of practising austerities and by believing in a Supreme Lord of the Universe.

---

* See Colebrooke's Miscellaneous Essays Vol. I. pp 239-401; also Maxmuller's Six Hindu Darsanas; also Manning's Medæival India Vol. I.

† See *Sarva Darsana Sangraha* by Madhavacharya; and also Colebrooke's Essays, Vol. I. p 402-460.

Later than Sankhya is the Nyaya, of which the very name seems to imply that it is its counter-part. Sankhya means something analogous to speculation or synthetic reasoning. The word comes from Sankhya (*Sam* together—*khya* reasoning,) indicating that it is a philosophy, based on *synthetic* reasonings. The Nyaya, however, takes the other course and gives a philosophy founded on *analytical* reasonings. And thus while the Sankhya builds up a system of the Universe, the Nyaya dissects it into categories and enters into its component parts.* "Entering into" appears to be the literal rendering of Nyaya, a word which aptly describes a system which enters into the whole contents of the Universe. Goutama, the author of this system, took special note of man's mental powers and the uses to which such powers may be applied. The Vaisesika system, attributed to Kanada, is a fuller and probably later development of the Nyaya. It is remarkable for its peculiar doctrine of atomic individualities or *Viseshasa* from which its name is derived.† The Mimansas are but mere supporters in a philosophical way of the Brahmanas and the Upanishadas. Charvakas and others, on the other hand, are emphatically the overthrowers of the Vedic ritualism as well as of the Vedic Theism. Thus did both orthodox philosophers and religious preachers with their sects increase in scores all over the country.

"The paths of deliverance by which these masters led their believers in quest of salvation were a legion; there were ascetics who lived in self-mortification, denied themselves nourishment for long periods, did not wash themselves, did not sit down, rested on beds of thorns; there were adherents of faith in the purifying efficacy of water, who were intent on purging by continued ablutions all guilt which clung to them, others aimed at conditions of spiritual abstraction,

* See Goldstucker's Panini.

† See Miss Manning's Medæival India, Vol. 1. pp 152-153.

and sought while separating themselves from all perception of external realities to combine themselves with the feeling of the "Eternity of Space" or of the "Eternity of Reason," of "not anything whateverness" and whatever else these conditions are called."*

Ashwa Ghosa, the great biographer of the Buddha, thus describes the various sects that were flourishing in India when Goutama left his home to search for the great truth."†

---

* See Oldenberg's Buddha, pp. 67-68.

† This is of course the version from the sides of the Buddhists and therefore they cannot reasonably be called impartial. It would be intersting to know what the Vedic Hindus thought of the non-Vedic Buddhists and others. We therefore quote a passage from the Vishnu Purana, Part. III. See XVII—XVIII. "The Rig, Yayus and Sama Vedas are the three-fold covering of the several castes, and the sinful wretch who throws off this is called Nagna (naked, appostate). There took place in the days of yore a battle between the gods and the demons in which the gods were defeated. The celestials who were defeated fled away to the nothern shore of the milky ocean where they engaged in austerities and prayed to Vishnu. They then saw Hari and asked him to save them from the demons. When the glorious Vishnu heard their prayers, he emitted from his body an illusory form which he gave to the celestials and said, "This illusory form shall so deceive the Daityas, that being astray from the path of the Vedas, they shall be slain; for those gods, demons and others who shall transgress the authority of the Vedas shall perish." Shaven and carrying a bunch of peocock's feathers, the illusory figure then went to the Asuras and thus addressed them, gently, "O lords of Daitya race,—why do you practise these devout penances? Do you expect rewards in this world or in the next?' The Asuras said, "O thou of great mind, we have been engaged in these penances with a view to reap fruits in the next world. Do thou tell us if thou hast got anything to say on this." The deceptive figure said, "If you are desirous of final emancipation, hear my words, for you will obtain the revelation which is the door to final happiness. The instructions, superior to which there is nothing, that I will give you, are the secret path to final emancipation. If you follow them, you shall either obtain

"The Brahmacharins, holding the rules of deer, following the deer wandering through the mountain glades, deer course of nature with flushing eyes, regard the prince with fixed gaze.

---

heaven or exemption from future births. O ye gifted with mighty strength, you are worthy of these instructions."

Thus did the illusory figure mislead the Daityas from the teachings of the Vedas by various pursuasions and many spacious arguments, teaching that the same thing might be for the sake of virtue and of vice; might be and might not be; might or might not lead to final emancipation; might be the supreme object and not the supreme object; might be effect and not be effect; might be manifest and not be manifest; might be the duty of those who go naked and who go richly dressed. And thus were the Daityas led astray from the path of their duties by the continued teachings of their illusory teacher, keeping up the equal truth of contradictory teachings. And those were called Arhatas from the phrase he had employed of "Ye are worthy (Arhatha) of this great teaching," that is of the false teachings which he induced them to follow. Thus did the illusory figure lead away the Asuras from the teachings of the Vedas. And being impressed by those teachings the Asuras initiated others in all those doctrines. They in their turn became teachers of the same false doctrines and converted others. And thus communicating their doctrines to each other, they were all led away from the teachings of the Vedas.

Then putting on garments of red colour, with collyrium in his eyes, the illusory figure addressed others of the same family in sweet and mild accents, "O ye demons, gifted with strength, if ye wish for heaven or final rest, desist from the sinful massacre of animals and hear from me what you should do. The whole universe is composed of discriminative knowledge; understand my words well for they have been uttered by the wise. The world is without stay and is perpetually revolving in the straits of existence being engaged in the pursuit of erroneous knowledge and sullied by passions and others."

In this wise exclaiming to them "Know (Budhyadwam) and they saying (Budhyate) it is known," those Daityas were led away from their own religion. They thus renounced their respective duties being impressed by the reasonings and arguments of that illusory figure. O Maitreya, they, thus impressed, pursuaded others to do the same and thus the heresy spread. and many abandoned the practices laid down by the Vedas and Smritis. O twice-born one, with various

That twice-born in reply to Buddha explained in succession all the modes of painful descipline and the fruits as their results.

How some ate nothing brought from inhabited places but that produced from pure water, edible roots and tender twigs, fruits and flowers fit for food,

Each according to the rules of his sect, clothing and food in each case different; some living amongst bird kind and like them capturing and eating food;

Others eating as the deer the grass and herbs; others living like serpents inhaling air, others eating nothing founded in wood or stone; some eating with two teeth till a wound be formed;

Others again begging their food and giving it in charity taking only the remnants for themselves; others again who

---

other erroneous teachings, the illusory figure converted many other Daityas. Deluded, the Asuras, in no time abandoned the doctrines and rites laid down by the three Vedas. Some of them, O twice-born one, spoke ill of the Vedas and others villified the celestials. Some spoke against the Vedic rites and sacrifices, and others calumniated the Brahmans. "The precepts', they preached, " that lead to the sacrifice of animals, are highly culpable. To say that throwing clarified butter in fire produces rewards is simply childishness. If any one, after having obtained god-head by multiplied ceremonies, is fed along with Indra upon the wood used as fuel in holy fire, he is lower than a brute which feeds upon leaves. If a beast, being sacrificed, attains to heaven, why does not sacrificer slay his father in a sacrifice? If a dead person is satisfied if another is fed at a Sraddha, then why does not the food offered by his son reach him who resides at a distance? All these words therefore depend upon individual respect, so it is better for you to neglect them and appreciate mire. The words of authority, O mighty Asuras, do not fall from heaven; reasonable words only are to be accepted by persons like yourselves. "By these and similar reasonings, the Daityas were led away, and none of them any longer acknowledged the authority of the Vedas."

After the Daityas were thus led away, the celestials easily defeated them.

let water continually drip on their heads ; and those who offer up with fire.

Others who practise water-dwelling like fish. Thus there are Brahmacharins of every sort, who practise austerities that they may at the end of life obtain a birth in heaven.

Goutama then beheld their rites in connection with sacrifice to fire, the drilling for sparks and the fanning into flame ;

Also the sprinkling of the butter libations ; also the chanting of the mystic-prayers (the Veda) till the sun went down.*

Oldenberg says :—

"At this time of deep and many sided intellectual movements which had extended from the circles of Brahmanical thinkers far into the people at large, when amateur studies of the dialectic routine had already given up out of the arduous struggles of the past age over its simple profound thoughts, when dialectic scepticism began to attack moral ideas,—at this time, when a painful longing for deliverance from the burden of being, was met by the first signs of moral decay,—Goutama appears upon the scene."

——:o:——

CHAPTER VII.

THE BUDDHAS.

BUT Siddharta Goutama was not the only Buddha that was ever born in this world. He was neither the first nor the last Buddha ; there were many Buddhas that came before him, and there will be many more who will come after him.†

* This is a quotation from the Chinese work *Fo-Sho-Hing-Tsan-King* which is a translation of the Sanskrit *Buddha Charita* by Ashwa Ghosa.

† In the Bhagavad Gita, Chap IV. Slokas 7-8. ; Srikrishna said :—

When-soever, O Bharata, virtue languishes and sin predominates, I create myself.

I take birth age after age for the protection of the good and the destruction of the wicked and the establishment of true religion.

BUDDHA said :—" The all-subduing, the all-knowing am I in everything, that I am without a spot, I have given up every thing. I am without a desire,—a Delivered One. By my own power I possess Knowledge; whom should I call master? I have no teacher; no one is to be compared to me. In the world including heavens there is no one like unto me. I am the Holy One in the world; I am the Supreme Master. I alone am the perfect Buddha; the flames are extinct in me. I have attained the Nirvana."*

HIS FOLLOWERS say :—" The exalted One is the bringer of joy, the dispenser of joy, whose organs of life are placcid whose spirit is at rest, the Supreme Self-subduer and Peace-possessor, the Hero who has conquered self and watches himself, who holds his desires in check."

" He appears in the world for salvation to many people, for joy to many people, out of compassion for the world, for the blessing, the salvation, the joy of gods and men."†

Thus have the Buddhas of by-gone ages appeared; thus shall the Buddhas of coming ages appear. " The names of twenty-four of these Buddhas who appeared previous to Goutama have been handed down to us; and when after 5000 years‡ shall have elapsed since his re-discovery of the Truth under the Bo-tree, the religion of Goutama shall be forgotten, a new Buddha will again open the door of Nirvana to men, his name being *Maitreya Buddha*—the Buddha of Kindness."§

---

* See Mahavagga I. 6·8.

† See Anuguttara Nikaya, Vol. I.

‡ Buddha said to his beloved disciple :—" Five hundred years, Ananda, will the doctrine of the Truth abide." See Cullavagga X. 1. 6. Dr. Oldenberg remarks, " Later on, when his prophecy was contradicted by events, the numbers were naturally made greater." See Oldenberg's Buddha p. 327, and also Koppen, I. 327.

§ See Rhys David's Buddhism, p. 180.

We shall now briefly sketch the lives of these previous Buddhas.*

Dipanker was the First Buddha.† Next to the Dipanker Buddha, after the lapse of one *Asankheyya*, the teacher Kondanna appeared. The city of Kondanna Buddha was Rammavati; the Kshatriya Sunada was his father; his mother was queen Sujata; Bhadda and Subhadda were his two chief disciples. Anuraddha was his servitor; Tissa and Upatissa his chief female disciples. His Budhi-tree was the Salakalyain; his body was eight cubits high, and the duration of his life was a hundred thousand years.

After him at the end of one *Asankheyya*, in one and the same cycle, four Buddhas were born,—namely Mangala, Sumana, Revata and Sobhita.

---

* The *Buddhavansa*, the last book of the Khuddaka Nikaya in the second Pitaka, gives the lives of all the previous Buddhas. The Pali commentary on the Jatakas also gives certain details of these 24 Buddhas. See Fansboll's Jataka p.p. 2-44, and Sutta Nipata p. 40; also Turner's Mahavansa p. 1, and Hardy's Manual of Buddhism p. 49. We give here the accounts of the Buddhas from the *Nidana Katha* as translated by Rhys Davids.

† We find the following 55 names of the previous Buddhas in *Lalita Vistara*, Chap. I.

1. Padmauttara; 2. Dharmaketu; 3. Dipankara; 4. Gunaketu; 5. Mahakara; 6. Rishideva; 7. Sretaja; 8. Satyaketu; 9. Vajrasanhat; 10. Sarvavion; 11. Hemvarna; 12. Attuchagami; 13. Probahsaya; 14. Puspaketu; 15. Vararupa; 16. Sulochona; 17. Rishigupta; 18. Ginabaktra; 19. Unnata; 20. Puspita; 21, Urnitaja; 22. Puskara; 23. Sarasmi; 24. Mangala; 25. Sudarsana; 26. Maha Sinhataja; 27. Sthitabudhidatta; 28. Basantagandhi; 29. Satwadharmabipulakirti; 30. Pushya; 31. Visternavida; 32. Ratnakirti; 33. Ugrataja; 34. Brahmataja; 35. Sugosha; 36. Supushya; 37. Sumanagnaghosa; 38. Suchastarupa; 39. Prahasitanatra; 40. Gunarashi; 41. Maghaswara; 42. Sundarvarna; 43. Ayustaja; 44. Salilagajagemi; 45. Lokavilasita; 46. Jitasatru; 47. Sampujita; 48. Bipaschita; 49. Shikhi; 50. Vishwavu; 51. Krukuchhanda; 52. Kanakmuni; 53. Sumana Kashyapa. 55. Sidharta Goutama.

The city of Mangala Buddha was called Uttara; his father was the Kshatriya Uttara; his mother was Uttara. Sudeva, and Dhamasena were his two chief desciples; Palita was his servitor; Sivali and Asoka his two chief female disciples. The Naga was his Bodhi-tree; his body was eighty-eight cubits high. When his death took place, after he had lived ninety thousand years, at the same instant ten thousand worlds were involved in darkness, and in all worlds there was a great cry and lamentation of men.

And after the Mangala Buddha had died, shrouding in darkness ten thousand worlds, the Teacher Sumana appeared. The city of this Buddha was named Khema; Sudatta was his father; Srimana his mother; Sarana and Bravitatta his chief disciples; Adina his servitor; Sona and Upasona his chief female disciples. The Naga was his Boodhi tree; his body was ninety cubits high and his length of his life ninety thousand years.

After him the Teacher Revata appeared. The city of this Buddha was called Sudhannavati; his father was the Khattrya Vipula; his mother Vipula; Varuna and Brahmadeva his chief disciples; Sambhava his servitor; Bhadra and Subadra his chief female disciples, and the Naga-tree his Bo-tree. His body was eighty cubits high and his age sixty thousand years.

After him appeared the Teacher Sobhita. Sudharma was the name of the city of this Blessed One; Sudhamma the king was his father; Sudhama was his mother; Asama and Suneta his chief disciples; Anoma his servitor; Nakula and Sujata his chief female disciples, and the Naga-tree his Bo-tree. His body was eighty cubits high and his age sixty thousand years.

After him when an *Asankheyya* had elapsed, three Buddhas were born in one Kalpa—Anomadarsin, Padama, and Narada. The city of Anomadarsin, the Blessed One, was called Càndavati; Yasana, the king, was his father; Yosodhara was his mother; Nisabha and Anima his chief disciples; Varuna his chief servitors; Sundari and Sumana his chief female disciples; the Arjuna tree his Bo-tree; his body was fifty-eight cubits high, and his age a hundred thousand years.

After him appeared the Teacher named Padama. Now the city of Padama, the Blessed One, was called Champaka; his father was Paduma the king; his mother Asama; Sala and Upasala were his chief disciples; Varuna was his servitor; Rama and Uparama his chief female disciples; the Crimson tree his Bo-tree; his body was fifty-eight cubits high, and his age was a hundred thousand years.

After him appeared the Teacher named Narada. The city of the Blessed One was called Dhamavati; his father was Sumedha, the warrior; his mother Anomabuddasala; and Jittamila his chief disciples. Vissetta his servitor; Uttava and Peggumis his chief female disciples; the great Crimson tree his Bo-tree; his body eighty-eight cubits high and his age was ninety thousand years.

After Narada the Buddha, a hundred thousand cycles ago, there appeared in one Kalpa only one Buddha called Padumuttara. His city was called Hansavati; his father was Ananda the warrior; his mother Sujata; Devala and Sujata his chief disciples; Sumana his servitor; Amita and Asama his chief female disciples; the Sala tree his Bo-tree; his body was eighty-eight cubits high; the light from his body extended twelve leagues; and his age was a hundred thousand years.

After him when thirty thousand world cycles had elapsed, two Buddhas, Sumeda and Sujata, were born in one Kalpa. The city of Sumedha, the Blessed One, was called Sudasana: Suddatta the king was his father; Sudatta was his mother; Sarana and Sabbakama his two chief disciples; Sagara his servitor; Rama and Surama his chief two female disciples; the great Champaka tree his Bo-tree; his body was eighty-eight cubits high, and his age was ninety thousand years.

After him appeared the Teacher Sujatta. The city of this Blessed one was called Sumangala; Uggata the king was his father; Pabhavati his mother; Sudarsana and Deva his chief disciples; Nanda his servitor; Naga and Nagasamala his chief female disciples; and the great Bambu tree his Bo-tree. This tree, they say, had smaller hollows and thicker wood than ordinary bamboos have, and in its mighty upper branches it was as brilliant as a branch of a peacock's tails. The body of this Blessed one was fifty cubits high, and his age was ninety thousand years.

After him, when eighteen hundred world cycles had elapsed, three Buddhas, namely Piyadassin, Atthadassin and Dhammadassin were born in one Kalpa. The city of Piyadassin was called Anoma; his father was Suduma the king; his mother Canda; Palita and Subbadassin his chief disciples; Sobhita his servitor; Sujjata and Dhammadasin his chief female disciples, and the Priyangu tree his Bo-tree. His body was eighty cubits high, and his age ninety thousand years.

After him appeared the Teacher Athadassin. The city of this Blessed One was Sobhita; Sagara the king was his father; Sudassana his mother; Santa and Apasanta his chief disciples; Abhaya his servitor; Dhamma and Sudhamma his chief female disciples; and the Champaka his Bo-tree. His body was eighty cubits high; the glory from his body always extended over a league, and his age was a hundred thousand years.

After him appeared the Teacher named Dhammadassin. The city of this Blessed One was called Sarana; his father was Sarana, the king, ; his mother Sunanda; Paduma and Phussadeva his chief disciples; Sunetta his servitor; Khema and Subbanama his chief female disciples; and the red Kuravatra, tree his Bo-tree. His body was eighty cubits high, and his age a hundred thousand years.

After him ninety-four world cycles ago, only one Buddha, by name Siddhattha appeared in one Kalpa. The city of this

Blessed One was called Vebhara; Jayasena the king was his father; Suphassa his mother; Sambala and Sumitta his chief female disciples; and the Kanikar tree his Bo-tree. His body was sixty cubits high, and his age was a hundred thousand years.

After him, ninety-two world cycles ago, two Buddhas, namely Tissa and Phussa by name, were born in one Kalpa. The city of this Blessed One was called Khema; Janasandha the warrior-chief was his father; Paduma his mother; the God Brahma and Udaya his chief disciples; Sambhava his servitor; Phussa and Sudatta his chief female disciples; and the Asana tree his Bo-tree. His body was sixty cubits high, and his age a hundred thousand years.

After him appeared the Teacher named Phussa. The city of this Blessed One was called Kasi; Jayasena the king was his father; Suma his mother; Surakkhita and Dhammasena his chief disciples; Sabhiya was his servitor; Cala and Upacala his chief female disciples; and the Amalaka tree his Bo-tree. His body was fifty cubits high, and his age ninety thousand years.

After him ninety world cycles ago, appeared the Blessed One named Vipasin. The city of this Blessed One was called Bandhumati; Bandhuma the king was his father; and Bandhumati his mother; Khanda and Tissa his disciples; Asoka his servitor; Canda and Candamitta his chief female disciples; and the Bignonia his Bo-tree. His body was eighty cubits high; the effulgence from his body always reached a hundred leagues; and his age was a hundred thousand years.

After him, thirty-one world cycles ago, there were two Buddhas called Sikhim and Vessabhu. The city of that Blessed One was Arunavati; Aruna the warrior chief was his father; Parbhavati his mother; Abhibhu and Sambhava his chief disciples; Khemankara his servitor; Makhila and Paduma his chief female disciples; and the Pundanha tree his Bo-tree. His body was thirty-seven cubits high; the effulgence from his body reached three leagues; and his age was thirty-seven thousand years.

After him appeared the Teacher named Vessabhu; the city of this Blessed One was called Anopama; Supatila the king was his father; Yasavati his mother, Sona and Uttara his chief disciples; Upasanta his servitor; Dama and Sumala his chief female disciples; and the Sal-tree his Bo-tree. His body was sixty cubits high; and his age was sixty thousand years.

After him in this world cycle, four Buddhas have appeared, namely Kakusanda, Konagamana, Kassapa, and one other Buddha. The city of Kukusanda the Blessed One was called Khema; Aggidalla the Brahman was his father; Visaha the Brahman woman his mother; Vidura and Sanjivas his chief disciples; Bhisodhya his servitor; Sama and Champaka his chief female disciples; and the great Sirisa tree his Bo-tree. His body was forty cubits high, and his age forty thousand years.

After him appeared the Teacher Konagammana. The city of this Blessed one was called Sobhavati; Yannadatta the Brahmana was his father; Uttarà the Brahman woman was his mother; Bheyyesa and Uttara his chief disciples; Silthija his servitor; Samudda and Uttara his chief female disciples; and the Udumbara tree his Bo-tree. His body was twenty cubits high, and his age was thirty thousand years.

After him the Teacher named Kassapa appeared in the world. The birth place of this Blessed One was called Benares; Brahmadatta the Brahman was his father; Dhanavati of the Brahmana caste his mother; Tissa and Bharadwaja his chief disciples; Sobbamitta his servitor; Anula and Uruvila his chief female disciples: and the Nigradha tree his Bo-tree. His body was twenty cubits high, and his age was twenty thousand years.*

* Shambhu Purana,—a Sanskrit work much revered by the Nepalese Budhists,—gives in brief the accounts of the last six Buddhas as follows.

1. *Bipaschita*.:—It is said that Nepal was originally a marshy

Now after Kassapa, there is no other Buddha beside the present Supreme Buddha. The Bodisat received a proficiency from each of the twenty-four Buddhas beginning at Dipankara.*

The last Buddha, Sidhartha Goutama, was born in the family of the Sakyas. Rhys Davids says :—"They were seated, about 500 years before the birth of Chirist, at a place called Kapilavastu† on the banks of the river Rohini, the modern Kohana,

---

waste; but the Buddha Bipaschita came here with a large number of followers and made it a beautiful and fertile land.

2. *Sikhi* the Buddha also came here and entered Nirvana.

3. *Vishwavu*, the Buddha, did exactly what the No. 2 did.

4. 5. 6. are almost the same as the three others. For fear of repetition we do not give any details of their life.

* Dr. Oldenberg says :—"It could scarcely be otherwise than that the historical form of the one actual Buddha multiplied itself under dogmatic treatment to a countless number of past and coming Buddhas."

Rhys Davids says :—" It is sufficiently evident that nearly all these details are merely imitated from the corresponding details of the legend of Goutama; and it is to say the least, very doubtful whether the tradition of these legendary teachers has preserved for us any grains of historical fact. If not, the list is probably later than the time of Goutama, for while it is scarcely likely that he should have deliberately invented these names, it may well have seemed to later Buddhists very ediying to give such lists and very reasonable to exclude in them the names held in the highest honour by the Brahmans themselves."

† Dr. Oldenburg in his Buddha pp 95-96 says :—"We can point out the native land of Buddha in the map of India with tolerable accuracy. Between the Nepalese lower range of the Himalaya and the middle part of the course of the Rapti, which runs through the north-eastern part of the province of Oudh there stretches a strip of level, fruitful land, some thirty English miles broad, well watered by the numerous streams that issue from the Himalayas. Here lay the not very extensive territory over which the Sakyas claimed supremacy and dominion. On the east the Rohini separated their lands from their neighbours; to this day this stream has preserved the name which it bore more than two thousand years ago. On the west and south the rule of the Sakhyas extended quite up, or nearly so, to the Rapti."

about 100 miles north-east of the city of Benares. That insignificant stream rose thirty or forty miles to the north of their settlement in the spurs of the mighty Himalayas, whose giant peaks loomed up in the distance against the clear blue of the Indian sky. The Sakhyas had penetrated further to the East than most of their fellow Aryans, but beyond them in that direction was the powerful confideration of Lichchavis and the rising kingdom of Magadha. To their north were rude hill tribes of Mongolian extraction, while behind them to the west lay those lands which the Brahmanas held most sacred. Their nearest neighbours to be feared in that direction were the subjects of the king of Sravasti (Kosala), the rival of the king of Magadha. It was this rivalry of their neighbours more than their own strength which secured for the Sakhyas a precarious independence; but their own hand was strong enough to protect them against the incursions of

---

The territory of the Sakhyas included, as far as it appears, according to the present divisions of the land, approximately the following circles belonging to the Gorukpur districts:—Binayakpur, Bacsene and the western half of pergunnah Havili.

See Cunningham's Geography of Ancient India; also Dr. Waddell's Note in I. R. A. S.

The city of Kapilavastu (in Pali, Kapilavastu), was long searched for by archæologists in vain, but is now identified by General Sir A. Cunningham and Mr. Carlleyle with Bhuila, a village surrounded by buried brickwork in the Basti district under the Nepal mountains about twenty five miles northeast from Faizabad, twelve northwest from Basti, and one hundred and twenty north of Benares. Both Fa-hien (Legge, 67) and Hiouen Thsang describe the neighbouring Lumbini (Lavani) garden where the Buddha was born from the right side of his mother. They also mention the Arrow-fountain where Goutama contended with others of his tribe in a shooting-match. The legend is that he gained the victory by shooting an arrow which passed through the target, buried itself in the ground and caused a clear spring of water to flow forth (Legge, 65—67; Beal II. 23—24). This name Sarakupa—"Arrow fountain"—has now been corrupted into Sar-kina, and the spot has been identified.—Sir M. William's Buddhism, p. 388—389.

roving bands from the hills and to sustain them in their quarrels with neighbouring class of the same standing as themselves. They lived from the produce of their cattle and their rice fields, their supplies of water being drawn from the Kohana, on the other side of which stream lived the Koliyans, a kindred tribe.* With them the Sakyas some-

---

* The Kailyans and the Sakhyas were united by marriage, before the birth of Goutama, for his mother was a Kailyan lady. We give below the Genealogical tables of these two clans.

Genealogical Tables of the Sakhyas and Koliyans.

FATHER'S SIDE.

- Jayasena of the Sakhyas.
  - Sinhahaun
    - Sudhadhana.
      - Nanda.
      - Rupananda.
      - Sidhartha Buddha. son of Maya of the Koliyans).
        - RAHULA.
    - Sukladhana
      - Devdatta (monk).
      - Ananda (monk).
    - Amritadhana.
      - Mahavansa.
      - Anuruddha
    - 2 others.
  - Yosadhara.

MOTHER'S SIDE.

- Devadaha of the Kolyans.
  - Anjana
    - Suprabudha.
      - Yosadhara. (wife of Goutama Buddha).
        - RAHULA.
      - Devdatta.
    - Dandapani.
    - MAYA.
    - PRAJAPATI.

      (wives of Sudhadhana).
  - Anusuha.
  - Kausana.

times quarreled for the possession of the precious liquid, but just then the two clans were at peace and two daughters of the raja or chief of the Kailyans were the wives of Sudhadhana, the Raja of the Sakhyas."*

* Sudhadhana was the father of Goutama Buddha. Dr. Oldenberg does not admit that he was a "king."—He says, "A widespread tradition represents Buddha as having been a king's son. At the head of this aristocratic community there must certainly have been some one having been appointed we know not by what rules with the title of king, which can have indicated more than the position of *puinus intor pases*. But the idea that Buddha's father Suddhadhana enjoyed this royal dignity is quite foreign to the oldest forms in which the traditions regarding the family are presented to us ; rather we have nothing more or less to contemplate in Sudhadhana than one of the great and wealthy landowners of the Sakhya race, whom later legends transformed into the great King Suddhadhana."

THE LIFE, TEACHINGS AND ORDER OF

BUDDHA.

PART I.

CHAPTER I.

THE BIRTH OF SIDDHARTHA.

Some two thousand and five hundred years ago in the Full-Moon-Day,' in the beautiful season of Spring, Siddhartha Goutama, the great Buddha, was born.* His father, Sudhadhana† was ever unhappy for the want of a child who would

* We shall try as much as possible to follow the original chroniclers of Buddha's life both in style and form in narrating the biographical portion of his life; for we believe it would be more interesting than what we can give in our own language. In describing the early portion of the great Prophet's life, we shall principally follow "Mahabiniskramana Sutra," (the Book of the Great Renunciation), of which Rhys Davids says:—" The date of this Sanskrit work is unknown; the translation into Chinese was made in the sixth century A. D. The English version by the Reverend Sameul Beal was published in 1875 under the title "Romantic Legend of Sakhya Buddha." It gives an account of Goutama's life down to the time when in his 30th year, he revisited his father's home after openly coming forward as a teacher."

† See Lalita Vistara, Chapter I.

be a glory to his clan and joy to his home.* His two wives, Maya and Prajapati, two affectionate sisters,† grew old, but did not show any sign of giving birth to a child. At last in the

* Following is Dr. Oldenberg's authority for his saying that Sudhadana was not a king. He says,—"The following leads me to deny the antiquity of the tradition which makes Buddha's father a king. When (as in the Sonadanda Sutta of Digha Nikhya) the external claims of Buddha to respectful consideration are discussed it is always admitted merely that he has come of an "*Uchakula,—Bhatteyakula, Addhakula.*" It is emphasized that he, when he entered on a spiritual career, forsook relatives and friends, gold and silver,—the kingly dignity of the family is not alluded to. If any where, it is with reference to a circumstance of this kind, which assuredly could not have been suppressed. To this another consideration must be added. Any one, who knows the uniform care with which the titulary appellation of persons appearing in the Pitakas is observed, will also find this difference decisive that Buddha's father is there merely Suddhadana Sakka (See Mahavagga I. 54; also Mahasakha Sutta); just as mention is made of Anuruddha Sakka, Upananda Sakkaputta &c., while Bhaddika who was really the king of the Sakkas—if we may call this petty Raja a king—is regularly introduced as Bhaddika Sahkaraja (Cullavagga VII. I. 3). Moreover Sudhadhana is addressed "Gotama" (Mahavagga I. c.), as the Mallas are called Vaseltha, the Koliyas Byagghapajja, but no one says to him "Maharaja" as to Bindasara or Pasanadi. The oldest evidence which attributes to Suddhadhana the kingly dignity, as far as I know, the only passage of the kind in the Tipitaka occurred in the Mahapadhana Sutta (Digha Nikaya), where a series of notices of the lives of the last seven Buddhas is thrown together. In a systematic manner, exactly as in the passage apparently modelled on this Sutta (Dipavansa XVII. 3), there is recorded the length of life, the parentage, home, tree of knowledge, Savaka Yaga &c., of these Buddhas. The three first were king's sons, the following three Brahmana's sons, the last is again a king's son, the son of Sudhadhana raja. Possibly similar is the statement also in the concluding portion of the *Buddhavansa*, it would be quite in keeping with the character of these texts: I regret not to be able to make any statement on this part of the said texts as it is not accessible to me at present. There is no need of enlarging to show that in any case evidence of this description must retire before the momenta previously brought to bear on this question."

† See our note in p. 9 Introduction, Chapter VII.

forty-fifth year of her age, Maya promised her husband a son. The news flew from house to house all over the good chieftain's domain, and every one was very happy.

Maya, in accordance to custom,* started for her parent's house. The ancient chronicler says†;—The king ordered that the whole extent of the road between Kapilavastu and Koli should be perfectly levelled and lined on both sides with plantain trees and adorned with the finest ornaments. Jars, full of the purest water, were to be deposited all along the road at short intervals. A chair of gold was made ready for conveying the queen; and a thousand noblemen, attended by an innumerable retinue, were directed to accompany her during her journey. Between the two countries an immense forest of lofty Engyin trees extended to a great distance. As soon as the *cortege* reached it, five water lilies shot forth spontaneously from the stems and the main branches of each tree, and innumerable birds of all kinds, by their melodious tunes, filled the air with the most ravishing music. Trees, similar in beauty to those growing in the seats of gods, apparently sensible of the presence of the incarnated Buddha, seemed to share in the universal joy.

On beholding this wonderful appearance of all the lofty trees of the forest, the queen felt a desire to approach nearer and enjoy the marvellous sight offered to her astonished eyes. Her noble attendants led her forthwith a short distance into the forest. Maya, seated on her couch, along with her sister Prajapati, desired her attendants to have it moved closer to an Engyin tree which she pointed out. Her wishes were immediately complied with. She then rose

---

* See Rhys Davids' Buddhism p. 26. But *Lalita Vistara* says that she went to a beautiful garden-house with the permission of her husband to pass some time there. See Lilata Vistara, Chap. I.

† We quote this description from the Burmese *Mallalinkava Woniho* as translated by Bishop Bigandet See "The Life and Legends of Goudama, the Buddha of the Burmese" pp. 32—33.

gently on her couch; her left hand, clasped round the neck of her sister, supported her in a standing position. With the right hand she tried to reach and break a small branch which she wanted to carry away. On that very instant as the slender ratten, heated by fire, bent down its tender head, all the branches bowed their extremities, offering themselves, as it were, to the hand of the queen who unhesitatingly seized and broke the extremity of one of the young boughs. By virtue of a certain power inherent in her dignity, on a sudden all the winds blew gently throughout the forest. The attendants, having desired all the people to withdraw to a distance, disposed curtains all round the place the queen was standing on. Whilst she was in that position, admiring the slender bough she held in her hands, the moment of her confinement happened, and she was delivered of a son.

Five days after the birth of Buddha,* a great festival was

---

* It is needless to say that all the ancient chroniclers, that write anything about the life of the great Buddha, have narrated innumerable miracles all through his life. They are too numerous to be quoted in this book. But to give an example we quote the following from Bishop Bigandet's excellent work.

"Four chief Brahmanas received the new born infant in a golden net-work and placed him in the presence of the happy mother, saying "Give yourself up, O queen, to joy and rejoicing, here is the precious and wonderful fruit of your womb."

"From the hands of the four chiefs of Brahmanas four chiefs of gods received the blessed child, whom they handed over to men who placed him in a beautiful white cloth. But to the astonishment of all, he freed himself from the hands of those attending upon him and stood in a firm and erect position on the ground; when casting a glance towards the east more than one thousand worlds appeared like a perfectly levelled plain. All the gods inhabiting those worlds made offerings of flowers and perfumes exclaiming with exultation :—'An exalted personage has made his appearance,—who can ever be compared to him, who has ever equalled him? He is indeed the most excellent of all beings.' Phralong (Buddha) looked again towards the three other directions. Raising his eyes upwards and then lowering them down, he saw that there was no

appointed in order that his name might be given; and 108 learned Brahmans were invited to attend; to each of whom the

---

being equal to him. Conscious of his superiority, he jumped over a distance of seven lengths of a foot in a northern direction exclaming "This is my last birth; there shall be to me no other state of existence. I am the greatest of all beings." He then began to walk steadily in the same direction."

Rhys Davids thus gives a summary of these miracles:—"Earth and heaven at his birth united to pay him homage; the very trees bent of their own accord over his mother, and the angels and arch-angels were present with their help."

"After seven days of fasting and seclusion, the pure and holy Maya dreams that she is carried by archangels to heaven and that there the future Buddha enters her right side in the form of a superb white elephant. On her relating her dream to her husband, he calls together five chief Brahmanas to interpret it. Their reply is that the child will be a son who will be a Chakravarti,—a universal monarch; or if he becomes a recluse, he will be a Buddha, who will remove the veils of ignorance and sin from the world."

"At the conception of Buddha thirty-two signs take place; the 10000 worlds are filled with light, the blind receive their sight, the deaf hear, the dumb speak, the crooked become straight, the lame walk, the imprisoned are set free and so on,—all nature blooming and all beings in earth and heaven being filled with joy, while by a bold figure of speech even the fires of hill are extinguished and the tortures of the dammed are mitigated. During the ten months of his life in the womb, the child is distinctly visible, sitting crosslegged unsoiled and dignified, and he preaches to the angels who guard him, stretching out his hand to do so without wounding his mother.

"As a dagoba holding sacred relics cannot be used to guard any less sacred objects, so his mother can bear no other child and on the seventh day after his birth she dies. When the child is born, it takes seven steps forward and exclaims with lion's voice, 'I am the chief of the world; this is my last birth; and again the thirty signs of joy appear in the earth and heaven.

An aged saint, who had retired for meditation to the Himalaya mountains seeing these signs, is guided to Kapilavastu and the child is brought in to do him reverence, but instead of doing so, its feet were miraculously placed on the matted locks of the ascetic. The sage then

king gave an offering of food.* The Brahmans collected at the festival said, "This prince will hereafter be a blessing to the world (Siddhartha)," in consequence of which he was called "Siddhartha."†

The 80000 relatives of the prince, who were present on the day he was named, reflected that if he were to become a Chakravati,‡ he would require a retinue, and that if he were to become a Buddha, he would be attended by royal priests; so that in either case, their children might through him obtain great

---

explains the wonder to the astonished father and prophesies that the child will become a Buddha and weeps that he himself will not live to see the day."

"On the fifth day the name-choosing festival takes place when 108 Brahmans learned in the three Vedas of whom eight were specially learned in divination, are feasted at the palace. Seven of the eight, after examining the marks in the child's body, hold up two fingers and prophesy that he will become either a Chakravarti or a Buddha, but one Kondanya, afterwards Gotamas' first disciple, holds up one finger and prophesies that he will assuredly become a Buddha, who will remove the veils of sin and ignorance from the world."

"Then comes the story of the ploughing festival. The great king Suddhadhana goes out to celebrate the opening of the season, and the prince is taken with him. In the rejoicing the baby is neglected. It then seats itself cross-legged on the couch and falls into the mystic trance of Dhyana. Though the shadows of all other trees had turned, the tree under which the child sat still shaded it."

* This is quoted from Hardy's Manual of Buddhism pp. 148—151.

† Rhys Davids says :—"Even the name Sidhartha, said to have been given him as a child, may have been a subsequent invention. His family name was certainly Gotama." See his Buddhism, pp 27. But we do not understand why such a common name as Sidhartha should have been an invention. We find in the Pali works, there were many others who were called Sidhartha. The followers of the great master gave him many other names, such as Sakhya Singha, Sakhya Muni, Sugata, (the happy are) Satha, (the teacher) Jina (the conqueror), Bhagava (the blessed one) Lokenath (the Lord of the world), Sarvajna (the omniscient) Dharmaraja (the king of righteousness) and many more too numerous to mention.

‡ Chakravarti means the king of all the kings.

advantage. They therefore sent their sons to be educated with him as his companions.

In order to procure a proper nurse for his son, Suddhadhana assembled the princesses of the two cities of Kapilavastu and Koli. "She was not to be tall, or else the neck of the infant would be stretched; nor too short, or his body would be bent; nor too large, or his legs would be contracted; nor too weak, or his body would not acquire firmmess; nor of too full a habit, or her milk would be hot and cause his skin to become red; nor of too dark a complexion, or her milk would be cold and cause his flesh to be in lumps in some parts hard and in others soft." One hundred princesses were at last chosen free from these faults.

——:o:——

CHAPTER II.

HIS YOUTH.

The great astrologers said, "The lot of one possessed of these marks will not be cast amidst the cares of household life. Verily he will become a Buddha."

And the king asked, "After seeing what, will my son forsake the world?"

"The four Visions," was the reply.

"What are they?" asked the King.

"A man worn-out by age," replied the Brahman,"—a man ill,—a dead body,—and a monk."

The King thought, "From this time let no such things come near my son. There is no good my son's becoming a Buddha. I should like to see my son exercising rule and sovereignty over the four great continents and the two thousand islands that surround them." So saying, he placed guards two miles apart in the four directions to prevent men of these four kinds coming to the sight of his son.*

The king went further. As soon as Siddhartha grew to manhood, he got him married to Yasodhara, the princess of Koli.† He made for him three royal palaces,—"one nine storeys high,—one seven storeys high,—and one five storeys high." So that his mind be immersed in pleasures, he provided him with forty thousand beautiful dancing girls.‡ And Siddhartha Goutama, surrounded by this troop of beauties, lived in the enjoyment of great luxury.

The ancient chronicler says:—"The King appointed Yasodhara to be the principal queen of Siddhartha; and placing the prince and the princess upon a throne of silver, he placed the veil of consecration upon them from three conchs,—one of gold, another of silver and the third of shell. Afterwards he bound upon their head the royal diadem and delivered on to them the whole of his kingdom. He then sent for all his relatives, commanding them to bring their princesses so that they might be the inferior wives of Siddhartha. The relatives replied:—"The prince is very delicate, he is also young. Even to this day he has not learnt a single science. If hereafter there should be any war, he would be unable to contend with the enemy. He has not the means of maintaining our daughters. We cannot, therefore, consent to send them to one who is so utterly destitute of every endowment that he ought to possess."

"When the prince heard this, he resolved to exhibit his real strength, and asked it to be proclaimed throughout the city by beat of drum, that whosoever might be wishful to see his powers was invited to come to the palace in seven

---

* See *Nidankatha* as translated by Rhys Davids in his "Buddhist Birth Stories" pp. 73—74.

† See Hardy's Manual of Buddhism pp. 152—153.

‡ They are called *Nataka-Stri*, literally dancing-woman, but it is evident that they were considered as inferior wives.

days from that time. On the day appointed, an immense pavilion was erected and a vast multitude assembled in the court of the palace. Surrounded by a countless retinue and in the presence of 160000 of his relations, he took a bow that required the strength of a thousand men to bend it, and placing the lower end in the nail of the great tow of his right foot, without standing up, he thrummed the string of the bow with his finger nail easily, as if it were merely the bow by which cotton is cleansed. The sound produced by the vibration of the strain was so loud that it rolled to the distance of a thousand *Yoyanas* and the terror seized hold upon the inhabitants of Jamvudwipa as they supposed that it thundered, though it was not the season of rain. After this he placed four plantain trees at the corner of a square. By one flight of the arrow he pierced them all. Even in the dark he could send the arrow with so steady an aim as to split a hair from which any thing was suspended. The prince also proved that he knew perfectly the eighteen *Shilpas* though he never had a teacher* and that he was equally well acquainted with many other Sciences. The relatives were thus convinced by what they saw and heard that he was no ordinary being, and soon afterwards 40,000 princesses were sent to remain in the apartments of the palace."†

---

* It is said in the *Malinda Prasna* that Sudanta became the preceptor of the Prince and that he was succeeded in his office by the learned Brahman Subbamitta upon whose hands the king poured water when he delivered him into his charge as a token that he was entirely resigned to his care until he had acquired the knowledge it was necessary for him to know; while in other works it is said that he had no teacher at the time of his marriage. Nagasena says he had five preceptors. (Hardy's Manual of Buddhism p. 153.) It is evident Buddha was under some Teacher or Teachers when he was a boy.

† Dr. Oldenberg says:—"We are told that the coming Buddha was married, but whether to one or to several wives is not known." But we find no reason to disbelieve the fact that he had but only one

wife. As Rhys Davids agrees with our views, we quote his note on the point in *extenso*.

"The Southern Buddhists agree in saying that Goutama had only one wife; they give different names, but mean the same person. She is called Yasodhara by Bigandet (see his Life and Legend of Buddha p. p. 24·54·124) and the same by Hardy who adds that she was the daughter of Suprabindha (See his Manual of Buddhism p.p. 146·152·206), but she is usually called simply Rahula Mata, the mother of Rahula, in the oldest authorities (see Jatakas 54, 6· 58, 18· 90, 24· Venaya Texts Vol. I, p. 108). The name of Subhadracansana is a mere mistake for Subhadrasansana and is there stated to be the same as Yasodhara.

"The Chinese Life gives three wives, *viz*. Yasodhara, the mother of Rahula, Goutami and Monohara. The Chinese editor significantly adds concerning the last, "Some Doctors of the Law say that the attendants on Monohara only knew her name, but never saw her presence," and this evidently mythical person is never mentioned elsewhere. Goutami is the name used only in one story which does not occur in any other authority and the epithet would be applicable of course to every member of the Goutuma clan, as Prajapati for instance is also called Goutami. Goutami is made the daughter of Dandapani, while Yasodhara, the only wife who appears throughout the book, is made the daughter of Mahanama.

"The Lalit Vistara speaks only of one wife Gopa, the daughter of Dandapani, and relates of her the stories which are related elsewhere of Yasodhara, but Fancaux in a Note to p. 152 of his work says that Goutama had three wives, namely Yasodhara, Mrigaya or Gopa and Utpalvarna; of the last he gives one detail which identifies her with Yasodhara, namely that she and Prajapati were the first Buddhist nuns.

—:O:—

CHAPTER III.

FOUR VISIONS.

One day Siddhartha Goutama, wishing to go to his pleasure gardens, told his charioteer to harness his chariot. The latter accordingly decked the gloriously beautiful chariot with all its trappings and harnessed to it four State horses. The future Buddha then ascended the chariot and went towards the beautiful gardens.

When he had gone a few steps, he saw before him an old man passing by with difficulty, borne down as he was by old age and decrepitude.* Seeing him, he thus asked the charioteer:—†

"O charioteer, who is this weak and lean man? His flesh has been withered away, his bones and arteries are visible under the covering of his skins, his hair is white, his teeth are gone, he goes tottering bent on his stick?"

"Finally Alexander Cosma, the great authority on Tibetian Buddhism, mentions three wives and names them Gopa, Yasodhara, and Utpalvarna, but states elsewhere that the first two are the same, and in another place that the name of the third was Mrigaya.

"All this seems to be explicable on a very natural hypothesis. The oldest accounts agree in giving to Goutama, one wife. (See Buddhism, pages 50—51). For the Genealogy of Yasodhara see page 57 Int.

* We give this chapter from *Lalita Vistara*. We shall quote the Gathas (verses) which Buddha said and the charioteer uttered in reply.

† किं सारथे पुरुषदुर्ब्बल अल्पस्थाम
उच्छुष्कमांसरुधिरत्वच स्नायुनद्धः ।
श्वेतशिरो विरलदन्तकृशाङ्गरूप
आलम्ब दण्डब्रजरेह सुखं स्खलन्त ॥

The charioteer thus replied :—*

"Sire, this is an old man. His body has grown debilated, his senses have become weak. He is now quite unfit for work and is thoroughly helpless. His friends and relatives have abondoned him as a withered tree by the birds and beasts."

The prince then said in great sorrow :—† "O charioteer, tell me truly, is this state his own individual occurrence, or is it the universal law? Tell me soon its real cause, so that I can think over this matter."

The charioteer replied :—‡ "Sire, it is the universal Law of Nature. Every man, woman or child would come to this state. Your parents, your relations, you yourself, all must come to it."

"Shame then to life!" Saying this, he ordered his charioteer to turn back towards home. He did not that day go to the pleasure gardens.

---

* एषोहि देव पुरुषो ज्वराभिभूतः
क्षीणेन्द्रियः सुदुःखितो बलवीर्य्यहीनो
बन्धुजनेन परिभूत अनाथभूतः
कार्य्यासमर्थं अपविद्ध वनेवदारु ॥

† कुलधर्म्म एष अयमस्य हितं भणाहि
अथवाऽपि सर्व्वंजगतोऽस्य इयं ह्यवस्था
शीघ्रं भणाहि वचनं यथभूत मेतच्छ्रुत्वा
तथार्थंमिह योनि सञ्चिन्तयिष्ये।

‡ नैतस्य देव कुलधर्म्म न राष्ट्रधर्म्मः सर्व्वे
जगस्य जरयौवन धर्षयति
तुभ्यंपि मातृपितृबान्धवज्ञातिसङ्घो
जरया अमुक्तं नहि अन्यगतिर्जनस्य।

When the king his father heard this, he asked, "Why does my son turn back so hurriedly?"

"He has seen an old man;" they said, "and having seen him, he has come back."

"By this you ruin me!" exclaimed the king, "Quickly get-ready concerts and plays. So long as he continues in the enjoyment of pleasure, he will not turn his thoughts to forsaking the world."

A few days later, Siddhartha again started for his pleasure gardens and again turned back. He saw before him a man lying ill on the way-side forsaken and abandoned by all. Seeing him he thus asked his charioteer:—*

"Charioteer, who is this man, who is a mere skeleton, in appearance lying in his own excreta, groaning so in pain?"

The charioteer replied:—†

"Sire, this man is ill; he is at the point of death and is now in great sufferings. There is no cure for him, and no hope for him; he will soon die?"

The prince came back to his palace morose and sad. A few days after he again went out and saw a large body

---

* किं सारथे पुरुषरूपविवर्णगात्र:
सर्वेन्द्रियेभिविकलो गुरुप्रश्वसस्त:
सर्वाङ्गशुष्क उदराकुलप्रासकृच्छ्रा
मूत्रे पुरीष स्वकि तिष्ठती कुत्सनीये ।

† एषो हि देव पुरुष: परमं गिलानो
व्याधिभयम् उपगतो मरणान्तप्राप्त:
आरोग्य तेजरहितो बलविप्रहीनो
अत्राण वीप्रशरणो ह्यपरायणश्च ।

of men carrying a dead body. On seeing it he asked :—* "Charioteer, what is this? Why are they carrying a man on a cot? Why are the people following him with dishevelled hair? Why are they weeping and crying striking their breast?"

The charioteer replied :—†

"Sire, this man is dead! He will never again see his parents, sons, friends and relations. He is gone for ever from this world."

On hearing this the prince sighed and said ;—‡

"Shame to youth which will end in old age! Shame to

---

* किं सारथे पुरुष मञ्चोपरि गृहितो
उद्धृत केशनखपांशुभिरे क्षिपन्ति
परिचारयित्व विहरन्तुवक्षाड़योन्तो
नानाविलापवचनानि उदीरयन्तः।

† एषो हि देव पुरुषो मृत्यु जम्बुद्वीपे
नहि भूय मातृपितृद्रक्ष्यति पुत्त्रदारां
अपहाय भोगगृहमातृमित्त्रज्ञातिसङ्ग
परलोक प्राप्तु नहि द्रक्ष्यति भूय ज्ञातिम्।

‡ धिगयौवनेन जरया समभिद्रुतेन
आरोग्य धिग्विविधव्याधिपराहतेन
धिग् जीवितेन पुरुषो नचिरस्थितेन
धिक् पण्डितस्य पुरुषस्य रतिप्रसङ्गैः!
यदि जर न भवया नैव व्याधिर्न मृत्यु
स्तथापि च महद्दुःखं पञ्चस्कन्धं धरन्तो
किं पुनः ज्वरव्याधिमृत्युनित्यानुबद्धाः
साधु प्रतिनिवर्त्त्य चिन्तयिष्ये प्रमोचं!

health which is surrounded by innumerable diseases! Shame to the learned man who plunges in pleasure!

He came back to his palace and did not see any one for days together. He then once more came out and went towards his pleasure gardens, but saw a monk passing by. On seeing him, he thus asked his charioteer.*

"Charioteer, who is this man clad in yellow clothes walking by peaceful, calm and gentle, never looking up or to any thing?"

The charioteer replied:—†

"Sire, he is a mendicant. He has abandoned all desires. He has left the world. He looks every one with equal eyes. He lives upon alms."

The prince said:—‡

"Yes, I like this. The learned men always praise such a life. This is the happiest of all lives,"

---

* किं सारथे पुरुष शान्तप्रशान्तचित्तो
न्योत्क्षिप्तचक्षु व्रजते युगमात्रदर्शी
काषाय वस्त्रवसनो सुप्रशान्तचारी
पात्रं गृहीत्वं स च उद्धत उन्नतो वा।

† एषो हि पुरुष इति भिक्षुनामा
अपहार कामरतय सुविनीतचारी
प्रवंज्य प्राप्त सममात्मन एषमाणो
संरागद्वेषविगतो तिष्ठति पिन्डचर्य्यां।

‡ साधु सुभाषितमिदं मम रोचते च
प्रव्रज्य नाम विदुभिः सततं प्रशस्ता
हितमात्मनश्च पवसत्वहितञ्च यत्र
सुखजीवितं सुमधुरनमृतफलञ्च।

He asked his charioteer to turn back, and he returned to his palace.*

---

* Dr. Oldenberg does not believe that the four visions as narrated by the ancient chroniclers did really take place. He says :—"A later age desired to see illustrated in concrete occurrences, how for the first time and with impressive power the thoughts of old age, disease and death crept over the young man, healthy and in the freshness of life, and how he was directed by some insignificant example to that path which leads away beyond the power of all suffering. Thus was invented or rather transferred to the youth of Goutama, a legend which was narrated of one of the legendary Buddhas of by-gone ages—the familiar history of the four drives of the youth, to the garden outside the town, during which the pictures of the impermanence of everything earthly presented themselves to him one after the other in the form of a helpless old man, a sick person and a dead body and at last a religious mendicant with shaven head wearing yellow garment meets him—a picture of peace and deliverance from all pain of impermanence. In that way later tradition concocted this narrative preparatory to the flight of Goutama from his home."

To substantiate his theory, Oldenburg quotes the following from the Pali Texts.

सुखुमालो आहां भिक्खाभे पारामासुखु मालो आक्कातासुखुमालो। मामा सुखुं भिक्काभे पितु निभेसेने पोख्खाराणिओ ह्मरियाका हस्ति, एकाट्टा पुन्नारिकं याभाड एभाम आट्टाहाया। नाखोपाना एस आहां भिख्खाभे खासिकां कानडानां धारेमि, कासिकां भिख्खाभे सु मि तं तेथानं हटि कासिखा कानसुखा कासिकां निभासानां कासिको उत्तरासाह्दो।

(See Anuguttara Nikaya Vol. I).

Dr. Oldenberg then remarks :—"Now follows the narrative, how the thought of old age, disease and death is awakened in him, therewith ends the part of that text bearing in this matter. Let it be observed that the origin of these thoughts is not here attributed to an external occurrence like the well-known four excursions. The history of these excursions has been transferred to the later legends as is almost expressly stated in the Jataka in page 59 from the Mahapadhanasutta

CHAPTER IV.

KISAGOTAMI AND THE DANCING GIRLS.

The ancient chronicler says:— Arrayed in all his splendours—the musicians exhibiting each one his peculiar skill, the Brahmans honouring him with words of joy and victory, and the men of lower castes with festive cries and shouts of praise,—Siddhartha Goutama ascended his superbly decorated car in order to return to the city from his pleasure grounds.

At that time Suddhadhana the king heard that Yasodhara had given birth to a son, and sent a message to him saying "Make known my joy to my son." The future Buddha, as he was ascending the chariot, heard this news aud said sadly, "An impediment has come into being—a new bond has come into existence!"

When the messenger returned, the king eagerly asked "What did my son say?" And the messenger replied, "The Prince said, "a Rahula (impediment) has come into being." On hearing this, the king gave this command, "Henceforth let Rahula be my grandson's name."

But young Goutama returned home thoughtful and sad. The villagers were delighted at the birth of the child, their king's only grandson. Goutama's return therefore became an ovation, and he entered Kapilavastu amidst a crowd of rejoicing clansmen. Among the sounds of triumph which greeted his ear, one specially is said to have attracted his attention!*

(Digha Nikaya) where it is introduced as referring to the Buddha Vipassi. Of Gotama Buddha the excursions are as far as I know never narrated in the Tripitaka."

* See Nidan Katha, Buddhist Birth Stories, pages, 80—82.

The original of the song is the following:—

निब्भूत नून समाता

A noble vergin, his causin, Kisa Goutami by name, had gone to the upper storey of her palace to see the prince pass by, and she beheld the beauty and majesty of Goutama. Pleased and delighted at the sight, she burst forth into this song of joy.

" Blessed indeed is that mother,
Blessed indeed is that father,
Blessed indeed is that wife,
Who owns this Lord so glorious !*

Hearing this, the young prince thought to himself, " On seeing such a one, the heart of his mother is made happy, the heart of his father is made happy, the heart of his wife is made happy. This is what she says ! She speaks of HAPPINESS ! But by what means this HAPPINESS and PEACE are gained ? Sweet is the lesson this song makes me hear !"

Then taking from his neck a string of pearls worth a hundred thousand, he sent it to Kisa Goutami. Delighted at this she thought, " Prince Siddhartha has fallen in love with me." But the prince took no further notice of her and went to his palace.

निब्भूत नून सपिता
निबृभूत नून सनारी
यस्य यन इ दिस पति ।

Nibbhuta means Nirvana as well as happiness.

* Rhys Davids thus comments on the verse recited by Kisa Goutami. "The force of the passages is due to the fullness of meaning which to the Buddhist, the words *Nibbuta* and *Nibbana* convey. No words in western languages cover exactly the same ground or conote the same ideas. To explan them fully to any one unfamiliar with Indian modes of thought would be difficult any where and impossible in a note ; but their meaning is pretty clear from the above sentences. See Buddhist Birth stories page 80.

Thereupon women, clad in beautiful attires, skillful in dance and song and lovely as heavenly virgins, brought their musical instruments, and ranging themselves in order danced and sang and played delightfully. But the Prince, his heart being estranged from all worldly matters, took no pleasure in them and fell asleep.

The women on seeing him asleep said, "He for whose sake we were performing is gone to sleep? Let us sleep too." They then laid aside their musical instruments and lay down to sleep.

At dead of night Siddhartha Goutama awoke and sat up; the lamps, fed with sweet-smelling oil, were just burning out. He saw before him a scene which filled him with disgust. He saw the women lay asleep scattered all over the room,—their hair dishevelled, their dress in disorder;—some foaming at the mouth, some grinding their teeth, some yawning, some muttering in their sleep, and some gaping.

Seeing this woful change in their appearance, he became very much disgusted with lust and luxury. To him that magnificent appartment seemed to be a charnel-house full of loathsome corpses. Life, whether in the worlds subject to passions, or in the worlds of form, or in the world formless, seemed to him like staying in a house that had become the prey of devouring flames. An utterance of intense feeling broke out from him. "It all oppresses me! It is intolerable!"

He got up and went to the door and called out, "Who is there?"

Channa, who had been sleeping in the ante-room, answered. "It is I, Sir, Channa."

"I am resolved, beloved Channa, to accomplish today the great renunciation—saddle me a horse."

Finding from his appearance that it was useless to stop him, Channa went to the stable yard and saw by the light of the lamp he carried the mighty steed named Kantaka standing quietly at a splendid spot. "This is the very steed I should saddle today," thought he and saddled Kantaka.

—:o:—

CHAPTER V.

HIS THOUGHTS.

What is the reason that led Goutama to abondon his home, his wife and child? Are the four visions,—the words of Kisa Goutami and the disgusting appearance of the dancing girls—the sole causes of his great renunciation? What were his thoughts before he left the house. Oldenberg says :—* "We can very readily understand how in the oppressive monotony of idle ease and satiated enjoyment, there may have come directly over an earnest and vigourous nature a mood of restlessness, the thirst for a career and a struggle for the highest aims and the despair at the same time to find anything to assuage that thirst in the empty world of transitory pleasure. Who knows anything of the form which these thoughts may have assumed in the mind of the youth and how far the impulse which pervaded that age and led men and women to leave house for an ascetic life, acting from without upon these inner predispositions may have influenced him also?"

Rhys Davids says :—† "The mere sight of an old man, diseased stranger, or even of a dead body, would be insufficient of itself to work so powerful an effect on the mind of

---

* See Oldenberg's Buddha, page 101.

† See his Buddhism pages 29—30.

one who was not already keenly sensible to the mysteries of sorrow and of death. But we find in this ancient tradition an expression of what in the main we must ourselves believe to be the true explanation of the cause which induced Goutama to abandon his family and his home. He was probably not the first,—he was certainly not the last,—who in the midst of prosperity aud comfort has felt a yearning and a want which nothing could satisfy and which has robbed of their charm all earthly gains and hopes. This vague disaffection deepens with every fresh proof of the apparent vanity of life and does not lose but gain in power when, as is reported in the case of Goutama, it arises more from sympathy with the sorrows of others than from any personal sorrow of one's own. At last the details of daily life became insupportable and the calm life of the hermit troubled with none of these things seems a haven of peace where a life of self denial and earnest meditation may lead to some solution of the strange enigmas of life."

Now let us see what Buddha himself said about his thoughts before his great renunciation. He thus spoke to his disciples after describing the luxuries that surrounded him in his palaces :—

" My disciples, with such wealth was I endowed and in such great magnificence did I live. Then these thoughts arose within me :—A weak minded, every day man, although he himself is liable to decay and is not free from the power of old age, feels horror, revulsion and disgust if he sees another person in old age ; the horror he then feels recoils on himself. I also am subject to decay and am not free from the power of old age. Should I also who am subject to decay and am not free from the power of old age, feel horrors, revulsion and disgust if I see another in old age ? This would not be becoming to me ?' Whilst I thus reflected, my disciples, in my own mind, all that buoyancy of youth which dwells in the young sank within me. While I, my disciples, thus reflected in my mind all that spirit of life which dwells in life, sank within me."

We who believe in Karma say that Buddha was led to the renunciation by the Karma of his previous births. He left home, because his Karma destined him to be the great Buddha. At the time when Buddha was born, India was passing through a great religious revolution.* The Vedic religion of the Brahmans had been much weakened by the metaphysics of the Upanishads. The Brahmans were engaged in Vedic Sacrifices, but there was another class of men,—from all the four castes,—who passed by these sacrifices,—engaged in meditation and found out the cause of the Universe and the nature of man. Various men of the class promulgated various means for salvation, for the cessation of pain and misery, and for the final emancipation from the bonds of rebirths. Amongst these the abandonment of home and family and renunciation of the world were the most prominent. Men, young as as well as old, fled from their homes and passed their times in the recesses of the deep forests or in the caves of inaccessible hills and mountains. They passed their life either in meditation or in austerities in the hope of finally acquiring Salvation.

Buddha was not the only prince of his time who left luxury and pleasure behind and lived the life of a beggar to get eternal Peace. In fact when Buddha was born, it was the rage of the time;—it had almost grown to be a fashion for men to don the garb of an ascetic and roam over the country. When Siddhartha Goutama left his wife and child, his palace and abundance, he had no idea,—no ambition,—to be the Buddha,—to be the Saviour of Mankind. He was disgusted with worldly luxuries and pleasures, he felt keenly the existence of the miseries that visit man at every step. He was alarmed of the old age, disease and death, and fled

---

* See Introduction.

from his house to escape, and if possible, to get rid of them. And he met with disappointment after disappointment in his search for Eternal Peace. It was then that his thoughts turned towards Buddhahood which he finally attained.

Thus it was that circumstances led him to what he became. Thus it was that Karma of his previous births made him in this birth the great Buddha which he was in course of becoming through many previous births.

——:o:——

CHAPTER VI.

THE GREAT RENUNCIATION.

Whilst Channa was absent in the stable preparing the horse, Siddhartha thought of seeing his wife and child for the last time. He went to the apartment of Yasodhara, and opening the door he saw his beloved wife lying on a couch surrounded by flowers. She was asleep,—her hand embracing the infant. The prince saw that in order to take up his son, he must remove the mother's arm which would cause her to awake. He knew if she awoke, she would beseach him, tears in her eyes, not to abandon her. This might shake his resolution. He therefore remained on the threshhold, took a last loving look of his wife and child, and withdrew his foot from the door. He then descended to the courtyard of the palace.

Riding on the steed Kantaka, he left the city at the dead of night, Channa accompanying him. He did not stop till he arrived at the bank of the Aroma. At this place, he presented the horse together with all his ornaments to Channa and gave him permission to return. But Channa expressed his desire to accompany him and to abandon the world. Siddhartha promised to fulfill his wishes at some future date and strongly urged him to go back to Kapilavastu. "Go, Channa," said he, "and inform my father, my mother Prajapati, my wife, and the people of the city that I have become an ascetic. Ask them not to be sorry for me." The noble Channa began to weep, but he was at last prevailed upon by the prince to return to the city, and he went away weeping.

The prince then cut off his hair by his own sword, and meeting a poor man on the road exchanged his robe with him. Then as a beggar and a mendicant he walked on towards the city of Rajagriha.*

Round this city, the Capital of the kingdom of Magadha,—one of the biggest and most important city then in India,—were many hills,† on which lived some of the most famous Brahman philosophers and learned men,—men who knew all about religion, and professed to point out the path of Salvation. When he arrived at Rajagriha, his appearance created a great sensation. He was every inch a prince,—both in look and in

---

* For the description of Rajagriha, See General Cunningham's Ancient Geography of India pp. 462—468. Hamilton's Gazetteer says :—"This place is still known by the name of Rajgir and is situated about sixteen miles south of the town of Behar. It was abandoned by Asoka, and when visited by Fa Hian was entirely desolate and uninhabited, though a few Buddhistical remains could be traced. The surrounding country is covered with a great variety of ruins. It is a celebrated place of Hindu pilgrimage and is also honoured by the Jains who every year resort thither in great numbers, and have built temples in the five hills by which the valley is surrounded. In 1811 there was a Hindu hermit here who had seated himself in the open gallery of a thatched hut where he sat all day in the posture in which Buddha is represented, without motion or speech."

† The city of Rajagriha was surrounded by five hills which were called ni the Mahabharata Vaihara, Varaba, Vrishava, Rithi-Giri, and Chaitaka.

mein. However meanly garbed he was, the attention of the people was naturally drawn towards him.

The people talked among themselves ; some said, "he was Indra, the king of gods ;" the others said, " How do you talk ? How could he be Indra ? Where are his elephant and discus ? He must certainly be the Maha Brahma"*

The citizens then went to their king Bimbasara and informed him that a mysterious being had arrived in the city. The king went to the place where Buddha was then staying and asked him who he was. When he was informed that he was but a poor mendicant ascetic, he offered him immense wealth and invited him to live in his city. But Buddha declined his kind offer with thanks, and leaving the city he went to the hill where the learned Brahman philosophers lived.†

——:o:——

CHAPTER VII.

THE GREAT STRUGGLE.

He attached himself first to one of these great Brahman Teachers, named Alara ; but soon finding that he had only learning, and not salvation to give away to his pupils, he went to another named Udraka. He learned under him all that the

---

* See Hardy's Manual of Buddhism, pp 161—162.

† When Goutama left home to lead a hermit's life, he was 29 years of age. His chroniclers says :—

" The ascetic Goutama has gone from home into homelessness while still young, young in years, in the bloom of youthful strength, in the first freshness of life. The ascetic Goutama, although his parents did not wish it, although they shed tears and wept, has had his hair and beard shaved, has put on yellow garments and has gone from his home into homelessness."

Brahman Philosophy had to teach about this world or the next.

RHYS DAVIDS writes:—"One of the most frequently inculted tenets of the Brahmans was a belief in the efficacy of penance as a means of gaining superhuman power and insight, and when Goutama, after studying the systems of Alara and Udraka, was still unsatisfied, he resolved to go apart and see what progress he could himself make by this much-vaunted method. He withdrew accordingly into the jungles of Uruvela,* and there for six years, attended by five faithful disciples,† he gave himself up to the severest penances until he was wasted away to a shadow by fasting and self-mortification."‡

The ancient chronicler says:—The prince reflected that by living in this easy manner, he was not taking the proper course and that he must endure hardships of a kind much more severe. "If I receive," he thought, "as much food as a Sessamum seed in size, it would be sufficient. I require nothing more." By rejecting all solid food, his body became of a dark colour and the thirty-two signs disappeared. From the same cause, though he had previously the strength of ten kotis and ten thousand elephants, he was now so reduced as to be unable to stand; and one night, after walking and meditating until the third watch, he fell senseless to the ground.

He then gave up all penances. He found that penances and austerities could not lead a man to Salvation. Disappointed and disgusted,—with pain and sorrow,—he gave up his hard penances; and the labours of six long years came to naught.

---

* Uruvela is near modern Buddha Gaya.

† Their names were Kowdanya, Bhaddaj, Mahanama, Wappa, and Assaji.

‡ See Rhys Davids' Buddhism, p. 34—35.

When he was almost dying of starvation, a villager's daughter named Sujata came to him and nursed him with food. Buddha never forgot her kindness and said in his dying moment that her food was the best that was ever offered to him, for after pertaking of her food, he attained to Buddhahood.

When he regained his strength, he again took up his bowl and robes. Seeing this, his five followers, who stuck to him for the last six years, left him in disgust, saying among themselves, Goutama has fallen from the path of righteousness; he has become a heretic.

"When sympathy would have been most welcome, he found his friends falling away, his disciples leaving him. On the very day when his followers had gone, he wandered out towards the banks of the Niranjana,* receiving his morning meal from the hands of good Sujata. He sat himself down to eat it under the shade of a large tree† to be known from that time as the Sacred Bo-tree.‡

---

* This river is now called Falgu.

† Ficus religious &c.

‡ See Rhys David's Buddhism pp. 38—39. It stood in modern Buddha Gya. Hamilton's Gazetteer says:—"This country was afterwards called Buddha Gya. It was completely deserted when visited by Fa Hian who calls it Kia—Ye. Hieung Thsang says that the town is situated in a very strong position, but he found very few inhabitants. A few hundred yards west of the Niranjana river in a plain of great extent, about five miles from Gya proper, there are remarkable remains, that now consist of confused heaps of brick and stone exhibiting traces of having been once regularly arranged. There is a building called the temple of Buddha, built of brick and lofty, resembling at a distance a huge glass-house (probably a dagoba) and now so honey-combed with age as to excite surprise that it continues erect. The religion of Buddha may be considered as completely extinct in this neighbourhood, but a few pilgrims came occasionally from distant countries to visit its monuments. On the terrace behind the temple, a Pipul tree is growing which the Hindus suppose to have been planted

by Brahma. It is supposed by the Buddhists that it is exactly in the centre of the earth. In 1812 this tree was in full vigour and appeared to be 100 years of age, but a similar one may have existed in the same place when the temple was entire;—a circular elevation of brick has been raised round its root in various eccentric circles, and on one end of these has been placed a confused heap of images and carved fragments of stone taken from the rivers. Indeed the number of images scattered about this place for 15 or 20 miles in all directions is almost increditable, yet they all appear to have originally belonged to the great temple or its vicinity which seems to have been the grand quary for the whole, and carried from thence to different places. Many of these are now worshipped by the Brahmanical Hindus. Besides inscriptions establishing the Buddhist origin of many of these images, they may be distinguished by the enormous size and destension of their ears and also by a mark on the palm of the hand and soles of the feet."

Asiatic Researches Vol. X X writes :—" In 1833 Buddha Gya was visited by two Burmese Envoys from the king of Ava accompanied by Captain G. Burney. In the 20th Vol of the Asiatic Researches there is a translation of an inscription in the Burmese language discovered at that time in the court of the monastry called Guru Mat. The translation is by Captain Burney who transmitted it to the Bengal Asiatic Society with a translation of the Report made by the Vakils to the king together with a copy of a picture representing the Pipul tree and the surrounding scenery made by a Burmese painter in the suite of the Vakils. A *fac simile* of the inscription appears in the Researches, but the picture is not given. The Vakils write to the king thus :—" Proposing to invite a piece from the western branch of Buddha's excellent tree to proceed to the Burmese kingdom to the spot where religion shines and the protector of religions dwells, your Majesty's slave Mengyee-Maha-tsee-thoo, walked round the tree from the right to the left and poured out some rose-water, when owing to the great virtues of your Majesty, worthy to be styled the Protector of Religion, your slave beheld within the brick platform of five gradations which surround the body of the tree as high up as the branches strike off, what was wonderful, having never happened before, most curious and most excellent, and what contradicts the common saying that a small Pipul tree does not grow under a large one; it was a Buddha's adorable tree, of the size of a Chinese needle, with only four leaves and evidently produced by and of the same constituent part as the large Buddha's excellent tree. Delighted with joy, your Majesty's slave repeated his solemn appeal and carefully gathered this plant. It is growing in your slave's possession, but in consequence of the stem and leaves being very tender, it cannot now be forwarded to your Majesty." The Junior Envoy says in his Journal :—"The principal guardian of the tree, Mahunt Jogee, told me that the Engliish Chief has given him 27 villages contiguous to Buddh's tree and that he lives on the revenue derivable from the same. He occupied a three storeyed brick house all his disciples and subordinate Jogees living in the lawn and uppermost portions of it. On asking him how many disciples and followers he had, he said upwards of 500, some near him and some at a distance. The circumference of Buddh's tree on a line with the top of the encircling brick platform of five gradations which forms its throne and and is 35 cubits high, measured 19 cubits and 10 finger's breadh. The tree rises 44 cubits above the brick platform. From the top of the tree to the terrace on the ground on the eastern side may be 80 cubits or a little more, apparentlythe boughs and small branches which once grew upwards, have in consequence of the great age of the tree spread out literally, and this is the reason why the present height of the tree does not correspond with that mentioned in the Scriptures." Rhys Davids thus writes about the great Bo-Tree :—"This Tree came to occupy much the same position among the Buddhists as the Cross among the Christians. Worship was actually paid to it. An offshoot from it is still growing on the spot where the Buddhist pilgrims found it and where they believed the original tree had grown in the ancient temple at Buddha Gya, built about 500 A. D. by the celebrated Amarsinha. A branch of it planted at Anuradhpura in Ceylon in the middle of the third century B. C. by the daughter of Asoka and sister of Mahendra is still growing there."

Of the Bo-tree at Anuradhapura Sir Emerson Tennent writes thus :—"The Bo-tree of Anuradhpura is in all probability the oldest historical tree in the world. It was planted 288 years before Christ and hence is now 2167 years old. Ages varying from one to four thousand years have been assigned to the *Boabas* of Senigal, the *Eucalyptus* of Tasmania, the *Dragon tree* of Orotava, the *Willingtonia* of California and the Chestnut of Mount Etna. But all these estimates are matter of conjecture and such calculations, however ingenious, must be purely inferential, whereas the ages of the Bo-tree is matter of record. Its conservency has been an object of solicitude to successive dynasties and the story of its vicisitudes has been preserved in a series of continuous Chronicles among the most authentic that have been handed down by mankind."

——:0:——

CHAPTER VIII.

MARA.

DISENCHANTED and dissatisfied Goutama had given up all that men value most to seek Peace in secluded study and Self-denial. Failing to attain his object by learning, the wisdom of others and living the simple life of a student, he had devoted himself to that intense meditation and penance which, all the philosophers of the time said, would raise men above the Gods. Still unsatisfied, longing always for a certainty that seemed ever just beyond his grasp, he had added vigil to vigil and penance to penance, until, when to the wondering view of others, he had become more than a Saint. His indomitable resolution and faith had suddenly and completely broken down. Then when sympathy would have been most welcome he found his friends falling away and his disciples leaving him. The philosophy he had trusted seemed to be doubtful; the penance he had practised so long had brought no Certainty, no Peace, and all his old temptations came back upon him with renewed force.*

Thus sitting underneath the great Bo-tree, disappointed and dejected, Siddhartha Goutama was overwhelmed with temptations,—temptations to go back to his kingdom, to live in pleasures and luxuries,—to be a king of all kings. These were the thoughts that filled his mind. It was indeed a great struggle to get rid of these thoughts, to avoid these temptations,—to defeat and to destroy the great Temptor, Mara, the Evil Tendency of the mind.†

---

* See Rhys Davids' Buddhism p. p. 38—39.

† Rhys Davids thus speaks of Mara :—"There now ensued a second struggle in Goutama's mind, described in both the Southern and the Northern accounts with all the wealth of Poetic imagery of which the Indian mind is master. The crisis culminated on a day, each event of

which is surrounded in the Buddhist lives of their revered Teacher with the wildest legends in which the very thoughts passing through the mind of Goutama appear in gorgeous descriptions as angels of darkness or of light. Unable to express the struggle of his soul in any other way, they represent him sitting sublime, calm and serene, during violent attacks made upon him by a visible Tempter and his wicked angels armed by all kinds of weapons," (See Buddhism, p 36.)

Oldenberg writes :—"The toil by which the spirit seeks purity, rest and deliverance, pictures itself to the religious consciousness of Buddhism as a struggle against a hostile power. This power of the evil, of the sorrow which opposes a resistance to man's escape from its shackles—whence comes it? Buddhist thought holds aloof from this problem. To be curious about the origin of evil and of sorrow would amount to nothing less than prying into the origin of the Universe, for the innermost essence of the world according to Buddhism consists in this that it is subject to evil, that it is a state of continual sorrow.

It is not, therefore, as the one by whom evil has come into the world, but rather as the Supreme Lord and as the chief sources of evil thought, word and deed, that the creed of the Buddhas looks upon Mara as the Evil One, the Prince of Death, for Mara means Death. The kingdom of this world with its pleasures is the kingdom of death. In the highest of the spheres of the universe which are given over to the dominion of pleasure, he rules with his hosts as a powerful god; thence he comes down to earth, when it is his object to attack the kingdom of Buddha and his saints. To simple faith Mara is a personal existence,—a personality limited by the confines of time and space every one of which is as real as Buddha, as all men and all gods."

This is what Buddha himself said of Mara. (See Mahavagga, Sutta Nipata, Sacred Books of the East, Vol. X. p 69—71.)

"To me whose mind was intent upon exertion near the river Niranjana, having entered myself and given myself to meditation for the sake of acquiring Nibbana, came Namuchi (Mara) speaking words full of compassion: "Thou art lean, ill-favoured; Death is in thy neighbourhood. A thousandth part of thee is the property of Death; only one part belongs to life. Living life, O thou venerable one, is better. Living thou wilt be able to do good works. When thou livest a religious life and feedest the sacrificial fire, manifold good works are woven to thee. What dost thou want with exertion? Difficult is the way of exertion, difficult to pass, difficult to enter upon." Saying these verses Mara stood near me."

His poet-biographers then describe in glowing terms his great battle with the Evil One.* Mara thus addressed Buddha, "O Kshatriya, rise up quickly, for you may well fear;—your death is at hand." But Bodhisattwa's heart remained unmoved; no fear was there. Mara instantly discharged his arrows, but the Bodhisattwa regarded not the

---

To Mara thus spoke I :—"Go, O thou friend of the indolent, thou wicked one, for what purpose hast thou come here? Even the least good work is no use to me, and what good works are required, Mara ought to tell. I have faith and power, and understanding is found in me. While thus exerting myself, why do you ask me to live? This burning wind will dry up even the current of the rivers: should it not by degrees dry up my blood while I am exerting myself? While the blood is drying up, the bile and the phlegm are dried up, while the flesh is wasting away, the mind gets more tranquil and my attention, understanding and meditation get more steadfast.

While I am living thus, having felt the extreme sensations, my mind does not look for sensual pleasures. Behold a being's Purity.

Lust thy first army is called,—Discontent thy second,—thy third is called Hunger and Thurst,—thy fourth Desire,—thy fifth is called Sloth and Drowsiness,—thy sixth Cowardice,—thy seventh Doubt,—thy eighth Hypocrecy and Stupor, Gain, Fame Honour and what Celebrity has been falsely obtained,—and he who exults himself and despises others, this O Namuchi, is thine, the black one's,—fighting army." (This evidently shows that by Mara Buddha meant not a separate Being as Satan, but simply a mental state,—the Tendency of the Mind to evil.) None but a hero conquering it and after conquering it obtains joy."

Radha, one of Buddha's disciples, asks :—"Mara, Mara, thus people say, O Sire. Wherein, O Sire, consists the Being of Mara?" To him Buddha thus replied :—Where there is corporal from, O Radha, there is Mara, or he who kills or he who is dying. Therefore, O Radha, look upon corporal form as being Mara, or that it is he who kills, or he who is dying, or sickness, or an abscess, or a wounding dart, or impurity, or impure existence. Whoever regards it thus understands it correctly. (See Samyutta Nikaya, Vol. II.)

* See *Buddha Charita,* 13th Sarga, and Fo-Sho-Hing-Tsan-King as translated by Samuel Beal in the Sacred Books of the East, Vol. XIX. pages 147—156.

arrows. "Now I must assemble my army host and press him sore by force"; he having thus thought, Mara's army suddenly assembled round. "Each assumed his own peculiar form; some were holding spears, others grasping swords, others snatching up trees, others wielding diamond maces,—thus were they armed with every sort of weapon. Some had heads like hogs, others like fishes, others like asses, others like horses, some with forms like snakes, or like the ox, or the savage tiger, some lion-headed and some dragon-headed and some like other kinds of beasts. Some had many heads on one body-trunk, with faces having but single eye, and then again with many eyes; some great-bellied, mighty-bodied, and others thin and skinny, belly-less, others long-legged, mighty-kneed, others big-shanked and fat-calved; some dancing and shrieking, some jumping onwards with their feet together; some striking one another as they went; others flying and leaping between the trees; others howling, or hooting or screaming or whining with their evil noises shaking the great earth. Thus did this wicked goblin troop encircled on its four sides the Boddhi Tree. Some were bent on tearing his body to pieces, others in devouring it whole. But not a hair of Buddha's head was moved, and Mara's host was filled with sorrow. Filled with fear, Mara took his way to his own abode, and all his host overwhelmed with grief and disappointment fled away. The mind of Bodhisattwa remained peaceful and quiet."*

When the conflict began between the Saviour of the world and the Prince of Evil, a thousand appalling meteors fell; clouds and darkness prevailed. Even this earth, with the oceans and mountains it contains, though it is unconscious, quaked like a conscious being—like a fond bride when forcibly torn from her bridegroom—like the festoons of a vine shaking under the blasts of a whirled-wind. The ocean

* See the *Madhuratha Vilasini.*

rose under the vibration of this earth-quake; rivers flowed back towards their sources; peaks of lofty mountains, where countless trees had grown for ages, rolled crumbling down to the earth;—a fierce storm howled all around; the roar of the concussion became terrific; the very sun enveloped itself in awful darkness; and a host of headless spirits filled the air."*

—:o:—

CHAPTER IX.

THE BUDDHA.

THE sun had not gone down when the Prince overcame Mara. At the tenth hour, he received the Wisdom by which he knew the exact circumstances of all the beings who have ever existed in the endless and infinite worlds. At the twelvth hour, he received the Divine Eyes by which he saw all things within the space of the infinite *Sakwalas* as clearly as if they were close at hand. At the tenth hour again, he received the Knowledge that unfolds the causes of the repitition of existence, and at that time he received also the knowledge, by which he was enabled to investigate these causes from their end to their source, and from their source to their end; the great earth of the ten thousand *Sakwalas* called out in approbation by sections of twelve and twelve, a hundred and twenty thousand times, and said "Sadhu!" After this Buddha obtained in order the privileges of the Four Paths and their

* We purposely quote *in extenso* in this Chapter and in the next the form of the narrations as the immediate followers of Buddha left us, so that our readers may have an idea of their quaint style and phraseology.

fruition. Then at the dawn of the next day, every remain of evil desire being destroyed, the beings in the endless and infinite worlds, who had not before possessed this previlege, saw a supreme Buddha, and as they manifested great satisfaction, the six coloured rays from his body were extended to them. Then the rays, without staying for so short a period as the snapping of the finger and thumb, passed onward from *Sakwala* to *Sakwala*, resembling as they proceed (for they continue to spread, rejoicing the beings that see them in their beauty) a blue cloud, rock rose, a white robe, a red garland and a pillar of light. Those who see the rays exclaim, "See what splendid colours!" and from their satisfaction merit is produced, from which they obtain birth in this favoured world, and having the opportunity of seeing a Buddha, they are released from the repetition of existence. The thirty-two wonders that presented at his conception and birth were this day repeated. Not even a hundred thousand mouths could innumerate the offerings now made to Buddha or repeat the wonders that were performed!

At the moment the Prince became Buddha, like a vessel overflowing with honey, his mind overflowed with the Ambrosia of the Dharma, and he uttered the following verse.

This various transmigrations
I must travel, if I do not discover
The Builder whom I seek.
Painful are repeated transmigrations!
I have seen the Architect, (and said,)
"Thou shalt not build me another house,
Thy rafters are broken,
Thy roof timbers scattered;
My mind is detached (from all existing objects,)
I have attained to the non-existence of desire.*

* See Harvy's Manual of Buddhism, pages 179—180.

This is M. Gorgerly's translation. M. Turnour translates the verse thus :—" Performing my pilgrimage through the eternity of count-

Thus under that great Bo-Tree Siddhartha Goutama became the great Buddha. He had tried all existing religious paths to reach the goal where there is no death, no rebirth, no disease, old age, pain or misery;—but he had not been successful. Disappointed and disgusted, he gave up the means

---

less existences, in sorrow have I unremittingly sought in vain the Artificer of the abode. Now, O Artificer, art thou found? Henceforth no receptacle of sin shalt thou form—thy frames are broken, thy ridgepole shattered; my mind, emancipated from liability to transmigration, has annihilated the dominion of passion."

The following is the original of the verse supposed to have been uttered by Buddha—

अनेकजति संसारं
सन्ध द्रस्स अनिभिसां
गहकारकाङ्ग विसान्त
दुःखयाति पुनः पुनं।
गहकारक दितोसि
पुनगेहा नाकहसि
सभाते का सुखभाग्यः
गह कुटं विसां खिटां
विसां खारगतां चित्तं
उनहानकं खाया मभ्मगा।

The Reverend Spence Hardy translates it thus—

"Through many different births
I have run (to me not having found)
Seeking the Architect of the desire-resembling house,
Painful are repeated births,
O House-builder, I have seen this.
Again a house thou canst build for me,
I have broken thy rafters,
Thy central support is destroyed,
To Nirvana my mind is gone,
I have arrived at the extinction of evil desire.

which the teachers of those days called the path of salvation. He sat there under that tree,—passed the whole day in thought and meditation,—through many temptations,—through severe mental struggles. Was he to go to his wife and child,—to wealth and luxury? Is there no hope for him to discover the Path of Salvation? He thought and thought till at last the Light suddenly doomed upon him,—he found the true path to Nirvana. He became the great Buddha.

Even then he was not safe. He was tempted to die at that moment,—thus depriving the world of the great Ambrosia which he discovered. He thus spoke of the state of his mind at that time.

"Then came Mara, the wicked one, unto me. Coming up to me, he placed himself at my side. Standing at my side Mara, the wicked one, spoke unto me saying—" Enter now into Nirvana, Exalted One, enter Nirvana, O Perfect One." As he thus spoke, I replied to Mara, the wicked one, " I shall not enter Nirvana, thou wicked one, until I shall have gained monks as my desciples who are wise and instructed, intelligent hearers of the Word, acquainted with the Doctrine, experts in the Doctrine and the second Doctrine, versed in the Ordinances, walking in the Law, to propagate, teach, promulgate, explain, formulate, analyse what they have heard from their Master, to annihilate and exterminate by their knowledge any heresy which arises, and preach the Doctrine with wonder-working. I shall not enter Nirvana, O wicked one, until the life of holiness, which I point out, has been successful, grown in favour, and extended among all mankind and is in vogue and thoroughly made known to all men."

Then again this thought appeared in the mind of the Buddha. Into the mind of the Exalted One while he retired in solitude came this thought.* "I have penetrated this deep Truth which is difficult to perceive and difficult to

---

* See Mohavagga, 1, 5, 2.

understand, peace-giving, sublime, which transcends all thought, deeply significant, which only the wise can grasp. Man moves in an earthly sphere ; in an earthly sphere he has his place and finds his enjoyment. For man who moves in an earthly sphere and has his place and finds his enjoyments in an earthly sphere, it will be very difficult to grasp this matter, the Law of Casualty,—the Chain of Causes and Effects, and thus also will be very difficult for him to grasp the extinction of all confirmations,—the withdrawal from all that is earthly, the extinction of desire,—the cessation of longing,—the end, the Nirvana. Should I now preach the Doctrine, and mankind not understand me, it would bring me nothing but fatigue; it would cause me nothing, but trouble."

And there passed unceasingly through the mind of the Exalted One this voice which no one had ever before heard.

Why reveal to the world what
  I have won by a severe struggle?
The truth remains hidden from him
  Whom desire and hate absorb.
It is difficult, mysterious, deep,
  Hidden from the coarse mind.
He cannot apprehend it, whose mind
  Earthly vocations surround with might.*

When the Exalted One thought thus, his heart was inclined to abide in quietitude and not to proclaim the Doctrine.

Thus the Great Truth, though discovered, was at the point of remaining buried in the bosom of the great Buddha, but it is said Brahma Sahampati, the chief of the gods, came down from heaven and entreated him to preach the Doctrine

* It is said the following verse was sung by Brahma Sahampati.

"In the land of Magadha, there arose before
A doctrine of impure beings, sinful men,
Open thou, O Wise One, the door of eternity.
Let be heard what thou, O sinless one, discovered,
Who stands above high in the mountains' rocky summit,

Brahma repeated his request three times, and at last Buddha granted it.

As on a lotus-stalk some water rises, and the water damps not their blossoms, so likewise when the Exalted One surveyed the universe with the glance of a Buddha, he saw beings whose souls were pure, and whose souls were not pure, with noble natures and with ignoble natures, good hearers and wicked hearers, many who lived in fear of the world to come and of sin. When he saw this, he uttered this verse.

> Let opened be to all the Door of Eternity,
> He who hath ears let him hear the Word and believe.
> I thought of affliction to myself, therefore have I
> Not yet proclaimed the Noble Word to world.*

> His eye looks afar over all people,
> So mount thou also, O Wise One, up where on high,
> Far over the land stand out the battlements of Truth.
> And look down, Painless One, on mankind,
> The suffering creatures whom birth and old age torture.
> Rise, rise, thou valiant hero, rich and victorious,
> Go through the world, sinless preacher of the path,
> Raise thy voice, O Sire, many shall understand thy Word.

* The quotations in this Chapter are generally made from Mahavagga as translated by Dr. Oldenberg.

—:0:—

CHAPTER X.

HIS FIRST SERMON.

"To whom shall I preach the Doctrine first?" thought the Great Buddha, "Who will understand this Doctrine easily?"* And the Blessed One thought, there is Alarakama;† he is clever, wise and learned. He will easily understand the Doctrine. But he learnt, Alarakama was dead. He then thought of Uddaka Ramaputra,‡ but he too was dead. He then thought of his five old companions in austerities,§ and and directed his steps towards the holy city of Benares where they now lived.|| Upaka, the naked ascetic,¶ saw the Blessed

---

* From the day on which the Buddha, after attaining Buddhahood, started for Benares till he left Rajgriha, as his doctrines became unpopular there, we have a connected narrative in the Vinaya Pitaka, namely in the first portion of Mahavagga. Dr. Oldenberg and Mr. Rhys Davids say:—"It contains the oldest version accessible to us now, and most probably for ever, of what the Buddhist fraternity deemed to be the history of their master's life in its most important period." (See Sacred Books of the East., vol. xiii). We give the translation of Mahavagga in this portion of the biography of the Buddha.

† Alarakama was the teacher to whom Goutama first attached himself after he left his home.

‡ Uddaka was the next teacher to whom Goutama went.

§ These five ascetics were his companions in austerities. They left him when he gave up austerities.

|| It is probable that Goutama first went to Benares to preach his religion, because Benares was the chief seat of Brahmanism. The Mrigadwa wood or Deer Park is represented by a fine wood, which still covers an area of about half a mile and extends from the great town of Dhameh on the north to the Chaukundi mound on the south. See Cunningham's Archeological Reports, vol. I, p. 107.

¶ We have seen that when Buddha appeared, there was a sect of ascetics who roamed over the country completely naked.

One travelling on the road between Gya and the Bodhi Tree; and when he saw him, he said to the Blessed One, 'Your countenance, friend, is serene. Your complexion is pure and bright. In whose name, friend, have you retired from the world? Who is your teacher? Whose doctrine do you profess?" "I have overcome all foes," replied Buddha, "I am the Enlightened. I am free from stains in every way; I have left every thing and have obtained Emancipation by the destruction of Desire. Having myself gained knowledge, whom shall I call my Master? I have no teacher; no one is equal to me; in the world of men and of gods, no one is equal to me. I am the Holy One in this world; I am the highest Teacher; I alone am the absolute Sambuddha. I have gained Peace and have obtained Nirvana. To found the Kingdom of Rightiousness, I go to the holy city of Benares. I will beat the Drum of Immortality in the darkness of this world."

"You profess then, friend," said Upaka, "to be the holy, absolute Jina?"*

"All Jinas," replied Buddha, "who have reached the extinction of *Asawas* are like myself. I have conquered all states of sinfulness; therefore, friend, I am the Jina." "It may be so, friend," said Upaka. He shook his head, took another road and went away.

Then the Blessed One, wandering from place to place, came to Benares, and went to the Deer Park where the five ascetics, his old companions, lived. They saw the Blessed One coming from a distance. When they saw him, they thus spoke to one another, "Friends, there comes the Sramana Goutama who now lives in luxury and who has given up his austerities. Let us not salute him, nor rise from our seats, nor take his bowl and his robe from his hands. But let us put here a seat. If he likes, let him sit down."

---

* Jina literally means "the Victorious One."

But when the Blessed One gradually approached near unto these five ascetics, they would not stick to their promise; they went forth to meet the Blessed One. One took his bowl and his robe, another prepared a seat; another brought water for the washing of his feet, the fourth a footstool, and the fifth a towel. Then the Blessed One sat down and washed his feet. Then they asked, "Whence are you coming, friend Goutama?" "Do not address, O ascetics," said Buddha, "the Tathagatha* by his name and as a friend. The Tathagatha is the holy absolute Sumbuddha. Listen to what I say, O ascetics. I have acquired Immortality. I will teach you,—to you I will preach the Doctrine. If you walk in the way I show you, you will soon acquire the Truth, having you yourselves known it and seen it face to face."

"By those observances you performed," said they, "by those practices, O friend Goutama, by those austerities,—you have not been able to obtain power surpassing that of men, nor the superiority of full and holy knowledge and insight. How will you now living in luxury,—having given up your austerities,—be able to obtain power surpassing that of men and the superiority of full and holy knowledge and insight?"

"The Tathagatha," replied Buddha, "does not live in luxury; he has not given up exertion; he has not turned to an

---

* "The term *Tathagatha* is in the Buddhistical literature exclusively applied to *Sammasambuddhas*, and it is more specially in the Pitakas when the Buddha is represented as speaking of himself in the third person as the Tathagatha. The meaning "sentient being" which is given to the word in the Abhidhanapindeha and in Childer's Dictionery is not confirmed, as far as we know, by any passage of the Pitakas. This translation of the word is very possibly based merely on a misunderstanding of the phrase often repeated in the Sutta Pitakas. *Note Tathagatha Parem Marana*, means "Does a Buddha exist after death?" In the Jaina Books we sometimes find the term Tathagatha (he who has attained the world of emancipation) applied to the Jinas as opposed to other beings who are *Johagatha* (he who lives in this world).

abundant life. Do you think, O ascetics, I ever spoke to you in this way before this day?" "No, you have not," they said. "Then, O ascetics," said he, "listen to me." There are two extremes which the man who has given up the world ought not to follow:—* (1) the habitual practice, on the one hand, of those things whose attraction depends upon the passions and specially of sensuality—a low and pagan way of seeking satisfaction,—unworthy, uuprofitable, and fits only for the worldy-minded;—(2) and the habitual practice, on the other hand, of asceticism or self-mortification which is painful, unworthy and unprofitable.

There is a Middle Path avoiding these two extremes discovered by the Tathagatha,—a path which opens the eyes and bestows understanding which leads to Peace of Mind, to the Higher Wisdom, to Full Enlightenment and to Nirvana.

What is then that Middle Path? Verily it is this noble Eight-fold Path; that is to say—

1. Right Views.
2. Right Aspirations.
3. Right Speech.
4. Right Conduct.
5. Right Livelihood.
6. Right Effort.

Considering the close relation in which the dogmatical terms of the Jainas stand to those of the Buddhas, it is difficult to believe that *Tathagatha* and *Tathagya* should not originally have conveyed very similar ideas. We think that on the long way from the original Magadhi to the Pali and Sanskrit the term Tathagatha (he who has arrived where there is emancipation) may very easily have undergone the change into Tathagatha which would have made it unintelligible were we not able to compare its unaltered form as preserved by the Jainas." Rhys Davids and Oldenberg in the Sacred Books of the East. vol. xiii, pp. 82-83.

* We possess the complete version of Buddha's first sermon in the Pali Sutra called Dhamma-Chakka-Pavattana-Sutta or *Dharma-Chakra-Pravarthana-Sutra*; the translation of some passages from this

7. Right mindfulness.
8. Right Contemplation.

Birth is painful; decay is painful; disease is painful; death is painful. Union with the unpleasant is painful; the separation from the pleasant is painful. In brief, the five aggregates which spring from attachment (the conditions of individuality and their causes) are painful.

This is the Noble Truth concerning Suffering. Now this (namely the following) is the Noble Truth concerning the Origin of Suffering.

Varily it (the origin of suffering) is that thirst or craving causing the renewal of existence, accompanied by sensual delight, seeking satisfaction now here and now there, that is to say, the craving for the gratification of the passions, or the craving for a future life, or the craving for success in the present life.

Now this (the following) is the Noble Truth concerning the Destruction of Suffering.

Verily it is the Destruction of this very thirst in which no passion remains,—the laying aside of, the getting rid of and being free from the harbouring no longer of this thirst.

Now the Noble Truth concerning the means which lead to the destruction of sorrows is the Eight-fold Path.*

Sutra is given here. Rhys Davids says:—"It would be difficult to estimate too highly the historical value of this Sutra. There can be no reasonable doubt that the very ancient tradition accepted by all Buddhists as to the substance of the discourse is correct, and that we really have in it a summary of the words in which the great Indian Thinker and Reformer for the first time successfully promulgated his new ideas. And it presents to us in a few short and pithy sentences, the very essence of that remarkable system which has had so profound an influence in the religious history of so large portion of the human race."

* See Rhys David's Buddhism pp. 49-50. Hardy, (Manual p. 187) and Turnour (Journal, Bombay Asiatic Society vii p. 815) only men-

That this was the Noble Truth concerning Sorrow, the Origin of Sorrow, Destruction of Sorrow and the Means of Destruction of Sorrow, were not among the Doctrines handed down, but there arose within me the eye to perceive them,—there arose the knowledge of their nature,—there arose the understanding of their cause, there arose the wisdom to guide in the path of tranquility,—and there arose the light to dispel darkness.

So long as my knowledge and insight were not quite clear regarding each of these four Noble Truths, in this Triple Order, in this Twelve-fold Manner, so long was I uncertain whether I had attained to the full insight of that wisdom which is unsurpassed in the heavens or in earth among the whole race of Sramanas and Brahmanas, or of gods and men.

But as soon as my knowledge and insight were quite clear regarding each of these four Noble Truths, in this Triple Order, in this Twelve-fold Manner, then did I become certain that I had attained to the full insight of that wisdom which is unsurpassed in the heavens or in earth among the whole race of Sramanas and Brahmanas, or of gods and men.

And now this knowledge and this insight has arisen within me. Immoveable is the Emancipation of my Heart. This is my last existence. There will now be no re-births for me."

It was the aged Kondanya who first openly gave in his adhesion to Buddha; but the others also, after many talks with him,—sometimes separately and sometimes together,—soon accepted in its entirity his Plan of Salvation.*

---

tion here the conversation of Kondanya which all the accounts agree, Foncaun p. 396 and Bigandet p. 97.

* See Maha Pari Nibbana Sutra II, 2, 3 and IV, 7, 8, and Dhammapada, verse 191.

——:o:——

CHAPTER XI.

HIS FIRST CONVERTS.

THE next man who accepted the religion of the great Buddha was the son of the richest Banker of the holy city of Benares. Thus did the ancient chronicler describe this event.*

"There was in Benares a noble youth, Jasa by name, the son of a great Banker. He had three palaces,—one for the winter, and one for the summer, and one for the rainy season. In the palace for the rainy season he lived during the four months of rains surrounded by female musicians.

Now one day Jasa fell asleep, and the females also fell asleep. But Jasa awoke sooner than the others and saw his attendants sleeping. One had her lute leaning against her armpit, one had her tabor leaning against her neck, one had her hairs dishevelled; one had her saliva flowing from her mouth; and they were all muttering in their sleep. One would think it was a cemetery into which he has fallen.

When Jasa saw this scene before him, he felt the evil of the life he led. He exclaimed, "Alas, what distress! Alas, what danger!" He immediately left his palace and went straight to the Deer Park where the great Buddha lived. He had heard of him; he was told that the Goutama of the Sakya race had found the means of salvation; he was the man who could save one from the sufferings of the world. He met him and exclaimed, "Alas, what distress! Alas, what danger!" "Here is no danger," said the Blessed One, "here is no distress! Come here, friend, and sit down; I will teach you the Truth."

---

* See Mahavagga—as translated in the Sacred Books of the East, vol. xiii.

And Jasa, the noble youth, became glad and joyful. He went near the place where the Blessed One was. Having respectfully saluted him, he sat near him. Then did the Blessed One preach to him the Truth. He spoke of the merits obtained by alms-giving, and of the duties, of morality, of heaven, of the evils, of the vanity and sinfulness, of desires, and of the blessings of the abandonment of desires.

When the Blessed One saw that the mind of Jasa was prepared, then he preached the principal Doctrines of the Buddha, namely Suffering, the Cause of Suffering, the Cessation of Suffering, and the Path to obtain Nirvana. The noble youth Jasa was then ordained a Bhikshu.*

Very soon after, Jasa's father, the rich Banker, also his mother and his wife, accepted the religion of Buddha and were ordained as lay-disciples.† Four of Jasa's best friends

* Those that accepted the Path of Salvation preached by the Buddha had to cut off all connections with the world. He had to give up his home and earthly possessions,—his wife, children, relatives and friends;—strict "chastity and Poverty" were the great Moto of the Order. He had to live on alms and outside of towns and villages. When a man was thus ordained he was called a Buddha. See the particulars later on in the description and history of the Order.

† Many men became lay-members of Buddha's religion, and were called *Upasaka* (Male votaries). And *Upasika* (female votaries). We shall here quote what Dr. Oldenberg says about these men and women (see Buddha, p. 382—384). " Without a laity which proposed a faith in Buddha and Buddha's teachings and evinced this faith in pious offices, above all in works of helpful beneficence, an Order of Bhikshus could not be thought of. But while there was framed from the beginning for the Monastic Church an organization, clothed with strict forms of spiritual procedure, there was no attempt made at creation of similar kind for the quasi-church of lay-brothers and lay-sisters. Certain custom of spiritual life and practical benificence must obviously have risen even here, if definite institutions have not followed. There was not so much as any sharply drawn line between the laity who are to be regarded as adherents of the Order of Buddha and those who stood aloof therefrom. Entry into

Vimala, Subahu, Punnaji, and Gavurpati, followed his example and became Buddhist Monks. In the course of three months fifty others, receiving the Truths from the Blessed One, shaved their head, took the yellow robe and turned Bhikshus. Thus

---

the circle of votaries was dependent on no qualification and followed regularly upon a form fixed by custom, but not determined by law, namely upon the person taking the step declaring in the presence of a monk, either on his own behalf alone or jointly with wife, children, and servants, that he takes his refuge in the Buddha, in the Dharma and in the Sangha. Then there was also, it is true, inculcated on the lay disciples in the part of the Order the observance of certain duties of temperence and rectitude, but neither was the profession of a formal vow by them insisted upon, nor did the Church keep watch in any way whatever over the actual fulfilment of these duties. A formal excommunication of unbelieving unworthy or scandalously living lay-brothers there was not, and as a result of circumstances, there could not be. The only procedure prescribed in the regulations of the Church against laity, who had given cause of complaint, shows clearly how little the ideas of admission and expulsion had been applied to this relation, namely the order might resolve to withdraw the alms-bowl from such a layman and "refuse their company to him at table." If after this he reformed and conciliated the Order, then by a new resolution the alms-bowl would be again presented to him and the company of the Order at table be granted to him. It is entirely in keeping with the manner and method in which the position of the lay-brothers has been treated, that regular spiritual gatherings were not instituted for them, and much less were they admitted to be present at the ceremonious proceedings of the Order, or even to a share of any kind whatsoever in the administration of the business affairs of the Order. The daily begging excursions of the monks maintained the usual contact between them and the believing laity and gave a natural opening for attentions of a pastoral kind. The laity also on their part came to the parks of the community, near the gates of the town with gifts of every kind, with food and medicine, with garlands and and perfumes; there they paid their respects to the monks and listened to the exposition of the sacred discourses and sayings. Or they erected buildings for the uses of the Order and invited the monks to the dedicatory and opening celebrations."

at that time there were sixty-one Arahats* (including the Buddha) in the world.

The Blessed One, one day, thus spoke to his sixty Bhikshus, "I am delivered, O Bhikshus, from all fetters, human and divine. Go ye now and roam over the country for the welfare of the many, for the good, for the gain and for the benefit of gods and men. Let not two of you go the same way. Preach, O Bhikshus, the Doctrine which is glorious in the beginning, glorious in the middle, glorious at the end, in the spirit and in the letter. Proclaim a consummate, perfect and pure life of holiness."

Thus ordered the first missionaries of the great master scattered over the country. Jasa remained in Benares and the Buddha directed his steps towards Uruvela. But a difficulty soon arose. The Bhikshus had to take long journeys to find out the great Buddha, so that he might ordain the man whom they had converted. Therefore he thus addressed the Bhikshus one day, "I grant you, O Bhikshus, this permission. Confer henceforth in the different regions and coun-

---

* There are four classes of saintly men in the Buddhist Order. The lowest is Sotapanna. Of them it is said, 'By the annihilation of the three ties, they have attained the path,—they are not liable to rebirth in the lower world such as hills, spirit worlds, world of lower animals &c. They are sure of deliverence, they shall attain the highest knowledge." The next higher class is that of Sakadagami. Of them it is said, "By the annihilation of the three ties, by the suppression of desire, hatred and frivolity, they have become once-returning. When they have returned once only to this world they shall attain the end of sorrow." The next higher class is Anagami. Of them it is said, "By the annihilation of the five first ties they have come to be beings, who originate of themselves (*i. e.* who enter upon the state of being without being begotten or born; this is the case of the higher worlds of the gods); they attain the Nirvana up there (in the worlds of the gods); they are not liable to return from that world." The highest of the four stages is that of the Arahats.

tries the Pabbajya and Upasampada* Ordinations yourselves on those who desire to receive them. And you ought, O Bhikshus, to confer the Pabbajya and Upasampada Ordinations in this way. Let him first have his hair and head shaved off; let him put on yellow robes; adjust his upper robe so as to cover one shoulder; salute the feet of the Bhikshus present with his head and sit down squatting. Then let him raise his joined hands, and thus tell him to say :—

I take my refuge in the Buddha.
I take my refuge in the Dharma.
I take my refuge in the Sangha.†

Let him repeat this three times.

When the Bhikshus departed, the great master went away towards the kingdom of Magadha and reached Uruvela in due time.

——:o:——

CHAPTER XII.

KASSYAPA, UPATISSA, SARIPUTRA.

THESE were the three famous men in the kingdom of Magadha,—famous as great ascetics, vast scholars, and respected teachers; each had a large following of disciples. Kassyapas were three brothers. The eldest of them was known as

* Pabbajya is going out from a prior state, from the lay life or from a monastic sect holding another faith.

The Upasampada is the entry into the circle of the Bhikshus, the fully accredited members of the Buddhist Order. See Buddha, page 347.

† The Order of Bhikshus that Buddha established was called the *Sangha.*

Jatila Uruvela Kassyapa,* the second one as Nadi Kassyapa† and the third as Gaya Kassyapa.‡

Goutama lived with the eldest all through the winter and at the end the venerable Kassyapa asked the Buddha to ordain him as one of his monks. "You Kassyapa," said Buddha, "are chief, leader, foremost, first and highest of five hundred Jatilas. Go first and inform them of your intention, and let them do what they think fit."

The Jatila Kassyapa then went to his disciples and said, "I wish, Sirs, to lead a religious life under the direction of the great Sramana Goutama; you may do, Sirs, what you think fit."

"If you," replied they, "will lead, Sir, a religious life under the great Sramana's direction, we will also lead a religious life under the great Sramana's direction."

Then the Jatilas shaved their hair and beard, flung the things for the Agnihotra Sacrifice§ into the river, and went to the place where the Blessed One was. "Lord," said they, "let us receive Pabbajya and Upasampada Ordination from the Blessed One."

"Come, O Bhikshus," said Buddha, "lead a holy life for the complete extinction of suffering."

Thus those venerable persons were all ordained. Their example was soon followed by the Nadi Kassyapa and Gaya Kassyapa with all their followers. Thus within a very short

---

* *Jatila* means matted lock. Jatila Uruvela Kassyapa means Kassyapa who had matted locks on his his head and who lived in the village of Uruvela. After Buddha's death Kassyapa was elected in his place to become the chief of the Order.

† Nadi Kassyapa means one who lived on the banks of the river.

‡ Gaya Kassyapa means Kassyapa who lived in the village of Gaya.

§ Every Aryan used to keep a fire always burning in his home. Every morning and evening it was his duty to worship this fire. This fire was his God and the Emblem of his religion. This was called Agnihotra.

time Buddha became the leader of more than one thousand monks. With them all—a grand and majestic procession,—he went on towards Rajagriha,—the capital of the kingdom of Magadha.

In Rajagriha lived the other two very celebrated men,—Sariputra and Upatissa,*—two great religious devotees and scholars,—men of brilliant parts and extraordinary abilities. Though they had not as yet assumed the position of teachers, they being still then the disciples of one Sanjaya,—yet they had a large following,—in fact only for their sake Sanjaya had innumerable disciples.

One day, Sariputra met one of the Bhikshus of the great Buddha named Assagi and said, "Your complexion is pure and bright. In whose name, friend, have you retired from the world? Who is your teacher? Whose Doctrine do you profess?"

"There is, friend," replied Assagi, "the Sramana Goutama,—an ascetic of the Sakya race. In His, the Blessed One's name, have I retired from the world. He is my Teacher and His, the Blessed One's, Doctrine do I profess."

"And," asked Sariputra, "what is the doctrine, Sir, which your Teacher holds and preaches to you?"

"I am only a young disciple, friend," replied Assagi, "I have but recently received the Ordination, and I have newly adopted this Doctrine and Discipline. I cannot explain to you the Doctrine in detail, but I will tell you in short what it means" "Well, friend," said Sariputra," "tell me much, or tell me little as you like, but tell me the spirit of the Doctrine."

---

* Sariputra and Upatissa were both Brahmans. They soon became most prominent members of the Order founded by the Buddha. Upatisa Sutra and Sariputra Sutra are still now the two most sacred books of the Buddhist Canon. These two books containing the teachings of the great master were most probably edited by these two gifted monks. After Buddha's death Sariputra and Upatissa had places in the Order next to Kassyapa.

Then the venerable Assagi said, "Of all objects which proceed from a Cause, the Tathagatha has explained their Cessation also. This is the Doctrine of the great Buddha."

Then Sariputra went to his frend Upatissa and told him of his meeting with the Bhikshu Assagi. They made up their mind to place themselves under the teaching of the great Sramana Goutama. When they took the yellow robe, all the followers of their late master Sanjaya followed their example. This created a great sensation all over the country. Monks, ascetics, learned Brahmans, as well as lay men, poor and rich, all flocked to see the great Buddha who was then living with thousands of followers in the Jastivana.*

——:o:——

CHAPTER XIII.

HIS POPULARITY AND UNPOPULARITY.

The popularity of the great Buddha was extreme all over the Magadha country. The king himself came and paid the highest respect to him. The ancient chronicler says:—The Magadha king, Bimbasara, surrounded by twelve myriads of Magadha Brahmans and householders, went to the place where the Blessed One was. Having approached him he respectfully saluted him and sat down near him.

Now these twelve myriads of Brahmans and householders thought,—" Has the great Sramana Goutama placed himself under the spiritual direction of Uruvela Kassyapa, or has Uruvila Kassapa placed himself under the spiritual direction of the great Sramana?"

* See Cunningham's Archæological Reports Vol I pl XIV.

And the Blessed One, who understood in his mind the reflection which had arisen in the minds of those twelve myriads of Brahmans and householders, addressed the venerable Kassyapa thus:—"What knowledge have you gained that has induced you, who were renowned for your penances, to forsake your sacred fire?"

"It is visible things, and sounds, and also tastes, pleasures, and women that the Sacrifice speaks of;" replied Kassyapa. "Because I came to know that whatever exists is filth, I took no more delight in sacrifices and offerings."

"But," said Buddha, "if your mind found no delight either in visible things or sounds or tastes, what is in the world of men and gods in which your mind now finds delight? Tell me that."

"I have seen," replied "Kassyapa, the state of peace (Nirvana) by which the basis of existence (Upadhi) and the obstacles to perfection (Kinchana) have ceased."

Then the venerable Uruvela Kassyapa rose from his seat, adjusted his upper robe so as to cover one shoulder, prostrated himself inclining his head to the feet of the Blessed One and said:—"My teacher, lord, is the Tathagatha; I am his pupil." Then the Blessed One delivered a discourse.

The king most respectfully invited the Blessed One to his palace with all his followers, and served and offered with his own hands excellent food to the Bhikshus with the Buddha at their head. When the Blessed One had finished his meals and cleansed his bowl and hands, the king sat down near him and thus spoke:—"I give up my Veluvana Garden* to the

---

* Rhys Davids says:—Curiously enough while Jastivana has been identified by General Cunningham in his ancient Geography of India, p 461 and map XII, the site of Veluvana has not yet been discovered. It must have occupied about the position where the ancient basements marked K. K. K. I. G. in Cunningham's map of Rajagriha (PL XIV Reports Vol. I) were found by him.

Bhikshus with the Buddha at their head." The Blessed One accepted the gift.

"This enthusiasm of the people seems to have cooled down as rapidly as it rose, for there were no other conversions besides those of Sariputra and Uptissa and their pupils. The members of the Society began even to complain to Goutama that when they went out to beg their daily food, they were received with abuse and redicule on the ground that the new teaching would deprive householders of their supports and depopulate and ruin the country."*

The ancient chronicler says :—

"At this time many distinguished and noble youths of the Magadha territory joined themselves to the Buddha to lead a pure life.

The people were annoyed, murmured and became angry. They said :—"The Sramana Goutama causes fathers to beget no sons; he causes wives to become widows and families to become extinct. Already he has turned thousands of hermits into his disciples, and he has made two hundred and fifty mendicant followers of Sanjaya his disciples, and now these distinguished and noble youths of the Magadha kingdom are betaking themselves to the ascetic Goutama to lead religious life."

The people taunted the Bhikshus with this couplet, when they saw them walking by their houses.

"The great Bhikshu came in his travels to the capital of Magadha.
Seated on a hill he has converted all Sanjaya's followers.
Whom will he draw after him to-day?"

When the great Buddha learnt the state of the public feelings from his followers, he said :—"This excitement, O disciples, will not last long. But, if they taunt you, O Bhikshus, answer them with these words."

* See Rhys Davids' Buddhism, p 63.

"The Heroes, the Perfect Ones, convert by their true discourse.
Who will reproach the Buddha who converts only by the power of truth?"*

But this was not all the unpleasantness that the great Master had to meet at the very start of his righteous work.

The high position which Goutama assigned to Sanjaya and Upatissa created some ill-feeling among the older members of the Sangha, which Goutama allayed by calling together his followers and addressing them at some length on the means requisite for Buddhist salvation, which he summed up in the celebrated verse.

To cease from all wrong-doings to get virtue.
To cleanse one's own heart,—this is the religion of the Buddha.†

At the same time he laid down the first rules for the guidance of the Society, the simple law being called Patimokha, that is the Disbursement, a word afterwards applied to a book containing a summary of the more complex system of laws, as it had been elaborated at the time of Goutama's death. This meeting of mendicants, at which the Society was first so to speak, incorporated, is known as the Savakasamipata or the assembly of the disciples.‡

---

* See Oldenberg's Buddha. He asks.—"Have we really here a pair of those rhymes before us such as they were probably bandied at that time between the friends and the foes of the young teachers among the gossiping populace of the streets of the capital of Magadha?"

† This verse is the verse 183 of the Dhammapada. Hardy says,—"The verse above quoted constitutes the discourse called *Patimokha*. We have now a complete Buddhistic sacred book named Patimokha, the first portion of the *Vinaya*."

‡ See Buddhism, page 62, also Jataka page 85, Hardy, p. 198. Turnour, Journal Bombay Asiatic Society, VII. page 106.

——:o:——

CHAPTER XIV.

ARRIVAL AT KAPILAVASTU.

When the great Goutama was residing in the Velubana Mat near Rajgriha,* a messenger came from Kapilavastu with an urgent request from his father to go and see him and his dear relatives only for once. The messenger thus spoke the words of his father:—"It is my wish to see you, therefore come to me. Others have the benefit of the Dharma, but not your father and your other relatives. It is now seven years since we saw you?"

Buddha thought of once going to see his parents and relatives. When Buddha commenced his journey, he was attended by 10000 priests of Anga and Magadha and by 10000 priests of Kapilavastu. Each day he proceeded sixteen miles, and as it was sixty *yoyanas'* distance between Rajgriha and Kapilavastu, he accomplished the whole in two months.

The King prepared the garden called Nigrodha for the reception of Buddha. In the procession appointed by the king to receive Buddha on his approach to the city, there were first 500 princes and princesses about 12 years of age and afterwards the King with 16,000 attendants carrying perfumes and flowers. On reaching the garden, Buddha sat upon a throne surrounded by the 20,000 priests.

The next day all the members of the royal family being beside themselves from joy, no one remembered that food was to be provided for Buddha. In the morning he cleansed his teeth and washed his face; after which he went to a retired place and performed the exercise of Dhyana. At the time at which it was proper to set out to receive alms, he took

* We follow Hardy's translation in this chapter and the next.

his bowl and set out from the Nigrodha garden surrounded by the 20,000 priests. He then went a-begging from house to house.

When the king, his father heard this, he went to him in haste. "Why do you disgrace me thus?" Exclaimed he. "If you had been accompanied even by all the kings of Jambudwipa, could I not have supplied the whole with food! How much easier thus is it for me to supply you and your 20,000 priests!" "It is the custom of my race." Buddha replied. But the king said, "How can this be? You are descended from Mahasamanta; none of your race ever acted in this manner. Some of your ancestors could stamp for food, and they received whatever they wished." Buddha then informed his father that he spoke not of the race of Samanta, but of the race of the Buddhas. He continued:—"When any one found a hidden treasure, it was his duty to make an offering of the most precious of the Jewels to his father in the first instance." He then therefore opened the mine of Dharma.* He who listens to the Dharma will attain prosperity." On hearing this, the king entered into the Second Path.

The king then sent to inform Yasodhara that she also might come and worship Siddhartha; but she replied, "Surely if I am deserving of any regard, he will come and see me. I can then worship him." Buddha went to her apartments. As he was going, he told Maggalan and others, "I am, free from evil desire, though the princess is not so. From not having seen me for so long a time, she is exceedingly sorrowful. Unless this sorrow be allowed its course, her breast will cleave. She will take hold of my feet, but as the

* That is, he delivered to him a discourse. "Do not procrastinate; listen to the excellent Dharma. He who thus listens will attain prosperity. The king, whilst listening to this discourse, entered the first path. Buddha then repeated another stanza. Practice that which is enjoined in the Dharma. Avoid that which is forbidden in the Dharma."

result will be that she and the other princesses will embrace nunhood, you must not prevent her."

When Yasodhara heard that the Buddha was coming to see her, she was, from the abundance of her affection, like an overflowing vessel unable to contain herself. And forgetting that she was a mere woman and that Buddha was the Lord of the world, she held him by the feet and wept. But remembering that Suddhadhana was present, she felt ashamed and rose up;—after which she reverently remained at a little distance. It is not permitted even to Maha-Brahma to touch the body of Buddha. The king apologised for the princess and said, "This arises from her affection; nor is it a momentary display. For seven years that you were absent from her, she had lamented for you thus. When she heard that you had shaved your head, she did the same. When she heard that you had put on mean garments, she put on the same. When she heard that you had left off the use of perfumes and ornaments, she left off the same. Like you she has eaten only at appointed times and from an earthen bowl, and like you she has renounced high seats. Therefore grant her forgiveness."

Buddha gave his blessings to his wife and went away to the place outside the town where his followers were encamped.*

---

* A few years after Yasodhara became a Buddhist nun and the head of the Order of Female Bhikshunis. See below.

——:o:——

CHAPTER XV.

CONVERSION OF HIS SON AND RELATIVES.

THE next day* Buddha went from the Nigrodha garden to a festival that was held in honour of Nanda, the son of Maha Prajapati† the sister of Maya Devi and the wife of Sudhadhana. It was a three-fold festival as on this day he was to be elevated to a new office,—to enter upon a new residence,—and to be married. Buddha went with his Arhatas‡ to the festival hall that he might release Nanda from the sorrows of existence. When seated upon the throne that had been prepared for him, he repeated the following stanza.

"The destruction of evil desire, the keeping of the Brahmacharja, the knowing of the Four Truths, and the comprehending of Nirvana,—these constitute the greatest festival."

Having in this manner made him willing to follow the the advice he received, Buddha put his alms bowl in his hand which he took, though at that time he was arrayed in the richest ornaments. Buddha then rose from the throne and went to the Vihara, and Nanda followed him. The betrothed princess, Janapada-kalyani, called out to him from the window to enquire where he was going, but he gave her no reply.

On arriving at the Vihara, Buddha said to Nanda, "Regard not the honors of the Chakravati; become a priest like me." The thoughts of the prince, however, still wandered after his betrothed wife, but the great master drove away those evil thoughts from his mind and Maggalan admitted him to the Monkhood.

---

* We follow Hardy's trauslation.

† Nanda was Buddha's step-brother.

‡ Buddhist monks.

On the seventh day after the arrival of Buddha at Kapilavastu, Yasodhara arrayed her son Rahula, now seven years old, in all the splendour of a prince, and said to him pointing out to Buddha who was passing by the palace in his usual daily rounds for alms:—"This monk, whose appearance is so glorious, so that he looks like Maha-Brahma, is your father. He possesses four great mines of wealth. Since he went away, I have not seen them. Go to him and entreat him to put you in possession of these mines of wealth and the seven treasures of the Chakravati. The son ought to inherit the property of his father." Rahula said:—"I know of no father, but the king Sudhadhana. Who else is my father?" The princess took him in her arms and from the window pointed to Buddha and said, "That monk is your father."

Rahula then went to Buddha, and looking up in his face said without fear and with much affection, "My father, my father!" Buddha was then engaged in taking his meals. When he finished his repast and given his blessings to his host, he went away,—and Rahula followed him, calling him "father" and asking him to have his inheritance. None of the people did anything to stop him, nor did Buddha himself.

At last Buddha reached the Vihara. So long he did say nothing,—not a word—to his son. Now he suddenly turned towards Sujat and said, "My son asks for his inheritance. I will not give him that which is connected with the sorrows of existence. I will give him the inheritance of Buddhahood,—the benefit arising from which does never perish. Sujat, shave this boy's head and take him into the Order."

The princely costume of Rahula was taken away,—the yellow robe of the monk was given to him,—and his head was shaved; and Rahula was greatly blessed.* When Sudhadhana heard what had been done, he became excessively

* Rahula was taken as an apprentice in the Order, for he was then a minor. When he grew to be eighteen years of age, he was formally ordained a member of the Order.

sorry. By Buddha's renunciation he lost his one son, by Nanda's conversion the other. Now he lost his only grandson. He hastened to Buddha weeping; he prayed that henceforth Buddha should not ordain a son without the consent of his parents; and Buddha gave his word.

On his way he stayed for sometime at Anupiya on the banks of the Aroma in a mango grove near the spot where he had sent Channa back on the eventful night of the Renunciation. And whilst he was there, the Order received several important accessions, chiefly from his clan, or from that of his relatives the Kolyans. Among those Ananda, Devadatta Upali and Anuruddha deserved especial mention. The first became the most intimate friend of his cousin, Goutama, as will specially appear in the account of the Teacher's death. The second, also his cousin, became afterwards his rival and opponent. The third Upali was a barber attached to the household of Sudhadhana. His deep religious feelings and great intellectual powers made him afterwards one of the great most important leaders in the Order. The last Anuruddha became the greatest master of Buddhist metaphysics.

—:o:—

CHAPTER XVI.

HIS MISSION WORK.

The rest of the long life of the great master was spent from year's end to years' end in mission works, in preaching his great religion, in increasing the number of his Order, and in promulgating the laws of humanity and peace. Thus did he establish the Kingdom of Righteousness.*

* We have no connected, nor authenticated history of Buddha from the 4th to the 20th year of his mission. We can gather a few facts only

The following is a short summary of his mission works from the 4th year of his Buddhahood till the 20th year.

4th year :—In the fourth year Goutama admitted the rope-dancer Ugrasena* to the Order, and then crossing the Ganges into Vesali, he lived for a time in the Mahavana grove. Whilst there he heard of a quarrel between the Sakhyas and Kolyans about the water in the boundary river Kohana. He went to Kavilvastu, reconciled the two clans, returned to Mahavana and spent the rainy season there.

5th year :—In the middle *Was*, he heard of the illness of Sudhadhana and again returned to Kapilavastu and was present at the death of his father, then ninety-seven years old at sunrise of Saturday, the full moon-day of the month of August in the year of the Ectzana Era 107.† After comforting his relatives and carrying out the cremation of the body with due ceremony, Goutama returned to the Kutagara Vihara at Mahavana. He is there followed by his father's widow Prajapati, his wife Yasodhara and other Sakhya and Kolyan ladies who earnestly asked to be allowed to take the vow. He was very unwilling to admit them to the Order, but at last yielded to the earnest advocacy of Ananda and laid down certain rules for female mendicants.‡ He then retired to the hill Makula at Kusambi near Allahabad.

---

from the Dhammapada and Jataka Commentaries, but how far they are historically based cannot be confidently said. Bigandet and Hardy record certain tales, but do not mention their sources. They are probably derived from the Jatakas or from the different Commentaries on the utterances of the Buddha. The summary given here is after Rhys Davids. See Buddhism.

* Told by Bigandet in his Manual.

† Bigandet's Manual of Buddhism, page 19.

‡ The queen mother Prajapati said to Buddha that as Sudhadhana was dead and Rahula and Nanda (her son) were priests, she had no wish to reside alone in Kapilavastu, and therefore requested that with Jasodhara and other princesses she might be admitted into the Order. He replied, "Ladies, do not seek to enter my Order." Then did she

6th Year.—After spending the rainy season at Makula, Goutama returned to Rajgriha, and whilst there admitted Kshema, the queen of Bimbasara, to the Order. One of his disciples, gaining a *patra* (bowl) by the display of miraculous powers, Buddha had the *patra* broken to pieces and forbade any miracles.

7th Year.—While he was living in the Jituvana Vihara near Sarvasti, his opponents induced a woman named Chincha to accuse him of a breach of chastity, but her deceipt was exposed.*

---

pray to be admitted into the Order, and thrice were they refused. Buddha then left Kapilavastu and went away to Vesali.

Prajapati then said to the other princesses, "The great Buddha has thrice refused to admit us into the Order. Let us take it upon ourselves, and then go to him, and he cannot but receive us." On hearing this advice, they were pleased; and then all of them cut off their hair, put on the yellow robe and taking earthen alms-bowls in their hands departed from their homes. They went walking,—those that never knew what walking meant. In consequence of their extreme tenderness, their feet were soon covered with blisters. The distance from Kapilavastu to Vesali was fifty one Yoyanas. It was evening when they arrived at the Vihara in which Buddha was residing. They did not enter within, but remained outside. When Ananda saw them with bleeding feet, his eyes were filled with tears; and he said, "Why have you come?" Prajapati replied, "We have become nuns in the name of the great Master." On hearing this Ananda requested them to remain there whilst he went and informed Buddha of their arrival. To the sage he described all that he had seen, but the great Bnddha merely said, "Ananda, seek not to have women admitted into the Order."

After repeated requests from Ananda and pressure from many of his disciples, the great Master at last reluctantly agreed to admit the princesses into the Order, and thus a new Order of Female Mendicants was created, at the head of which was placed Prajapati. After Prajapati's entering Nirvana, Yasodhara, the wife of Buddha, became the head of the Order, but she too died long before Buddha's death.

* Regarding this matter, the following story is narrated. There were certain Thirthakas who were envious when they saw the

8th Year.—He spends the Was on the rock Sansumara near Kapilavastu. Conversion of the father and mother of Nakula of Moggali took place here.* Goutama then returned to Kusambi near Allahabad.

---

numbers who received the instructions of Goutama. They therefore thus cried out to the people in the corners of the streets, "What is it that you are doing? Is Goutama the only Buddha? Are not we also Buddhas? If he imparts Nirvana, do not we enable you to receive the same?" They then consulted together to see if they could not destroy the influence of the sage by a stratagem. There was at that time in Sewet a young female, named Chinchi, an ascetic. One day she went to the residence of the Thirthikas and worshipped them, but they remained silent. At this she became fearful, thinking that she must have done something wrong; and after worshipping them thrice, she asked what fault she had committed. The Thirthikas informed her that they wished to hinder the success of Buddha in which she would be able to assist them. She enquired in what way, and they told her what to do. Chinchi was well-versed in all kinds of female devices. The people of Sewet were accnstomed to resort to Buddha in the evening that they might hear *bana.* She proceeded from her residence just at that time, arrayed in a crimson robe with flowers and perfumes. The people asked her where she was going at that time and she said it was no business of theirs. She passed the night near the place where Buddha was residing. In the morning when the Upasakas were coming at an early hour that they might worship Buddha, she returned towards the city. When they enquired where she had slept, she told them that she had spent the night in the appartment of Goutama.

One day when Buddha was saying *bana*, she entered the hall making a big belly with a piece of wood as if she were in advanced pregnancy. She said, "I am with chiid by you; you have appointed no place for my confinement." At this time a sudden gust of wind removed her cloth and exposed the piece of wood. The assembled people, when they saw the falsity of the accusation she had brought against Buddha, took her by the hands and feet and drove her away. (See Hardy's Manual, p 276.)

* Buddha generally converted men and women by parables. Here is a beautiful one.

Kisagotami is the name of a young girl whose marriage with the

9th year :—Moggali stirred up enmity against Goutama, and Ananda urged him to go elsewhere, but he refused. A dissension then broke out in the Order and Goutama in vain exhorted the two parties to patience, union and charity, and then sorrowfully left his disciples and went alone to the Pareleyaka.

---

only son of a wealthy man was brought about in true fairy tale fashion. She had one child, but when the beautiful boy could run alone, it died. The young girl in her love for it carried the dead child clasped to her bosom and went from house to house of her pitying friends asking them to give her medicines for it. But a Buddhist mendicant, thinking 'she does not understand', said to her, "My good girl, I myself have no such medicine as you ask for, but I think I know of one who has." "O tell me who that is," cried Kisagotami. "Buddha can give you medicine, go to him," was the answer. She went to Goutama and doing homage to him said, "Lord and master, do you know of any medicine that will be good for my child?" "Yes, I know of some," said the Teacher. Now it was the custom for patients or their friends to provide the herbs which the doctors roquired, so she asked what herbs he would want. "I want some mustard seed," he said; and when the poor girl eagerly promised to bring some of so common a drug. he added, "You must get it from some house where no son, husband, or parent, or servant has died." "Very good," said the girl and went to ask for it still carrying the dead child with her. The people said, "Here is mustard seed, take it;" but then she asked, "In my friend's house has any son died or a husband or a parent or a servant? "They answered," Lady, what is this you say? The living are few, but the dead are many." Then she went to other houses, but one said, "I have lost a son," another, "We have lost our parents," and another, "We have lost our servants." At last not being able to find a single house where no one had died, her mind began to clear and then moving up resolution, she left the dead body of her child in a forest and returning to Buddha paid him homage. He said to her, "Have you the mustard seed?" "My Lord," she said, "I have not. The people tell me that the living are few, but the dead are many." Then he talked to her on that essential part of his system,—impermanency of all things.—Then her doubts were cleared away and accepting her lot she became a disciple and entered the First Path. (See Buddhism, pp. 133-34).

10th year :—There in a hut built by the villagers, he spent his 10th rainy season. The refractory medicants sought him out to ask pardon, and were well received and forgiven. He told them, "Outsiders who know not the littleness of all things might indeed quarrel, but they should have been wiser. He who has found prudent, sober, wise companions may walk happy if he be considerate; but rather than be with the unwise let him walk alone without sin and with few wishes like the lovely elephant." He then wished the repentant desciples to return to Sravasti, and he then went on to Magadha.

11th year :—In a village near Rajagriha he converted the Brahmana Bharadwaja by the parable of the sower.* After spending the rainy season there, he returned to Kosola to a town called Satiabia.

12th Year :—Thence he went to the neighbouring town of Veranja and spent the rainy season. After it was over, he

---

* This is the parable referred to.

A wealthy Brahmana named Bharadwaja was looking his harvest home when the Teacher came and stood by with his bowl. Some of the people went by and paid him reverence, but the Brahmana was angry and said, "Sramana, I plough and sow, and having ploughed and sowed, I eat. It would be better if you were in like manner to plough and sow, and then you would have food to eat.'

"O Brahman," replied Buddha, "I too plough and sow, and having ploughed and sown, I eat."

"You say you are a husbandman," said the Brahman, "but we see no signs of it. Where are your bullocks, and the seed and the plough ?"

Then the teacher answered "Faith is the seed I sow and good works are as the rain that fortilizes it: wisdom and modesty are the parts of the plough and my mind is the guiding rein. I lay hold of the handle of the Law, earnestness is the goad I use and deligence is my draught ox. Thus this ploughing is ploughed, destroying the weeds of delusion. The harvest that it yields is the ambrosia fruit of Nirvana, and by this ploughing all sorrow ends.

took the longest journey he had yet made, penetrating as far as Mantala returning via Benares and Vesali to Sarvasti in Kosala preaching in all the places he visited. On his return he preached the Maharahula Sutra to his son Rahula.

13th Year:—Goutama then went to Chaliya where he spent the rainy season and returned to Sarvasti.

14th Year:—In this year Goutama ordained at the Jituvana Vihara in Sarvasti his son Rahula, delivering on this occasion the Rahula Sutra. He then travelled to Kapilavastu.

15th Year:—He spent the 15th year at the Nigradha grove near Kapilavastu. He addressed to his cousin Mahanama who had succeded Badraha, the successor of Sudhadhana, in the headship of the Sakhya clan, a discourse. He then returned to the Jituvana Vihara. He dilivered here a discourse on the superiority of righteousness to alms-giving.

16th Year:—Goutama next went to Alawi where he converted a mythical monster who used to eat all the children of the district.

17th Year:—During the 17th rainy season which he spent at Rajagriha, Goutama preached a Sermon on the occasion of the death of Srimati, a courtezan, and in the fine weather returned through Sravasti to Alwi, preaching in all the places he passed through. At Alawi he refused to preach to a hungryman until he had been well-fed.

18th Year.—He spent the Was at Chaliya near Sravasti and while there the Teacher comforted a weaver who had accidently killed his daughter. Goutama then went to Rajagriha.

19th Year.—After spending the rainy season in the Veluvana Vihara, Goutama travelled through Magadha preaching in all the villages, On one occasion, finding a deer caught in a net he released it, and sitting down under a tree near by became absorbed in meditation. The angry hunter tried to shoot him, but failed. Buddha then preached to him and to his family who all became his lay-disciples. He then went on to Sravasti.

20th Year.—Here he spent the rainy season, and having been twice contemptuously treated by mendicants who used to carry his alms-bowl he appointed Ananda to be his constant companion. Then went he to a forest near Chalya and succeeeded in overcoming by kindness a famous robber, named Angulimala who became a monk.*

---

* This is the story of Angulimala as given by Hardy in his Manuel of Buddhism, pp. 250-252.

The priest of the king of Kosala had a son named *Ahingsaha*, but by the freak of fate he became a great robber who murdered every one he got hold of and cut off his fingures, thus getting the name Angulimala (the garland of fingures). At this time Buddha was residing in Jetuvana Vihara. He had to make a journey through the country in which the terrible robber lived. The herdsmen informed him that no one could pass that way alone, that men were obliged to go in companies in forty and fifty and that even then they were sometimes murdered. Buddha went on and soon he was seen by the robber. He hastened towards him and ran after him, but ran as much as he could, he failed to come to the great Prophet. "I have run after elephants, horses, chariots," thought the robber, "and have overtaken them, but this priest outstrips me." He then called out to the priest to stop, and Buddha did so and commanded him to remain where he was and not come nearer. He then gave him good advice, telling him to be kind to all beings, by which he would be able to save himself from hell. His words so impressed the robber that he fell at his feet and prayed to be taken into his order. Buddha ordained him a monk, and thenceforth he became one of the holiest of holy monks of the Buddhist Order.

From the 21st year till the year of his death, we have no records of Buddha's mission.

—:o:—

CHAPTER XVII.

HIS FRIENDS.

EVERY great man that had been ever born in this world had friends innumerable as well as enemies countless. The great Buddha was no exception. He was adored and worshipped by thousands of men and women; and thousands again were jealous of him; they slandered him, they tried in various ways to injure him. Amongst his friends and supporters,—two prominently stood over all, namely the great merchant Anatpinda of Sravasti and the wealthy lady Visaka of Visali. Amongst his enemies none was so bitter as his own cousin and disciple Devadatta. We shall give the story of Anatpinda and Visaka as well as Devadatta.

There resided in Rajagriha a rich merchant; Anatpinda the great merchant of Sravasti was his friend, and every year he used to visit him when the merchant of Rajagriha went out many miles from the city to receive him. One day Anatpinda approached Rajagriha, but there was no friend to meet him. He came to the city, but saw no one to welcome him as had been usual. When he entered the house, his friend was there, but his greeting was hurried and brief. At night, however, he came to him to inform him of the reason of his conduct. He expected Buddha and his monks the next day to receive an alms-offering at his dwelling, and he had been too much engaged in making the necessary preparation to show him the accustomed courtesy.

Anatpinda determined to see Buddha, but he thought, "There are many now who say that they are the Buddha and I may be deceived. There was a name given to me Sudatta by my parents which is known only to them and me. If Goutama tells me what it is, I will believe in him." Early in the morning Buddha himself went to meet him and on seeing him said, "Sudutta, come hither." On hearing his words, the faith of Anatpinda became firm, and he promised to stick to his teachings to the end of his life.

He returned to Sravasti inviting Buddha to honour his house with a visit and the great master promised to do it. On returning to Sravasti, Anatpinda bought the best garden in the suburbs of the city by paying an immense amount of money to the prince to whom it belonged. He then began the erection of the Vihara. Round it were houses for the monks, offices that were suitable for the day and others for the night, an ambulatory, tanks and gardens of fruits and flower trees, and round the whole extending 4,000 cubits was a wall 18 cubits high. The whole of these erections cost 18 *kotis* of *masuraus* (gold coins).

When all was furnished, Buddha was invited to visit the place; and he set off by easy stages, sixteen miles each day, so that he was forty-five days in travelling from Rajgriha to Sravasti. On his approach to the city, he was met by a splendid procession composed of different companies with 800 persons in each, carrying appropriate vessels and emblems of the most costly descriptions. One company was headed by Anatpinda's two daughters. Anatpinda escorted Buddha to the Vihara, and there enquired of the sage unto whom it should be offered, and Buddha said, "Let it be offered to the Sangha (Order)." Then Anatpinda poured water from a golden vessel upon the hands of Buddha in token that he dedicated the Vihara to all the monks from whichever of the four quarters they might come.

Buddha passed many years of his life in this great Vihara, that Anatpinda dedicated to the Buddhist Order. Anatpinda spent his whole fortune—an immense one to the cause of Buddhism, and so long the great Religion of the great Master would exist in the world, the name of the noble Anatpinda will be ever associated with his name.

The next great friend and supporter of Buddha's religion was the very wealthy lady of Sravasti, named Visaka. Oldenberg says :—"She is a rich citizen-commoner at Sravasti, the chief town of Kosala, the mother of many blooming children, the grand-mother of countless children. Every one invites Visaka to sacrificial ceremonies and banquets, and the dishes offered first to a guest like her brings luck to the house. It is Visaka who is represented to have made the first liberal preparations in a large scale to provide for Buddha's disciples who came to Sravasti, the chief necessaries of life."

Buddha is one day dining with his disciples at Visaka's home. After dinner Visaka approaches him and says: "Eight requests, Sire, I make of Exalted One." Buddha replied, "The Perfect One, O Visaka, is too exalted to be able to grant you every wish."

Visaka said, "I pray to have what is allowable, Sire, and what is unblamable.

"Then, said Buddha, "speak, Visaka."

"I desire," said Visaka, "as long as I live, Sire, to give the Brotherhood clothes for the rainy season, to give food to the stranger-monks who arrive here, to give to monks food who are passing through, to this great city of Sravasti, to give food to the attendants on the sick, to give medicine to the sick, to distribute a daily dole of boiled rice, to give bathing-dresses to the sisterhood of nuns."

"What object," said Buddha, "hast thou in view, Visaka, that thou approachest the Perfect One with these eight wishes?"

"A monk," said Visaka, "who comes from foreign parts does not know the streets and lanes of this city and he goes about weary to collect alms. When he has partaken of the food which I shall provide for the monks who arrive, he may then, when he has enquired the ways and the streets, go about refreshed to collect alms. This end, Sire, I have in view.

Therefore, I desire as long as I live to give food to monks when they arrive. And again, Sire, a monk who is travelling through, if he has to seek for food for himself, falls behind his caravan or arrives late when he intends to rest, and he walks on his journey wearily. If he has partaken of the food which I shall have provided for monks who are passing through, he will not fall behind his caravan, and he will arrive in proper time at the place where he intends to rest and he will walk on his journey refreshed. This object I have in view, Sire. Therefore I desire as long as I live to give food to the monks who are passing through. It has happened, Sire, that nuns were bathing naked together in the river *Asiravati* at the same bathing place with the prostitutes. The prostitutes, Sire, mocked the nuns saying, "Most respected ones, what do you need of your holy life as long as you are young? Is it not proper to gratify desire? When you are old you may begin a holy life, so both will be yours;—this life and that which is to come!" When the nuns, Sire, were thus mocked by the prostitutes, they were put out of temper. Improper, Sire, is nakedness for a woman,—obscene and objectionable. This, Sire, I consider. Therefore I desire, as long as I live, to provide bathing-dresses for the sisterhood of nuns."

And Buddha said, "Good, Visaka? Thou doest well that thou, seeking this reward, askest the Perfect One for these eight wishes. I grant thee these eight wishes, Visaka." Then the Holy One praised Visaka in these words.

Who gives food and drink with generous readiness,
The follower of the Holy One, rich in virtues,
Who, without grudging, gives gifts for the reward of heaven,
Who puts an end to pain, is ever intent on bringing joy,
Obtains the reward of a heavenly life.
She walks the shining, commendable path;
Free from pain, she joyfully reaps for a long period

The reward of good deeds in the happy realm of heaven above.*

—:o:—

CHAPTER XVIII.

HIS ENEMIES.

THERE was no lack of enemies of Buddha, though perfectly good he was. The chief of them was Devadatta, his own cousin. Dr. Oldenberg writes:—"Stimulated by ambition he seems to have aimed at stepping into the place of Buddha who had already grown old and at getting the management of the community into his own hands. When Buddha does not permit this, he attempts in conjunction with Ajatsatru, the son of King Bimbasara of Magadha, who was then aiming at his father's throne, to put the Master out of the way. Their projects failed.† Miracles are related by which the holy one is preserved. The defeated murderers are attacked by fear and trembling. When they came near Buddha, he speaks gently to them and they are converted to the faith; the piece of rock which is intended to crush Buddha is interrupted by two converging mountain peaks so that it merely grazes Buddha's feet; the wild elephant which is driven against Buddha in a narrow street remains standing before him paralized by the magic power of his friendly thought and then turns back."

Failing to destroy the great Master, Devadatta attempted to obtain the leadership of the Order in another way. Deva-

* See Mahavagga, VIII. 15.

† See Kulavagga. VII.

datta, still professing himself a Buddhist, went with due solemnity to Veluvana Vihara where Buddha was then residing, and formally called upon him to insist on the stricter rules which he advocated. These were that the mendicants should live in the open air and not close to towns, should dress in cast-off rags, should always beg their food from door to door, that is,—never accept invitations or food sent to the Viharas, and should eat no meat. Buddha answered that his precepts could be kept in any place, that he had no objection to such members of the Order as wish to do so keeping stricter rules, but that they were not necessary, and could not be kept at all by the young or the delicate. As to food, the members of the Order might eat whatever was customary in the countries where they were, so long as they ate without indulgence of the appetite. It was possible to become pure at the foot of a tree, or in a house, in cast off clothes, or in clothes given by laymen, whilst abstaining from flesh, or whilst using it. To establish one uniform law would be a hinderance in the way of those who were seeking Nirvana which was his sole aim. Devadatta upon this returned to his own Vihara and founded a new and stricter Order which gradually grew in numbers and was openly supported by Ajatsatru.*

The ancient chroniclers thus describe the end of Devadatta.

"The requests made by Devadatta being all refuged, he retired to his own Vihara at the head of the river Gaya, with his four companions and was soon joined by other dissatisfied monks, so that the number of his disciples again amounted to 500. When Buddha saw that the time to reclaim the 500 monks had arrived, he commanded Sariputra and Magyalana to visit their Vihara and exert their influence for this purpose. On their arrival, Devadatta was in the

* Rhys Davids' Buddhism pp. 76—77.

midst of the followers saying *bana* in imitation of Buddha; and when he saw them, he gladly gave them permission to enter as he supposed they had come to join his party. But Kokilaka, his chief disciple, said that it would be better to require them to keep at a distance as it was most probable they had come to do him injury. The one was placed on the right hand of Devadatta and the other on his left, and Kokilaka occupied the place of Anyakondanya according to the arrangement when *bana* was said by Buddha. After he had proceeded a little, Sariputra said that he must be fatigued and began to say *bana* in his stead, but in such a manner that all the monks became Rahats with the exception of Devadatta who who had fallen asleep. When he awoke and found that all his followers were gone, he regretted that he had not followed the advice of Kokilaka and was so affected by this event, that he fell seriously ill and continued so for nine months.

After this period he resolved to go to Buddha and to entreat his forgiveness; and though his disciples tried to persuade him not to go as they said that Buddha would not see him, yet they were unable to induce him to alter his intention, as he knew that the great Master felt no enemity towards him. When they saw that he was determined, they took him in a litter as he was quite unable to rise, and conveyed him to Jetuvana Vihara.

When near the Vihara, the disciples put the litter upon the ground whilst they washed themselves in the tank. The eagerness of Devadatta to see Buddha was so great that he rose from the litter, though he had been unable to move for sometime past.* But when he put his foot to the ground, flames came from the hill and enrapped his body in their folds. He cried, " O Buddha, though I have done wrong to you, yet for the sake of my relationship, save me."†

* Most likely he died in his attempt to run towards Buddha.

† See Hardy pp. 328—329.

CHAPTER XIX.

HIS MODE OF LIFE.

CAN we gather any idea of how Buddha lived? The great disciples, who clustered round the master, such as Ananda, Upali, Sariputra Maggalana and others, completely resemble each other in the old narratives that have come to us in the Buddhist Sacred Texts. Their pictures are nothing else, but the invariably uniform copy of Buddha himself, only in a reduced scale. Thus we can very well form a picture in our mind of the great Teacher as he lived and preached 2500 years ago.

As the picture of the daily life of Buddha has been most magnificiently drawn by Oldenberg, we make no apology to quote him in *extenso**

"From year to year the change from a period of wandering to a period of rest and retirement repeated itself for Buddha and his disciples. In the month of June when after the dry scorching heat of the Indian summer, clouds came up in towering masses and the rolling thunders heralded the approach of the rain-bearing monsoon, Buddha every year kept *Vana* (rainy-season) for three months surrounded by his disciples who flocked together to pass the rainy season near their Teacher. Kings and wealthy men contended for the honour of entertaining him and his disciples who were with

---

* Buddha in his sojourn usually resided in the various *Viharas*, that were presented to the Order by the wealthy *Upasakas*; the most celebrated of them were the Veluvana Vihara in Rajgriha, presented by king Bimbasara of Magadha and Jetuvana Vihara in Sravasti, presented by the wealthy merchant Anatpinda. These were the two most favourite places of residence of the great Master. In fact he past most part of his long life in those places, sometimes alone and sometimes surrounded by his numerous disciples.

him as guests during this season in the Viharas and gardens which they had provided for the community."

The rain being over, the itinerating began. Buddha went from town to town and village to village, always attended by a great concourse of disciples.* The territory through which these wandering excursions generally extended was the circuit of the Eastern Land, *i.e.*, chiefly the old kingdoms of Kasi, Kosala and Magadha with the neighbouring free states and territories known at the present day by the name of Oudh and Behar.

In these frequent journeying, Buddha and his disciples were often invited to dinner by wealthy laymen. He permitted his consent by silence and attended it dressed in his long coat with alms bawl in his hand. After dinner he addressed the host and his assembled friends and relatives with a few words of spitritual admonition and instruction.

If the day be not filled by an invitation, Buddha, according to the rules of his Order, went round the village or town in quest of alms. He went from house to house and stood, alms bawl in hand, silently waiting until a morsel of food was thrown into it.

After taking his repast he passed a few hours in silent meditation, either within a cloister or underneath the shady branches of a banian tree. Thus did pass his life from years' end to years' end till at last he attained to the final Nirvana.

---

* See Cakkavatti Suttanta.

—:o:—

CHAPTER XX.

HIS MODE OF PREACHING.

BUDDHA always preached orally—written discourses he did not deliver. He spoke not in Sanskrit, but in the Vernacular of the land through which he journeyed.*

In the evening almost every day, if he was residing in a place and not journeying, he used to deliver his *bana* before his disciples and all those that came to hear him. These were long discourses, such as have come down to us in Pali Texts. We give below an extract from his celebrated Discourse on Fire.

"Every thing, O disciples, is in flames. And what everything, O disciples, is in flames? The eye, O disciples, is in flames, the visible is in flames, the knowledge of the visible is in flames, the contact with the visible is in flames, the feeling which rises from the contact with the visible, be it pleasure, be it pain, be it neither pleasure nor pain, this also is in flames. By what fire is it kindled? By the fire of desire, by the fire of hate, by the fire of fascination, it is kindled; by birth, old age, death, pain, lamentation, sorrow, grief and despair, it is kindled,—thus I say. The ear is in flames, the audible is in flames, the knowledge of the audible is in flames, the contact with the audible is in flames, the feeling which arises from the contact with the audible, be it pleasure, be it pain, be it neither pleasure nor pain, this also is in flames. By what fire it is kindled? By the fire of desire, by the fire of hate, by the fire of fascination, it is kindled; by birth, old age, death, pain, lamentation, sorrow, grief, despair, it is kindled;—thus I say," and so forth.†

---

* See Introduction.

† See Mahavagga, V. 1—15.

If a man came to him to be converted or to know what his Doctrine was, he began by admonishing him to the practice of virtues in worldly vocations, to generosity, to rectitude in every earthly occupation; he spoke of the heavens with their rewards which await him, who has led a life of earnest purpose here below. And as soon as he knew that his hearer or hearers was or were fit to receive some thing deeper, he proceeded to speak to them of that which,—as the Text says, —"is pre-eminently the revelation of the Buddhas," namely, the Doctrines of Sufferings and Deliverance."

The third mode of Buddha's teaching was by conversation and dialogue. We give an example.

"Buddha comes in his begging excursion to the house of his wealthiest and his most liberal admirer, the great merchant Anatpinda. He hears loud conversation and wrangling, and asks, "Why are the people screaming and crying in thy house? One would think fishermen had been robbed of their fish." And Anatpinda pours out his grief to Buddha:—a daughter-in-law of a rich house has come into his family who will not listen to her husband and her parents-in-law and declines to show due reverence to Buddha. Buddha says to her. "Come, Sujata." She answers, "Yes sire," and comes to Buddha. He says to her, "There are seven kinds of wives which a man may have, Sujata. What seven are they? One resembles a murderer, another a robber, another a mistress, another a mother, another a sister, another a friend, another a servant. These, Sujata, are the seven kinds of wives which a man have. Which kind art thou?"

And Sujata has forgotten all obstinacy and pride, and says defferentially, "O Sire, I do not understand the full meaning of that which the Exalted One has stated in brief; therefore, may the Exalted One so expound to me his doctrine that I may be able to understand the full meaning of that which the Exalted One has stated briefly." "Hearken, O Sujata, and take it well to heart; I shall state it to thee." And Buddha described the seven kinds of wives. "These, Sujata, are the seven kinds of wives which a man may have. What kind among these art thou?" "From this day forward," says Sujata, "Sire, I may be esteemed as one who is to her husband a wife who resembles a servant."

Another mode of Buddha's teaching was by similes. Here is an example. Buddha said,—

"As when, O disciples, in the forest on a mountain slope, there lies a great tract of low-land and water where a great herd of deer lives, there comes a man who devises hurt, distress and danger for the deer,—who covers over and shuts up the path which is safe, good, and pleasant to take,—and opens up a false path, a swampy path, a marshy track; thenceforward, O disciples, the great herd of deer incurs hurt and and diminishes. But now, O disciples, if a man comes, who devises prosperity, welfare and safety for this great herd of deer, who clears and opens up the path which is safe, good and pleasant to take, and does away with the false path and abolishes the swampy and the marshy track, thenceforward, O disciples, the great herd of deer thrives, grows and increases. I have spoken to you, O disciples, in a parable, to make known my meaning. But the meaning is this. The great low land and the water, O disciples, are pleasures. The great herds of deer, O disciples, are living men. The man, O disciples, who devises hurt, distress, and ruin is Mara, the Evil One. The false path, O disciples, is eightfold path, to wit, false path, false resolve, false speech, false action, false living, false effort, false thought, false conception. The swampy way, O disciples, is pleasure and desires. The swampy track is ignorance.*

---

* See Devdhavitaka Sutta. As we shall have to deal with Buddha's preachings and doctrines in *extenso* in Parts II and III, we do not dilate upon them here. We refer our readers to these Parts of the work.

CHAPTER XXI.

HIS LAST TOUR.

In the 8oth year of his age and 45th year of his mission* the great Buddha returned to Rajgriha from Sravasti and dwelled for sometime on the hill called Vulture Peak.† And whilst the Blessed One stayed there at Rajgriha on the Vulture's Peak, he held those comprehensive relegious discourses with the Bhikshus, namely the discourses on the nature of upright conduct and of earnest contemplation and of intelligence.

And now when the Blessed One had sojourned at Rajagriha as long as he pleased, he addressed the venerable Ananda and said, "Come, Ananda, let us go to Ambalithiha.

From this place the great Goutama with his followers

---

* From this Chapter till the end of the Chapter XXV., we give the incidents as we find them in the Pali work—Maha-Pari-Nibbana-Sutta. We have tried to keep up the quaintness of the original,—therefore we follow here the translations of Rhys Davids as he has done it in his *Buddha Suttas*, Vol. XI. of the "Sacred Books of the East." He says:—"At the time when our Book of the great Decease (Maha-Pari-Nibbana Sutta) was put into its present shape and still more so when a Book of the Great Decease was first drawn up, there may well have been some reliable traditions as to the events that took place and as to the subjects of his various discourses, in the Buddha's last journey."

Dr. Oldenberg says:—"Regarding the last months of his life on his last great journey from Rajgriha to Kusanagara, the place of his death, we possess a detailed account in a Sutta of the Sacred Pali Canon, *i.e.*, Maha-Pari-Nibbana Sutta. The external feature of this narrative bears for the most part, though perhaps not in every particular, the stamp of trustworthy traditions."

† Maha-Pari-Nibbana Sutta.

went to Nalanda and lived in the Pavarikȧ mango grove. Then the Blessed One proceeded with a great company of mendicants to Pataligama which afterwards became world-renowed by the name of Pataliputra.

Now the disciples at Pataligama heard of his arrival there, went to the place where he was, took their seats respectfully beside him, and invited him to their village rest-house, and the Blessed One consented. They then went away to their house, bowing to the Blessed One and keeping him on their right as they passed him. On arriving at the rest-house, they made it fit in every way for occupation, placed seats in it, set up a water-pot and fixed an oil lamp. Then they returned to the Blessed One and bowing stood beside him and said, "All things are ready now. It is time for you to do what you deem most fit."

And the Blessed One robed himself, took his bowl and other things, went with the Bhikshus to the rest-house, washed his feet, entered the hall and took his seat against the center pillar with his face towards the east.

Then the Blessed One addressed the Pataliputra disciples and said, "Five fold, O house-holders, is the loss of the wrong-doer through his want of rectitude. In the first place the wrong-doer, devoid of rectitude, falls into great poverty through idleness; in the next place his evil repute gets noised abroad; thirdly whatever society he enters, whether of Brahmans, nobles, heads of houses, or Sramanas, he enters shyly and confused: fourthly he is full of anxiety when he dies, and lastly on the dissolution of body after death, he is reborn into some unhappy state of suffering and woe. This, O house-holders, is the five-fold loss of the evil-doer?",

"Five-fold, O house-holders, is the gain of the well-doer; strong in rectitude, he acquires great wealth through his industry; in the next place, good reports of him are spread abroad; thirdly whatever society he enters, whether of nobles,

Brahmanas, heads of houses, or members of the Order, he enters confident and self-possessed; fourthy he dies without anxiety; and lastly, on the dissolution of body after death, he is reborn into some happy state in heaven. This, O house-holders, is the five-fold gain of the well-doer."

When the Blessed One had thus taught the disciples and and incited them and roused them and gladdened them far into the night with religious discourses, he dismissed them saying, "The night is far advanced, O house-holders; it is time for you to do what you deem most fit."

Buddha rose early in the morning and saw a fortress in course of construction in the village of Pataligrama. "Who is it, Ananda," asked he, "that is building a fortress in Pataligrama?" The venerable Ananda replied, "Sunidha and Vaisakara, my Lord, the chief ministers of Magadha, are building a fortress here to keep back the Vajjias."

And the Blessed One said, "Among famous places of residence and haunts of busy men will become the chief, this city of Pataliputra,—a centre for the interchange of all sorts of merchandise. But three dangers will hang over Pataliputra, that of fire, that of water and that of dissension."*

On hearing the arrival of the great Buddha, the two chief ministers of the king of Magadha hastened to him and bowing said, "May the venerable Goutama do us the honour of taking his meal together with his disciples at our house to-day." The Blessed One signified his consent by silence.

That day he took his meal in their house and then passed out of the village. The ministers followed him as he went, and when he departed, they said, "The gate the Sramana Goutama goes out by to-day shall be called *Goutama's Gate* and the ferry at which he crosses the river shall be called *Goutama's Ferry*."

---

* This prophecy was afterwards fulfilled.

Crossing the Ganges,* Goutama went on and reached Kotigrama. Thence he went to the village of Nadika where he stayed for some time. He then went to Vesali and took his stay at a mango grove belonging to a courtezan, named Ambapalli.

Now the courtezan Ambapalli heard that the Blessed One had arrived at Vesali and was staying at her mango grove.† She went in a carriage as far as the ground was passable for carriage; there she alighted, and she proceeded on foot to the place where the Blessed One was and took her seat respectfully on one side. And when she was thus seated, the Blessed One instructed, incited and gladdened her with religious discourses. Then she addressed the Blessed One and said, "May the great Lord do me the honour of taking his meal together with the brethren at my house to-morrow." The Blessed One gave his consent by silence.

The nobles‡ of Vesali, when they heard that the Great One had arrived in their city, they hastened towards the mango grove to invite him to dine at their place. But on their way they heard that the courtezan Ambapalli had secured that honour. They therefore went to her place and said, "O Ambapalli, give up this meal to us for a hundred thousand." But Ambapalli replied, "My Lords, were you to offer all Vesali, I would not give up this feast." Saying "we

---

* Here a miracle has been narrated in the Maha Pari Nirvana Sutta. We quote the passage. "The Blessed One went into the river. And at that time the river Ganges was brimful and overflowing, and wishing to cross to the opposite bank, some began to seek for boats, some for rafts of wood, while some made rafts of basket works. Then the Blessed One as instantaneously as a strong man would stretch forth his arm or draw it back again when he stretched it forth, vanished from this side of the river and stood on the further bank with the company of the brethren."

† This portion of the Maha Parinibbana Sutta is word for word the same as Maha Vagga Vol. VI. 30. 1 to VI. 30. 6.

‡ The nobles of Vesali were the Lichhavis.

are outdone by this Mango girl," they went to meet the Blessed One with depressed hearts. Bowing at his feet they said, "May the Blessed One do us the honour of taking his meal together with his disciples at our house." And the Blessed One replied, "I have promised to dine with Ambapalli the courtezan." The nobles went away disappointed and sad.

The Blessed One robed himself early in the morning and took his bowl and went with the brethren to the place where Ambapalli's dwelling house was, and when he had come there, he seated himself in the seat prepared for him. And Ambapalli, the courtezan, placed the sweet rice and cakes before the Order, with the great Buddha at their head, and waited upon them, and pressed food till they refused.

And when the Blessed One had quite finished his meal, the courtezan had a low stool brought and sat down at his side and addressed the Blessed One and said, "Lord, I present this mansion to the Order;" and the Blessed One accepted the gift.

When the great Buddha was in Vesali, the rainy season set in. He then thus addressed his followers, "O mendicants, do you take up your abode round about Vesali, each according to the place where his friends, intimates, and close companions may live for the rainy season of *Was*. I shall pass the rainy season at Beluva."

"So be it, Lord," said the Bhikshus. And they entered upon the *was* round about Vesali, each according to the place where his friends or intimates or close companions lived.

When his followers thus scattered round Vesali, the Blessed One said, "Come, Ananda, let us go to Beluva." And they two, the great master and the great disciple—lived all through the rainy season alone at Beluva.

——:O:——

CHAPTER XXII.

HIS LAST DAYS.

DURING the rainy season, when the great Buddha was quietly staying at Beluva with his beloved Ananda only as his companion and attendant, he for the first time fell ill. He grew daily worse and was almost at the point of death. Then he thus thought,—"It would not be right for me to pass away without addressing the disciples. Let me now, by a strong effort of will, subdue this illness."* Very soon after he began to recover. When he grew quite strong again, he came out of the monastry and sat on a seat which Ananda spread out for him. None of them talked for some time, till at last, the venerable Ananda thus spoke, "I have beheld, Lord, how the Blessed One was in health, and I have beheld how the Blessed One had to suffer. And though at the sight of the sickness of the Blessed One, my body became weak as a creeper and the horizon became dim to me and my faculties were no longer clear, yet notwithstanding I took some little comfort from the thought that the Blessed One could not pass away from existence until at last he had left instructions for the Order."

"What then, Ananda," said the great Goutama, "Does the Order expect of me? I have preached the Truth without making any distinction between exoteric and esoteric doctrine; for in respect of the truths, Ananda, Thathagata (Buddha) has no such thing as the closed fist of a teacher who keeps something back. Surely Ananda, should there be any one who thinks, "It is I who will lead the Brotherhood; the order is dependent upon me," it is only he who should lay down instructions concerning the Order.

* See Maha-Pari-Nibbana Sutta, Chap. II.

Now the Buddha, Ananda, does never think that it is he who should lead the Brotherhood or that the Order is dependent upon him;—why then should he leave instructions concerning the Order? I, too, Ananda, am now grown old and full of years; my journey is drawing to its close; I have reached my sum of days; I am turning eighty years of age. Just as a worn-out cart, Ananda, can only with much additional care, be made to move along, so the body of the Buddha can now be kept going only with much additional care. Therefore, O Ananda, be ye yourselves lamps unto yourselves. Be ye yourselves a refuge to yourselves. Hold fast to the Truth as a lamp. Hold fast as a refuge to the Truth. Look not for refuge to any one besides yourselves. And now, Ananda how, is a brother to be lamp unto himself, a refuge unto himself? It is by betaking himself to no external refuge. It is by holding fast to the Truth as a lamp, holding fast as a refuge to the truth, looking not for refuge to any one besides himself."

The Great Master stayed a few days more in Vesali, living in various charming *Chaityas*.* One day he said to his beloved cousin and disciple. "Go, Ananda, assemble all the Bhikshus that now reside in the neighbourhood of Vesali." Ananda immediately called them all together, and when they all assembled, the great Goutama addressed them thus.† "Brethren, I have made known to you the truths

* The *Chaityas* were places where the Bhikshus lived. There were many such places round about Vesali. The Buddha himself said, "How delightful a spot, Ananda, is Vesali: and the Udena Chetiya, and the Gotamaka Chetiya, and the Sattambaka Chetiya and the Bahuputta Chetiya, and Sarandada Chetiya, and the Kapali Chetiya." See Maha-Pari-Nibbana Sutta, Chap. III.

† This is the last sermon he delivered to his followers. Rhys David says: "It is of great interest to notice what are the points upon which Gotama in this last address to his disciples and at the solemn time when death was near at hand, is reported to have lain such emphatic stretch. Unfortunately we have only a fragment of the address, and as it would

that I have perceived. Having thoroughly made yourselves masters of them,—practice them, meditate upon them, spread them abroad, so that pure religion may last long and be perpetuated for the good and for the happiness of gods and men.

Which then, brethren, are the truths that I have made known to you? They are these—

The four earnest meditation,
The four-fold great struggle against sin,
The four roads to saintship,
The five moral powers,
The five bargains of spiritual sense,
The seven kinds of wisdom,
The noble eight-fold path."

After a few minutes' silence the Great Master said, "Behold now, Brethren, I exhort you, saying "All component things must grow old. Work out your salvation with diligence. The final extinction of the Tathagatha will take place before long. At the end of three months from this time, the Tathagatha will die.

My age is now full ripe, my life draws to its close.
I leave you, I depart, relying on myself alone.
Be earnest then, Brethren, full of holy thought;
Be steadfast in resolve, keep watch over your own hearts."

He then, bidding them all adieu, left Vesali and went with Ananda towards Pava,—a few of his most devoted followers accompanying him. When he arrived at Pava, a Smith named Chanda of that place came to him and said, "May the Blessed One do me the honour of taking his meal at my house." The Blessed One consented.

---

seem from its commencement, only the closing fragment. This summary of the Buddha's last address may fairly be taken as a summary of Buddhism which thus appears to be simply a system of earnest self-culture and self-control. See Sacred Books of the East, Vol xi, p. 62.

Chanda made ready in his house sweet rice and cakes and a quantity of dried boar's flesh, On seeing this, the Great Master said, "As to the dried boar's flesh you have made ready, serve me with it, Chanda. Give the sweet rice and cakes to the Bhikshus."

Leaving Pava, the Great Master went towards Kusinara, but on his way there fell upon him a dire sickness, the disease of dysentry, and sharp pain came upon him even unto death. But the Blessed One, mindful and self-possessed, bore it without complaint.*

The Great Master gradually grew worse. The Blessed One went aside from the path to the foot of a certain tree; and when he had come there, he addressed the venerable Ananda and said, "Fold the robe, I pray you, Ananda, and spread it out for me. I am weary, Ananda, and must rest a while." After little rest he said, "Fetch me some water I pray you, Ananda; I am thirsty, Ananda, and would drink."

He again rose and dragged himself to the bank of the Kukustha river,† went down into water and bathed and

---

* Dr. Oldenberg apparently does not find much historical basis concerning this cause of the Buddha's last iilness. He quotes from the Maha-Pari-Nibbana Sutta the following Gatha,

"Travel-worn came Buddha to the river Kukuotha
Peaceful, pure with clear waters;
Down into the water went the Master weary,
The supreme perfect one, without equal.
When he had bathed, the Master drank of the river,
And went up out of it with the bands of his disciple,
The holy master, the preacher of the truth,
The sage went on to the mango grove."

Then he remarks:—"These very old verses, which plainly and truly depict a plain situation, belong beyond all doubt to the most trustworthy reminiscences, which we have of Buddha's life." See Oldenberg's Buddha, p. 200.

† Kukustha is the small stream called Barhi, which flows to the Chota Gondak eight miles below Kasik. See Cunnigham's Ancient Geography, p. 435.

drank. Thus refreshed he again walked on and reached a Sal grove on the outskirts of Kushimaga.*

He said, "Go, Ananda, and prepare a bed for me between two twin trees with my head to the north. I am tired, Ananda, I shall lie down."

The Blessed One laid himself down on his right side, with one foot resting on the other; calm and self-possessed.

Then thus spoke Tathagatha to the venerable Ananda, "Although this is not the time of flowers, Ananda, yet there are two twin trees decked with blossoms, and the flowers are falling, showering down on the body of the Tattagatha. But to him belongs another honour, another glory, another reward, another homage, another reverence. Whosoever, Ananda, male or female Bhikshu or follower, lay brother, lay-sister, lives in the Truth, in matters both great and small, and lives according to the ordinance and also walks in the Truth in details, these bring to the Tattagatha the highest honour, glory, praise and credit."

As night came on, it became evident to the followers that their Great Master was passing away. They silently began to weep all around apart from the place where their dying master lay.†

---

* Now Kasia, east of Gorrukpur on the Chota Gundak. See Cunningham's Ancient Geography of India p. 430.

† Of his principal followers the following were present at the time of his death,—Ananda, Anurudha, Sariputra etc.

The great Kassyapa arrived when the Great Master had already passed away.

CHAPTER XXIII.

HIS LAST ACT.

The poor Ananda exclaimed:—"Vouchsafe, O Lord, to live during the Kalpa. Live on, O Blessed One, through the the Kalpa for the good and the happiness of the great multitudes, out of pity for the world, for the good and the gain and the weal of gods and men."

The Great Master smiled. The venerable Ananda then said:—"Let not the Blessed One die in this place in the midst of jungles. There are, O Lord, such great cities as Champa, Rajgriha, Sravasti, Saketa and Baranasi. Let the Blessed One die in one of them. There are in them many wealthy nobles, believers in the Tatatgatha, who will pay due honour to the remains of the Tattagatha."

The Great Master again smiled. The venerable Ananda then exclaimed:—"What are we to do, Lord, with the remains of the Tattagatha?"

The Great Master spoke:—"Trouble not yourselves, O Ananda, by honouring the remains of the Tattagatha. Be zealous, I beseach you, Ananda, in your own behalf. Be earnest, be zealous, be intent on your own good. There are wise men, Ananda, among the nobles who are firm believers in the Tathagatha, they will do due honour to the remains of the Tattagatha."

After a few minutes, silence, the great Goutama then spoke to Ananda, "After I am gone, tell Chanda that he will in a future birth receive very great reward, for having eaten of the food he gave me, I am about to pass away. Say, it was from my own mouth, you heard it. There are two gifts that will be blest above all others,—that of Sujata before

I attained Buddhahood and this of Chanda before I finally pass away."*

The venerable Ananda could no longer hold himself; he completely broke down and went aside to weep. Not seeing him by his side, the Great Master said :—" Where is Ananda, " Brethren ?" " The venerable Ananda, O Lord," replied they, "has gone aside and is weeping." " Go, bretheren," said the Master, " and call him to me."

Ananda came and sat by his side. Then the great Tattagatha slowly began :—"Do not let yourself be troubled, Ananda, do not weep. Have I not on former occasions told you that it is in the very nature of all things most dear and near unto us that we must separate ourselves from them, leave them, sever ourselves from them. Nothing can for ever exist, no such condition is possible. For a long time, Ananda, have you been very near to me by acts of love, kind and good that never varied and was beyond all measure. You have done well Ananda. Be earnest in effort and you too shall soon be free from the great evils, from sensuality, from individuality, from delusion, from ignorance."

As the night wore on, the great master gradually began to sink. At this time came there a Brahman,—a philosopher of Kusinagara named Subhadra. He met Ananda and said; I have heard that Sraman Goutama will pass away this night. Now a certain feeling of uncertainty has sprung up in my mind, and this faith have I in Sraman Goutama that he is

* These are the words spoken by the Great Master: " Now it may happen, Ananda, that some one should stir up remorse in Chanda the smith by saying ' This is evil to thee, Chanda and loss to thee in that when the Tathagata had eaten his last meal from thy provision, then he died!" Any such remorse, Ananda, in Chanda, should be checked by saying, ' This is good to thee Chanda and gain to thee in that when the Tathagatha had eaten his last meal from thy provision, then he died." See Maha-Parinibbana Sutta, Chap. IV.

able so to present the Truth that I may get rid of this feeling of uncertainty. O Ananda, allow me to see the Sramana Goutama." "Friend Subhadra," said Ananda, "trouble not the Tattagatha. The Blessed One is weary." But Subhadra again and again pressed the venerable Ananda. The Blessed One overheard this conversation and said to Ananda, "Beloved cousin, do not keep out Subhadra. Allow him to see the Tattagatha. Whatever Subhadra may ask of me, he will ask from a desire for knowledge and not to annoy me."

The Brahman Subhadra came and sat by the side of the dying Prophet. "The Brahmanas of saintliness, Goutama" asked he, "who are heads of various sects such as Purana Kasyapa, Makhali, Ajita, Kachayana, Sangaya, Belathic and Nigrantha*—have they all, according to their own assertion, throughly understood things, or have they not? Are then some of them who have understood and some who have not?"

"Subhadra," replied Buddha, "let this matter rest whether they according to their own assertion, have throughly understood things or not. This is not the time for such discussions. I will teach you, Subhadra, the Truth; pay attention to it."

Goutama then went on to declare that salvation could not be found in any system which ignored the virtuous life, the eight stages of the Path of Holiness which begins with purity and ends in love.*

"Most excellent, O Lord," said Subhadra, "are the words of your mouth. May the Blessed One accept me as a disciple, as a true believer from this day, as long as life endures."

"Whosoever, Subhadra "said Buddha" that has formerly been a follower of another dectrine and then desires to be

---

* Goutama gave Subhadra a summary of his teachings as given in Dhamma-Chakka-pavathana—Sutta,

received into the higher or the lower grade in this doctrine and discipline, remains on probation for the space of four months."

"I too then," replied Subhadra, "will remain on probation for the space of four months."

The Blessed One called the venerable Ananda and said, "Ananda, receive Subhadra into the Order." Then Ananda took him on one side, poured water over his head, made him repeat the formula of meditation on the impermancy of all things. He then shaved off his hair and beard, clad him in the yellow robes, made him repeat the three refuges,—*Buddha, Dharma* and *Sangha*—and led him back to the Blessed One. The Blessed One himself admitted him then into the higher rank of the Brotherhood and pointed out to him a subject for meditation."* This was the last act of the Great Master.

---

* This Subhadra or some other Subhadra was the man who first raised dissensions in the Order? We find in the Maha-Pari-Nibbana Sutta, Chap. vi, the following passage. "And Subhadra the old addressed the brethren and said, "Enough, brethren. Weep not, neither lament. We are well rid of the great Sramana. We used to be annoyed by being told, "This beseems you, this beseems you not." But now we shall be able to do whatever we like; and what we do not like,—that we shall not have to do."

Rhys Davids remarks:—" At p. xxxi of the Introduction to his edition of Mahavagga, Dr. Oldenberg identifies this Subhadra with Subhadra the last convert mentioned in Chap. V. of the Maha-Pari-Nibbana Sutta. They are different persons; the last convert being represented as a young man of high character incapable of the conduct here ascribed to this Subhadra. The last convert was a Brahman, traditionally supposed to be the younger brother to Anna Kondanna, the first convert. This Subhadra, however, had been a barber in the village Atuma."

—:O:—

CHAPTER XXIV.

HIS DEATH.

As the last watch of the night drew nigh, the Blessed One addressed the venerable Ananda and said:—* "It may be, Ananda, that in some of you the thought may arise, the the word of the Master is ended, we have no teacher more. But it is not thus, Ananda, that you should regard it. Let the truths and the rules of the Order which I have set forth and laid down for you all, be the teacher to you, after I am gone."

After a pause the dying Master thus again spoke to Ananda:—"when I am gone, Ananda, let the Order, if it so wish, abolish all the lesser and minor precepts."†

Then the Blessed One addressed the Bhikshus and said:— "It may be, bretheren, that there may be doubt or misgiving in the mind of some brother as to the Buddha, or the Truth, or the Path or the Way. Enquire, brethren, freely. Do not have to reproach yourselves afterwards with the thought, "Our teacher was face to face with us and we could not bring ourselves to enquire of the Tattagatha when we were face to face with him."

And when he had thus spoken, the brethren were all silent. And again the second and the third time the Blessed

* As it would be more interesting to read what the immediate disciples and followers of the great Buddha wrote about their Master's death in their own language than what we can possibly write ourselves, we quote in this chapter the whole of the 6th chapter of the Moha-Pari-Nibbana Sutta. We have followed Rhys Davids' translation.

† In Chula-Vagga XI. 1, 9, 10, is related how the Brotherhood formally considered the permission thus accorded to them and resolved to adhere to all the precepts laid down in the Buddha's life-time. See Sacred Books of the East, Vol. XI. page 112.

One addressed the brethren and asked them to enquire freely. And even the third time the brethren were silent.

Then the Blessed One addressed the Bhikshus and said :— "It may be, brethren, that you put no questions out of reverence for the teather. Let one friend communicate to another."

And when he thus spoke, the brethren remained silent. Then the venerable Ananda said to the Blessed One :— "Verily I believe that in this great assembly of the Bhikshus, there is no one brother who has any doubt or misgiving as to the Buddha, or the Truth or the Path."

"It is out of the fullness of faith thou hast spoken, Ananda," said the Blessed One.

Then after a pause the Great Master half rose and said :— "Behold now, brethren, I exhort you, saying,—Decay is inherent in all component things. Work out your salvation with deligence."

These were the last words of the Tattagatha.

Then the Blessed One entered into the first stage of deep meditation (Dhyana). And rising out of the first stage, he passed into the second. And rising out of the second, he passed into the third. And rising out of the third stage, he passed into the fourth. And rising out of the fourth stage of deep meditation, he entered into the state of mind to which the infinity of space is alone present. And passing out of the mere consciousness of the infinity of space, he entered into the state of mind to which the infinity of thought alone is present. And passing out of the mere consciousness of the infinity of thought, he entered into a state of mind to which nothing at all was specially present. And passing out of the consciousness of no special object, he fell into a state between consciousness and unconsciousness. And passing out of the state between consciousness and unconsciousness, he fell into a state in which the consciousness both of sensation and of ideas had wholly passed away.

Then the venerable Ananda said to the Venerable Anurudha, "Oh, my Lord, O Anurudha, the Blessed One is dead!" "Nay, brother Ananda," said Anurudha, "the Blessed One is not dead. He has entered into that state in which both sensations and ideas have ceased to be."

Then the Blessed One, passing out of the state in which both sensations and ideas have ceased to be, entered into the state between consciousness and unconsciousness. And passing out of the state of consciousness and unconsciousness, he entered into the state of mind to which nothing at all is specially present. And passing out of the consciousness of no special object, he entered into the state of mind to which the infinity of thought is alone present. And passing out of the mere consciousness of the infinity of thought, he entered into the state of mind to which the infinity of space is alone present. And passing out of the mere consciousness of the infinity of space, he entered into the fourth stage of deep meditation. And passing out of the fourth stage, he entered into the third. And passing out of the third stage, he entered into the second. And passing out of the second, he entered into the first. And passing out of the first stage of deep meditation, he entered into the second. And passing out of the second stage, he entered into the third. And passing out of the third stage, he entered into the fourth stage of deep meditation. And passing out of the last stage of deep meditation, he immediately expired.

When the Blessed One died, there arose at the moment of

his passing out of existence a mighty earth-quake, terrible and awe-inspering: and the thunders of heaven burst forth.*

When the Blessed One died, of those of the Bhikshus, who were not yet free from the passions some stretched, out their arms and wept, and some fell headlong on the ground, rolling to and fro in anguish at the thought, "Too soon has the Blessed One died? Too soon has the Happy One passed away from existence! Too soon has the light gone out in the world."

But those of the brethren who were free from the passions bore their grief collected and composed at the thought, "Impermanent are all component things."

---

* Maha-Pari-Nibbana Sutta says that the following two Gathas were respectively recited by Brahma—the Supreme One and by Sakra the Lord of the Gods at the moment the great Buddha passed away.

"They all, all beings that have life, shall lay
Aside their complex form—that aggregation,
Of mental and material qualities,
That gives them, or in heaven or in earth,
Their fleeting individuality!
E'ven as the Teacher—being such a one
Unequalled among all the men that are
Successors of the prophets of old time,
Might by wisdom and in insight clear
Hath died.

They 're transient all, each being's parts and powers,
Growth is their nature and decay.
They are produced, they are dissolved again,
And then is best, when they have sunk to rest.

—:0:—

CHAPTER XXV.

HIS REMAINS.

Then the venerable Anurudha said to the venerable Ananda, "Go now, brother Ananda, into Kusinagara and inform the Mallas* of Kusinagara that the Blessed One is dead."

The venerable Ananda went to the Mallas and said:—"The Blessed One is dead. Do whatever seemeth to you fit."

And when they had heard this saying of the venerable Ananda, the Mallas with their young men and their maidens and their wives were grieved and sad and afflicted at heart. And some of them wept, dishevilling their hair, and some stretched forth their arms and wept, and some fell prostrate on the ground, and some reeled to and fro in anguish at the thought:—"Too soon has the Blessed One died. Too soon has the Happy One passed away. Too soon has the light gone out in the world."

Then the Mallas of Kusinagara gave orders to their attendants saying, "Gather together perfumes and garlands and all the musical instruments and five hundred suits of apparel;" and went to the Sala grove where the body of the Blessed One lay. There they past the day in paying honour, reverence, respect, and homage to the remains of the Blessed One with dancing and hymns and music, with garlands and perfumes, and in making canopies of their garments preparing decoration-wreathes to hang thereon.†

---

* The people who lived in Kusinagara were called the Mallas.

† It is mentioned that the Mallas went on honouring the remains of the Blessed One for seven days. This was how they burnt the body.

The body of the Great Master was then burnt in due honour.* Then the Mallas of Kusinagara surrounded the bones of the Blessed One in their council Hall with a lattice

---

"Then the Mallas of Kusinagara wrapped the body of the Blessed One in a new cloth. And when that was done, they wrapped it in cotton and wool. And when that was done, they wrapped it in a new cloth,—and so on till they had wrapped the body of the Blessed One in five hundred layers of both kinds. And then they placed the body in an oil vessel of iron and covered that close up with another vessel of iron. And they built a funeral pile of all kinds of perfumes, and upon it they placed the body of the Blessed One."

As usual some miracles are narrated here.

* The following story is given.

Some years after the death of the great Master, a very great internal dissension broke out amongst the various clans that took possession of the Great Master's remains and built stupas over them. There was every likelihood, amidst these terrible wars and rapines, of these sacred stupas being destroyed and the remains of the great Buddha scattered to the winds. Therefore the old Kassapa went from one clan to the other who possessed these stupas and begged for the sacred remains. They could not refuse the venerable monk and handed him the remains keeping almost nothing for themselves.

Kassapa took them away and in the interior of the deep forest near Gya, he dug a deep well and built a temple within it. In this temple in a golden vessel covered with several silver and other metallic vessels, he placed the sacred remains,—covered over the whole with mud and and went away. It is said he left an inscripion on a gold-plate here on which he said, "One Asoka, king of Magadha, will seatter the sacred remains all over the world and build holy stupas over them all."

When Asoka became the great supporter of the religion, he became desirous to build one million stupas, but where could he get the sacred remains of the Great Master? He made many searches without any result, till at last a very old Bhikshu said, "When I was a boy, my old Teacher took me to a place in the deep forest and asked me to bow down my head there, saying "Do not forget this place." I believe the sacred remains are there." Asoka at once went to the place, dug up the whole forest, discovered the holy temple underneath the earth and took away the sacred remains. He raised innumerable stupas over them before he died.

work of spears and with a rampart of bows, and there for seven days they paid honour and reverence and respect and homage to them with dance and song and music and with garlands and perfumes.

Then the King of Magadha Ajatasatru sent a messenger to the Mallas saying, "The Blessed One belonged to the soldier caste;—I too am of the soldier caste. I am worthy to secure a portion of the remains of the Blessed One. Over the remains of the Blessed One, will I put up a sacred cairn and in their honour will I celebrate a feast."

The Lichhaves of Vesali sent a messenger to the Mallas with the same proposal. The Sakhyas of Kapilavastu did the same. The Bulis of Allakappa, the Koliyas of Ramgrama, the Brahmans of Vethadipa and the Mallas of Pava, all sent messengers praying for the remains of the Blessed One.

But the Mallas of Kusinagara spoke to the messengers thus:—"The Blessed One died in our village. We will not give away any part of the remains of the Blessed One." When they had thus spoken, Drona, the Brahman, addressed the Mallas thus:

"Hear, reverend Sirs, one single word from me;
Forbearance our Buddha was wont to teach.
Unseemly it is that over the division
Of the remains of him who was the best of beings
Strife should arise and wounds and war.
Let us all, Sirs, with one accord unite
In friendly harmony to make eight portions.
Wide spread let Sthupas rise in every land
That in the Buddha mankind may trust.

"Do thou then," said the Mallas, "O Brahman, thyself divide the remains of the Blessed One equally into eight parts with fair divisions."

And the Drona the Brahman divided the remains of the Blessed One equally into eight parts and gave each to the different messengers. Then he said:—"Give me Sirs, this vessel and I will set up over it a sacred cairn, and in its honour will I establish a feast." And they gave the vessel to Drona.

Then the Moriyas of Pipphalivana sent a messenger to the Mallas praying for a portion of the remains of the Blessed One. When they heard, "there is no portion of the remains of the Blessed One left over," they took away the embers.

The ancient chronicler thus concludes:—"Then the king of Magadha, Ajatsatru, the son of the queen of Videha, made a mound in Rajagriha over the remains of the Blessed One and held a feast.

And the Koliyas of Ramgrąma made a mound in Ramgrama over the remains of the Blessed One and held a feast.

And Vithadipa, the Brahman, made a mound in Vithadipa over the remains of the Blessed One and held a feast.

And the Mallas of Pava made a mound in Pava over the remains of the Blessed One and held a feast.

And the Mallas of Kasinagara made a mound in Kasinagara over the remains of the Blessed One and held a feast.

And Drona, the Brahman, made a mound over the vessel in which the remains of the Blessed One were kept and held a feast.

And the Moriyas of Pipphalivana made a mound over the embers and held a feast.

Thus were there eight Stupas (mounds) for the remains, and one for the vessel and one for the embers. This was how it used to be."

—:o:—

PART II.

DHARMA.

CHAPTER I.

BUDDHIST METAPHYSICS.

It is generally believed that the great Buddha did not recognise the existence of God and Soul, or more appropriately—of Paramatma and Atma, as the then Brahman philosophers used to term them.* All through the Buddhist Sacred Scriptures, there is not a single place in which Goutama has ever mentioned of God, or Paramatma, or the Supreme Cause of the Universe. There is the mention of Brahma, but He is described as the Chief of Gods,—a mortal being,—as all the Buddhist gods are mortal like man. Though there is no mention of a Supreme One, yet the Soul or Atma has been mentioned in more than one place, and the great Buddha impressed upon his followers that the Soul is not immortal, neither has it a separate existence. Notwithstanding Buddha's silence about the Supreme One and his difference of opinion about Atma with the Brahmanical idea of Atma, the great Goutama was not an atheist.† We shall show later on that he

* We are sorry we cannot agree with the views of those great oriental scholars who have written upon the doctrine and religion of the great Buddha. Our readers will find as we proceed where we have to differ from them.

† See Chapter III. of this Part.

believed in a Supreme Cause of the Universe, and he believed in the existence of man after death.

According to the Buddhist philosophy, man consists of an assemblage of different properties, or qualities. These are :—(1) *Rupa*, material qualities, (2) *Vedana*, sensations (3) *Sanna* abstract ideas, (4) *Sankhara*, tendencies of mind and (5) *Vinana*, mental powers. All these are called *Skandhas*.

1. The Rupa *i. e.* the material qualities, are twenty eight in number, namely

(a) Four elements *i. e.* Earth, Water, Fire and Air.

(b) Five organs of sense, *i. e.* ear, eye, nose, tongue, body.

(c) Five attributes of matter *i. e.* form, sound, smell, taste and substance.

(d) Two distinctions of sex, *i. e.* male and female.

(e) Three essential conditions *i. e.* thought, vitality and space.

(f) Two means of communications *e. i.* gesture and speech.

(g) Seven qualities of living bodies *i. e.* buoyancy, elasticity, power of adaptation, power of aggregation, duration, decay and change.

2. The *Vedana* (sensations) are divided into six classes according as they are received immediately by each of the five senses, or sixthly by the mind through memory; and further into eighteen decrees, as each of these six classes may be either agreeable, disagreeable or indifferent.

3. The *Sanna*, (abstract ideas) are divided into six classes corresponding to the six classes of sensations, for instance, ideas—blue and a tree—are classed under sight; the idea—sweetness—under taste and so on.

4. The Sankharas, (the tendencies or potentialities) are in fifty two divisions which are not however mutually exclusive. Some of them include, or are identical with, items in the previous classes, but whereas the previous groups are arranged

as it were from an objective, this group is arranged as it were from subjective point of view :—

1. Contest *(phana)*.
2. The resulting sensation *(Vedana)*.
3. Abstract ideas formed on sensation *(Sanna)*.
4. Thought, the regrouping of ideas *(Chitana)*.
5. Reflection, turning these groups over and over *(Manasikara)*.
6. Memory *(Sati)*.
7. Vitality *(Jivitendrya)*.
8. Individuality *(Ekaggata)*.
9. Attention *(Vitaka)*.
10. Investigation *(Vicara)*.
11. Effort *(Viriya)*.
12. Steadfastness *(Adhimoḥha)*.
13. Joy *(Piti)*.
14. Impulse *(Chanda)*.
15. Indifference *(Majjhattata)*.

16-17. Sleep and torper *(Thina* and *Midha)*.
18-19. Stupidity and intelligence *(Moha* and *Panna)*.
20-21. Covetousness and content *(Lobha* and *Alobha)*.
22-23. Fear and Rashness *(Ottapa* and *Anotappa)*.
24-25. Shame and Shamelessness (*Hiri* and *Ahirika*).
26-27. Hatred and affection (*Dwesa* and *Adwesa*).
28-30. Doubt, faith and delusion (*Vicikiccha, Sadha,* and *Ditthi*).
31-32. Repose of body and mind (*Pasidhi*).
33-34. Lightness and activity of body and mind (*Lahuta*).
35-36. Softness and elasticity of body and mind (*Maduta*).
37-38. Adaptability and pliancy of body and mind (*Kammanata*).
39-40. Dexterity of body and mind (*Pagunnala*).
41-42. Straightness of body and mind (*Ajjukta*).
43-45. Propriety of speech, action and life (*Saunma*).
46. Pity (*Karuna*).

47. Gladness (*Mudita*).
48. Envy (*Irsa*).
49. Selfishness (*Machareya*).
50. Moroseness (*Kakucca*).
51. Vanity (*Udohacea*).
52. Pridi (*Mano*).

5. Thought (reason) is the last Skandha and is an amplification from another point of view of the fourth of the last group which is inherent in all the others. It is divided from the point of view of the mind or demerit resulting from different thoughts into eight or nine classes."*

All these constitute the human body, but is there a Soul? The following conversation would give a clear idea of what the Buddhists thought about Soul.†

King Malinda says to the great sage Nagasena, "How art thou known, venerable Sire? What is thy name, Sire"?

The sage replied, "I am named Nagasena, O great king, but Nagasena, O great king, is only a name, an appellation, a designation, an epethet, a mere word. Here there is no *subject*."

Then said the king Malinda, "Well to be sure. Let this five hundred Yavanas and eighty thousand monks hear it. This Nagasena says,—here there is no *subject*. Can any one assent to this?"

And king Malinda went on to say to the venerable Nagasena, "If, O venerable Sire, there is no *subject*, who is it then that provides you with what you need,—cloths and food, lodging and medicines for the sick? Who is it that enjoys all these things? Who walks in virtues? Who expends labour upon himself? Who attains the path and the fruits of nobleness? Who attains Nirvana? Who kills? Who steals?

---

* Rhys Davids' Buddhism page 90—93.

† See Milindapasha page 25. We follow Oldenberg in translating the passages quoted in this chapter.

Who walks in pleasures? Who deceives? Who drinks? Who commits the five deadly sins? Thus there is then no good and no evil? There is no doer and no originator of good and evil actions,—good action and evil action bring no reward and bear no fruits. If any one to kill thee, *i.e.*, venerable Nagasena, even he would commit no murder. Sire, then asked the king, "are the hairs in your head Nagasena?"

"No, great king," replied the sage.

"Are nails, or teeth, skin or flesh, or bone Nagasena?"

"No, great king."

"Is the bodily form Nagasena?"

"No, great king."

"Are the sensations Nagasena?"

"No, great king."

"Are the perceptions, the conformations, the consciousness Nagasena?"

"No, great king."

"Or, Sire, the combination of corporeal form, sensations, the perception, conformations and consciousness, is this Nagasena?

"No, great king,"

"Or, Sire, apart from the corporeal form and the sensations, the perceptions, conformations, and consciousness, is there a Nagasena?"

"No, great king."

"Wherever I look then, I nowhere find a Nagasena. What is then Nagasena? Thou speakest false then, O venerable sage. There is no Nagasena at all."

Then thus spoke the venerable Nagasena to king Malinda:

"Thou art accustomed, O great king, to all the comforts of a princely life;—to the greatest comfort. If then, O great king, thou goest out on foot at midday on the hot earth, on the burning sand and treadest on the sharp stones, gravel and sand, thy feet are hurt, thy body is fatigued, thy mind is upset; there arises a consciousness of bodily condition associated with dislike. Hast thou, O great King, come on foot, or on a charioteer ?"

"I do not travel on foot, O Sire," replied the king, "I have come on a chariot."

"If thou hast come on a chariot, O king, then define the chariot. Is the pole the chariot, O great king ?"

"No, Sir."

"Is the ornamented cover the chariot? And the wheels the chariot? Are the reins the chariot? Are all these together the chariot? If you leave all these out, does there remain any thing of the chariot?"

"No, Sire."

"Wherever I look then, O great king, I nowhere find the chariot? A mere word, O great king, is the chariot;—what then is the chariot? Thou art, O great king, the suzereign of all India. Whom dost thou fear that thou speakest falsehood? Well to be sure? Let the five hundred Javanas and eighty thousand monks hear it: This king Malinda has said, 'I have come in a chariot.' "Then," I said, "If thou hast come in a chariot, O great king, then define the chariot." And he could not point out the chariot. Can any one assent to this?"

But king Malinda said, "I do not speak untruly, O venerable Nagasena. In reference to pole, axle, wheel, body and bar, the name, the appellation, the designation, the epithet, the word chariot, is used."

"Good indeed, O great king; thou knowest the chariot. And in the same way, O king, in reference to my hair, my skin, and bones, to corporeal form, sensations, perceptions, conformations and consciousness, the word Nagasena is used, but the subject in the strict sense of the word there is none. As in the case where the parts of a chariot come together the word chariot is used, so also where the five groups of Skandhas are come together, there is a person, a man, a human being.

The following incident would show that Buddha deliberately and intentionally avoided the discussion of God and Soul.

King Pasinada of Kosala on one occasion* in a journey between his two chief towns, Saketa and Savatthi fell in with a nun named Khema—a female disciple of Buddha, renowned for her wisdom. The king paid his respects to her and enquired of her concerning the Sacred Doctrine.

"Venerable lady," asked the king, "does the Perfect One (Buddha) exist after death?"

"The Exalted One," replied Khema, "O great king, has not declared whether the Perfect One exists after death."

"Then does the Perfect One exist not after death, O venerable Lady?"

"This also, O great king, the Exalted One has not declared."

"Thus, O venerable lady, the Perfect One does not exist after death and at the sametime does exist after death? Thus, O venerable lady, the Perfect One neither exists after death, nor does he not exist after death."

"O great king, the Perfect One has not declared whether he exists after death, or he does not exist after death."

"What is the reason, O venerable lady, what is the ground on which the Exalted One has not revealed this?"

"Permit me," answer the Bhikshuni, "now to ask a question, O great king; and do you answer me as the case to you stands. How think you thou, O great king? Have you an accountant, or a mint-master, or a treasurer who could count the sands of the Ganges, who could say there are so many grains of sand or so many hundreds or thousands or hundreds of thousands of grains?"

"No, venerable lady, I have not."

"Or have you an accountant, a mint-master or a treasurer who could measure the water in the great ocean, who could say there are therein so many measures of water or so many

* See Samyutta Nikaya Vol. II.

hundreds or thousands or hundreds of thousands of measures of water ?"

" No, venerable lady, I have not."

" And why not, O great king ? Because the great ocean is deep, immeasurable, unfathomable. So also, O great king, if the existence of the Perfect One, be measured by the predicates of the corporeal form these predicates of the corporeal form are abolished in the Perfect One; their root is severed, they are hewn away like a palm tree and laid aside so that they cannot germinate again in the future. Released, O great king, is the Perfect One from this, that his being should be gauged by the measure of the corporal world; he is deep, immeasurable, unfathamable, as the great ocean. 'The Perfect One exists after death,' this is not apposite. "The Perfect One does not exist after death :—this also is not apposite. The Perfect One exists and at the sametime does not exist is not also apposite. The Perfect One neither does nor does not exist, this is also not apposite."

On one occasion* the Bhikshu Vachagotta thus spoke to the Exhalted One. " How does the matter stand, O venerable Goutama? Is there the Atma (Ego or Soul) ?" When he said this, the Exalted One was silent.

" How then," asked the Bhikshu, is there then not the Atma ?"

And still the Exalted One remained silent. Then the Bhikshu Vachagotta rose from his seat and went away.

But the venerable Ananda soon said to the Exalted One, " Wherefore, O Sire, has the Exalted One not given an answer to the question put by the Bhikshu Vachagotta ?"

" If I, Ananda," replied Buddha, when Vachagotta asked me—" Is there the Atma ?"—had answered, " there is Atma," then that, Ananda would have confirmed the doctrine

* I bid.

of the Sramans and Brahmans who believe in *Permanence.** If I, Ananda, when the Bhikshu Vachagotta asked me "Is there not the Atma," had answered, "there is no Atma," then that Ananda would have confirmed the doctrine of the Sramanas and Brahmans who believe in annihilation.† If I Ananda, when Vachagotta asked me, "Is there Atma," had answered "there is Atma," that would have served my end Ananda, by producing in him the knowledge that all existences are non-ego?

"That it would not, Sire."

"But if, Ananda, when Vachagotta asked me "Is there not the Atma," I had answered "There is no Atma," then that Ananda, would only have caused the wondering monk Vachagotta to be thrown from one bewilderment into another."

One one occasion the venerable Malukya‡ came to the Master and expressed his astonishment that the Great Master's discourse left a series of the very most important and deepest questions unanswered. He said, "Is the world eternal or is it limited by the bonds of time? Does the Buddha live beyond death, does the Perfect One not live beyond death? It pleases me not that all this should remain unanswered, and I do not think it right; therefore I have come to the Master to ask him about these doubts. May it please the Buddha to answer them if he can. When any one does not understand a matter and does not know it, then a straightforward man says, "I don't understand this, I do not know that."

"What have I said to you before now Malukya," said the

---

* At the time when the Buddha was born, there was a class of Brahman philosophers who said the Supreme One was eternal, ever-existing, undying &c. &c. and the human soul is none else but the Supreme Soul. See Upanishadas.

† There were also another class of Brahman philosophers who declared that there remains nothing after death; complete annihilation comes as soon as a man passes away. See Charvaka Darsana.

‡ See Cula Malukya Oveda in Majjhima Nikaya.

great Master, "Have I said, come, Malukya, and be my disciple; I shall teach you whether the world is everlasting or not everlasting, whether the world is finite or infinite, whether the vital faculty is identical with the body or separate from it, whether the Perfect One lives on after death or does not live on, or whether the Perfect One lives on and at the same time does not live on after death, or whether he neither lives on, or does not live on?"

"Thou hast not said this, Sire."

"If a man were struck by a poisoned arrow and his friends and relatives called in a skillful physician, what if the wounded man said, I shall not allow my wound to be treated until I know who the man is by whom I have been wounded, whether he is a Kshatrya, Brahman, Vaisya or Sudra, or if he said, I shall not allow my wound to be treated until I know what they call the man who has wounded me, and of what family he is, whether he is tall, or small or of middle stature, and how his weapon was made with which he struck me, what would the end of his care be? The man would die of his wound."

It is evident the great Buddha avoided the discussion of all these crude points of metaphysics, for he considered them useless and mere waste of time. But at the same time he never meant that after death the Perfect One would meet with annihilation. We will later on find that so long a man is not the Perfeet One, he must pass through many births and deaths. Even when he becomes a Perfect One he does not meet annihilation. Those that believe in this were considered as heretics. The following incidents would clearly show this.

On one occasion* a Bhikshu named Yamaka had adopted the following heretical notion.—"I understand the doctrine taught by the Exalted One to be this that a Bhikshu who is free from sin, who has become perfect, when his body

---

* See Samyutta Nikaya Vol. I.

dissolves is subject to annihilation,—that he passes away, that he does not exist beyond death."

The venerable Sariputra removed his this heretical view. How thinkest thou, friend Yamaka, asked he, "that the Perfect One is identical with the corporeal form? Does the body of the Buddha represent his Ego? Dost thou hold this?"

"I do not, my friend."

"Is the Perfect One identical with the sensations, the perceptions, the conformations, the consciousness? Dost thou hold this?"

"I do not, my friend."

"Is the Perfect One separate from the corporeal form? Dost thou hold this?"

"I do not, my friend."

"Dost thou think, friend Yamaka, the corporeal form, sensations, perceptions, conformations and consciousness are the Pefect One. Dost thou hold this?"

"I do not, my friend."

"Dost thou think, friend Yamaka, is the Perfect One separate from corporeal forms, sensations, perceptions, conformations, and consciousness? Dost thou hold this?"

"I do not, my friend."

"Thus then, friend Yamaka, even here in this world the Perfect One is not to be apprehended by thee in truth. Hast thou therefore a right to speak, saying, "I understand the doctrine taught by the Exalted One to be this that a monk who is free from sin, when his body dissolves is subject to annihilation,—that he passes away, that he does not exist beyond death."

In one place the great Buddha thus spoke:

"There is, O disciples, a state where there is neither earth nor water, neither light nor air, neither infinity of space nor infinity of reason, nor absolute void, nor the co-extinction of perception and non-perception, neither this world nor that world, both sun and moon. That, O disciples, I term neither coming nor going, nor standing,—neither death nor birth. It is without basis, without procession, without cessation, that is the end of sorrow. There is, O disciples, an Unborn, Unoriginated, Uncreated, Unformed. Were there not, O disciples, this Unborn, Unoriginated, Uncreated, Unformed, there would be no possible exit from the world of the born, originated, created, formed." Is this atheism?

—:o:—

CHAPTER II.

KARMA AND TRANSMIGRATION.

We thus fiind the great Buddha avoided all discussions about the disputed metaphysical matters as useless and profitless. But he said,—all the visible universe is impermanent; every thing movable and immovable, mobile and immobile, is liable to change, decay and death; gods and men are both mortal, all would die, nothing would remain for ever. Thus he described the birth of man :—*

"From *Ignorance* comes conformations (*Sankhara*); from conformations comes consciousness (*Vinnana*); form conscious come name and corporeal form; from name and corporeal form come the six fields *i. e.* (five senses and mind); from six fields comes contact between the senses and their objects; from contact comes sensation; from sensation comes thirst or desire; from thirst comes clinging to existence (*Upadana*); from clinging to existence comes being (*Bhava*); from being comes birth; from birth comes old age and death,

* See Anguttara Nekaya.

pain and lamentations, suffering, anxiety and despair. This is the origin of the whole region of suffering."

The original cause of our being, according to the great Buddha, is Ignorance. What is this *Ignorance* then? What did the great Master mean by Ignorance. Sariputra says :—* "Not to know suffering, O friend, not to know the origin of suffering, not to know the extinction of suffering and not to know the path to the extinction of suffering, this O friend, is called Ignorance." Another great Bhikshu says :—† "Not seeing the four truths as they are I have wandered on the long path from one birth to another, nor have I seen them; the current of being is stemmed. The root of suffering is destroyed; there is henceforward no rebirth."‡

---

* See Sammaditthesunta.

† See Mahavagga VI 29.

‡ Dr. Oldenberg thus speaks of the Buddhist Ignorance (see his Buddha pp. 237—238). "If Ignorance be designated the ultimate source of suffering, the question must arise: who is here the ignorant? What is that of which this Ignorance is ignorant. It is tempting, by the place assigned to the category of Ignorance at the beginning of the whole line of causality, to allow one's self to be carried away by interpretations which see in this idea, as it were, a cosmogonical power working at the primitive foundation of things. Or one might be tempted to read in it the history of a crime preceding all time, an unlucky act by which *nonbient* had doomed itself to be *bient*, that is to suffer. The philosophy of the later Brahmanical schools speak in similar fashion of *Maya*, that power of delusion which causes the deceptive picture of the created world to appear to one, the uncreated as if it were *beent*. "He the knowing, gave himself up to confused fancies and when he fell into the slumber prepared for him by Maya, he beheld in amazement multiform dreams: I am, this is my father, this my mother, this my field, this my kingdom." Some have compared the Ignorance of Buddhism with this Maya of the Brahmanical theosophy; only with this note that as the Maya is the deceptive reflection of the true everlasting *bient*, so Ignorance is the reflection of that which, as they thought, took the place of the everlasting *bient* for the Buddhist, that is nothing".

Then it comes to this—Ignorance of the means of stopping rebirths is the cause of our births after births. Ignorance is the cause of our various births. The great Master said—"It is *Karma*,—our actions and doings of one birth cause our subsequent births. Thus it goes on till we can destroy our Ignorance and get rid of the bonds of rebirths."

He said:—* "If ignorance be removed by the complete extinction of desire, this brings about the removal of conformations; by the removal of conformations, consciousness is removed; by the removal of consciousness, name and corporeal form are removed; by the removal of the fields, contact is removed; by the removal of contacts, sensation is removed; by the removal of sensation, thirst is removed; by the removal of thirst, the clinging to existence is removed; by the removal of the clinging to existence, being is removed; by the removal of being, birth is removed; by the removal of birth, old age and death, pain and lamentation, suffering, anxiety and despair are removed. This is the whole realm of suffering."

Dr. Oldenberg beautifully describes the Buddhist idea of "being." We could do no better than quote him.† "No other picture was so perfectly adapted for Buddhism to express the nature of "being" as the figure of "flame" which remaining in apparently restful invariability is yet only a continuous self-production and self-consumption and in which at the same time is embodied with still more impressive reality for the Indians than for us, the tormenting power of heat, the enemy of blissful coolness, the enemy of happiness and peace. As where there is heat, coolness is also found, so also where there is the three-fold fire—the fire of love, hate and infatuation, the Nirvana—extinction of fire must—be sought."‡ Again "every thing, O disciples, is in

* See Anguttara Sutta.

† Oldenburg's Buddha pp. 260—262.

‡ See Buddhavansa.

flames. By what fire is it kindled? By the fire of desire, by the fire of hate, by the fire of infatuation it is kindled; by truth, old age, death, pain, lamentation, sorrow, grief, despair, it is kindled." And again "the whole world is in flames; the whole world is wrapped in smoke; the whole world is wasted by fire, the whole world quakes."* "Beings" resemble a flame; their state of being, their becoming, their re-born is a flaming cleaving of self, a feeding of self upon the fuel which the world of impermanence supplies. As the flame, clinging to the wind, borne by the wind, inflames distant things, so the flame like the existence of beings presses on in the moment of re-birth into far distances; here the being puts off the old body, there it clohes itself with a new body. As the wind carries on the flame, so the thirst which clings to being carries on the flame, so the thirst which clings to beings carries on the soul from one existence to others.

In the "Questions of Malinda,"† the conversation turns upon the problem of the identity or non-identity of the several existences. The sage Nagasena says:—"It is not the same being, and yet they are not separate beings which relieve one another in the series of existences."

"Give an illustration," says the king.

"If a man were to light a light, O great king," replies the sage, "would it not burn on through the night.?"

"Yes, Sire, it would burn through the night."

"How then, O great king, is the flame in the first watch of the night identical with the flame in the midnight watch?"

"No, Sire."

"And the flame in the midnight watch, is it identical with the flame in the last watch of the night?"

"No, Sire."

* See Samjutta Nikaya Vol. I.

† See Malindapaniha.

"But how then, O great king, was the light in the first watch of the night another, in the mid-night watch another, and in the last watch of the night another?"

"No Sire, it has burned all night long feeding on the same fuel."

"So also, O great king, the chain of elements of beings completes itself; the one comes and the other goes. Without beginning, without end, the circle completes itself; therefore it is neither the same being, nor another being, which presents itself last to the consciousness."

Being is the procession, regulated by the law of causality—of continuous being, at every moment self-consuming and anew begetting. What we term a souled being is one individual member in the line of this procession,—one flame in this sea of flame. As in consuming, the flame is always seeking fresh fuel for itself, so also this continuity of perception, sensation and suffering, which seems to the deluded gaze, diversed by the appearance of unbroken invariability, to be a being, a subject, maintains itself in the general influx of ever fresh elements from the domain of the objective world.

Thus we find *Karma* and *Transmigration* are the two great pillars on which the doctrine and religion of the Great Master stand.* Most probably Buddha borrowed the two principal stand-points of his religion from the philosophies of the Brahmans, for in fact even now the religion of the

---

* We are sorry no oriental scholar of Europe was able to induce himself to believe in Karma and Transmigration. All of them say that these two are the most weak points of Buddhism—nay also of Hinduism. Every one of them considers the belief in Karma and Transmigration as but superstitious. We do not venture to say that we shall be able in this little book to remove their this great misconception,—but we humbly submit he who does not believe in Karma and Transmigration can by no means understand the true import of the teachings of the great Buddha.

Hindus stands on the strong foundations of Karma and Transmigration.

We shall now quote a few passages from the Buddhist Sacred Scriptures concerning Karma and Transmigration.

Buddha said:—"It happens, my disciples, that a Bhikshu, endowed with faith, endowed with righteousness, endowed with knowledge of the Doctrine, with resignation, with wisdom, communes thus with himself. "Now then could I, when my body is dissolved in death, obtain rebirth in a powerful princely family?" He thinks this thought, dwells on this thought, cherishes this thought. The *Sankharas* and *Viharas* (internal condition) which he has thus cherished within him and fostered, lead to his rebirth in such an existence. This, O disciples, is the avenue, this the path, which leads to rebirth in such an existence."

"The Bhikshu communes thus to himself:—"Now then were I but able, by the destruction of sinful existence, to discover and behold for myself the sinless state of deliverence in action and knowledge even in this present life and find in it my abode!". He will, by the destruction of sinful existence, discover and behold for himself the sinless state of deliverence in action and in knowledge even in this present life, and will find in it his abode. That Bhikshu, O disciples, will never be reborn."*

The king Yama (Death) thus spoke:—"Hast thou, O man, when thou reachedst riper years and becamest old, not thought within thyself, 'I also am subject to birth, old age and death. I am not exempt from the dominion of birth, old age and death. Well then I will do good in thought word and deed?'

The man answers, "I was unable to do it, Sire. I neglected it, Sire, in my frivolity."

Then king Yama says:—"These thy evil deeds thy mother

* Sankharuppati Suttanta in Majjhima Nikaya.

hath not done, nor thy father, nor thy brother, nor thy sister, nor thy friends and advisers, nor thy connections and blood relations, nor ascetics, Brahmans and Gods. It is thou alone that hast done these evil actions. Thou alone shalt gather their fruits."*

"Whatsoever one does, to a corresponding state he attains. My action (Karma) is my possession, my action is my inheritance, my action is the womb which bears me. My action is the race to which I am akin; my action is my refuge."†

"What appears to man to be his body is in truth the action of his past state, which then assuming a form, realized through his endeavour, has become endowed with a tangible existence."‡

"Not in the heavens, not in the midst of the sea, not if thou hiddest thyself away in the clefts of the mountains, wilt thou find a place on earth where thou canst escape the fruits of thy evil actions.§

Karma you can never avoid. The Gita says :—

"Man does not attain freedom from action by not performing action. By asceticism also, he does not attain to final emancipation. None can remain for a moment without performing some actions. All perform actions impelled by the Laws of Nature. The deluded man who controlling his organs of actions ponders in his mind over the objects of senses is a hypocrite. But he who restraining his senses by his mind performs actions by the organs of actions is superior to all. Therefore always perform actions, for action is better than inaction and your body cannot be supported without performing action. The world is bound in by the laws of action; therefore being free from attachment, perform actions."

---

* See Devaduta Sutta.

† See Anguttara Nikaya in Panchaka Nipata.

‡ See Samyutta Nikaya Vol. I.

§ See Dhammapada, 127.

Every action (Karma) produces a result, visible or invisible. That again produces effects, and so on it goes in a cycle. After the dissolution of the physical body, it remains as if in a dormant state which is called *Samaskaras*. From this *Samskaras* new births are produced till Nirvana is attained.

—:o:—

CHAPTER III.

NIRVANA.

What is then this Nirvana? It is not annihilation, as those Bhikshus that held such a view were considered as heretics. Then what did the Great Buddha mean by Nirvana?—He said:—"Difficult will it be for men to grasp the *Law of Causality*—the chain of causes and effects. And this also will be very hard for them to grasp, the coming of all conformations to an end,—the loosing from every thing earthly, the extinction of desire, the cessation of longing, the end, the Nirvana."*

All the European scholars have unfortunately misunderstood the real import of Nirvana. It is quite natural, as none of them could believe in *Karma* and *Transmigration*. He who does not understand what Karma and Transmigration really mean, and who does not believe that Karma and its result Transmigration are realities, can not possibly form any idea of the Nirvana. Let us first see what the great oriental scholars of Europe say about the Nirvana.

Rhys Davids says:—† "What then is Nirvana which

* See Maha Dharmachakra Parivartana Sutra.

† See Rhys David's Buddhism.

means simply going out,—extinction; it being quite clear, from what has gone before, that this cannot be the extinction of a soul? *It is the extinction of that sinful grasping condition of mind and heart which would otherwise, according to the great mystery of Karma, be the cause of renewed individual existence.* That extinction is to be brought about by and runs parallel with the growth of the opposite condition of mind and heart and it is complete when that opposite condition is reached. Nirvana is therefore the same thing as a sinless calm state of mind, and if translated at all may best perhaps be rendered 'holiness'—holiness that is in the Buddhist sense perfect peace, goodness and wisdom.

Our word 'holiness' would often suggest the ideas of love to and awe in the full presence of a personal Creator,—ideas inconsistent with Buddhist's holiness. On the other hand, Nirvana implies the ideas of intellectual energy and of the cessation of individual existence of which the former is not essential to and the latter is quite unconnected with our idea of holiness. Holiness and Nirvana, and in other words, may represent states of mind not greatly different, but they are due to different causes and end in different results and in using the words, it is impossible to confine one's thought to the thing expressed, so as not also to think of its origin and its effect.

It is better, therefore, to retain the word Nirvana as one name of the Buddhist *summum bonum* which is a blissful state, moral condition, a modification of personal character, and we should allow the world to remind us, as it did the early Buddhists, both of the Path which leads to the extinction of sin and also of the break in the transfer of Karma which the extinction of sin will bring about. That this must be the effect of Nirvana is plain; for that state of mind which in Nirvana is extinct is precisely that which will, according to the great mystery of Buddhism, lead at death to the formation of a new individual to whom the Karma of the disolved or dead one will be transferred. That new individual would consist of certain bodily and mental qualities or tendencies enumerated in the five *Skandhas* or aggregates. A comprehensive name of all the five is *Upadi*, a word derived (in allusion to the name of their cause (Upadana) from *Upada* to grasp either with the hand or mind. Now when a Buddhist has become *Arahat*, when he has reached Nirvana, the fruit of the fourth 'Path,' he has extinguished *Upadana* and *Klesa*, but he is still alive; the *Upadi*, the *Skandhas*, his body with all its powers, that is to say the fruit of his former error, remain. These, however, are impermanent, they will soon pass away. There will then be nothing left to bring about the rise of a new set of *Skandhas* of a new individual and the Arahat will be no longer alive or existent in any sense at all; he will have reached Parinibhana—complete extinction.

The life of man, to use a constantly recurring Buddhist simile or parable, is like the flame of an Indian lamp,—a metal or earthern ware saucer in which a cotton wick is laid in oil. One life is derived from another as one flame is lit at another; it is not the same flame, but without the other it would not have been. As flame cannot exist without oil, so life-individual existence depends in the cleaving to low and costly things, the sin of the heart. If there is no fire in the lamp, it will go out, though not until the oil which the wick has drawn up is exhausted and then no new flame can be lighted there. And so the parts and powers of the perfect man will be dissolved and no new being will be born to sorrow. The wise will pass away, will go out like the flame of a lamp and their Karma will be individualized no longer.

Stars long ago extinct may be still visible to us by the light they emitted before they ceased to burn, but the rapidly vanquishing effect of a no-longer active cause will soon cease to strike upon our senses, and where the light was, will be darkness. So the living, moving body of the perfect man, is visible still, thus its cause has ceased to act, but it will soon decay and die and pass away, and as no new body will be formed, where life was will be nothing.

Freedom from the imperfections of finite being is then a result of but is not Nirvana. The Buddhist heaven is not death and it is not on death but on a virtuous life here and now, that the Pitakas lavish these terms of ecstatic description which they apply to Arahat ship the goal of the excellent way and to Nirvana as one aspect of it."

Spence Hardy says:—" Nirvana is the destruction of all the elements of existence. In this way. The unwise being who has not yet arrived at a state of purity or who is subject to future birth, overcome by the every evil desire rejoices in the Organ of sense, Ayatana and their relative object and commends them. The Ayatanas therefore become to him like a rapid stream to carry him onward towards the sea of repeated existence and they are not released from old age, decay, death, sorrow &c. But the being who is purified, perceving the evils arising from the sensual organs and their relative objects, does not rejoice therein, nor does he commend them or allow himself to be swallowed up by them. By the destruction of the 108 moons of evil desire he has released himself from birth, as from the jaws of an alligator; he has overcome all attachment to outward objects; he does not regard the unauthorised precepts, nor is he a sceptic and he knows that there is no Ego, no Self. By overcoming these four errors, he has released himself from the cleanging to existing objects. By the destruction of the cleaning to existing objects, he is released from birth whether as a Brahma, man or any other being. By the destruction of birth he is released from old age, decay, death sorrow &c. All the afflictions connected with the repetition of existence are overcome. Thus all the principles of existence are annihilated and that annihilation is Nirvana.

In the Asangkala Sutra, Goutame has set forth the

properties of Nirvana. It is the end of Sangsara or successive existence, the arriving at its opposite shore, its completion. Those who attain Nirvana are few. It is very subtle, and is therefore called Suksma; it is free from decay and therefore called Ajaraya. It is free from delay, the gradual development of events, and therefore called Niprapancha; it is pure, and therefore called Visudhi; it is tranquil, and therefore called Kshanta; it is firm and stable, and therefore called Sthira; it is free from death, and therefore called Amrita; its blessedness is great, and it is therefore called Siva; it is not made or created, but supernatural, and therefore called Arbhuta; it is free from Government or order and therefore called Aniti; it is free from sorrow, and therefore called Awyapaga; it is free from the evils of existence, and therefore called Tana.

It cannot be predicted of Nirvana, that it has ceased to be or that its existence is past; it is not a thing accomplished or a relation to past time: nor is it a substance.

The man who has not obtained Nirvana may nevertheless become acquainted with its character. That those who have their ears, noses, hands and feet cut off suffer great pain, may be known by those who have not undergone the same amputation of the limbs from their tears and from the cries that they utter. In like manner, from the joyful exclamations of those who have seen Nirvana, its character may be known by those who have not made the same attainment.

All sentient beings will not receive Nirvana. But if any one attain the knowledge that is proper to be acquired; if he learn the universality of sorrow; if he overcome that which is the cause of sorrow and if he practise that which is proper to be observed, by him the possession of Nirvana, Nirvana Sampati, will be secured. Nirvana is Dharma

Bhisamaya, the end, or completion of religion; its entire accomplishment."*

Dr. Oldenberg says:—† Does this end of the earthly existence imply at the same time the total cessation of being? Is it the nothing which receives the dying Perfect One into its dominion?

Some have thought to find the answer to this question contained in the word Nirvana itself, *i.e.*, extinction. It seemed the most obvious construction that extinction is an extinction of being in the Nothing. But doubts were soon expressed as to the propriety of so summary a disposal of this question. It is quite allowable to speak of an extinction in the case—and the term was most incontrovertibly used by the Indians in the case—where being was not annihilated, but where it, freed from the glowing heat of suffering, had found the path to the cool repose of painless happiness. Max-Muller has above all others maintained with warm eloquence the notion of Nirvana as the completion, but not as an extinction of being. His position is, that although later Buddhist metaphysicians have undoubtedly regarded the Nothing as the supreme object of all efforts, yet the original teaching of Buddha and the ancient Order of his disciples was different; for them the Nirvana was nothing more than the entry of the Spirit upon its rest; an eternal beatitude, which is as highly exalted above the joys as it is above the sorrow of the transitory world. "Would not,"

---

* See Eastern Monachism, pages 291—292. As the author, Spence Hardy, bases his explanation of Nirvana solely on Buddhist Sacred Texts, he approaches nearer to the true import of Nirvana. See below.

Burnouf, Goldstucker, Max Muller, Beal and the other scholars who have studied Buddhism have all defined Nirvana almost in the same way as is done by Hardy, Oldenburg and Rhys Davids as quoted above. See Burnouf's Introduction to the Histore Le Buddhism, also Goldstucker's Literary Remains. Max Muller's Selected Essays.

† See Oldenberg's Buddhism.

asks Max-Muller, "a religion which lands us at last in the Nothing cease to be a religion? It would no longer be what every religion ought to be and purports to be a bridge from the temporal to the eternal, but it would be a delusive gangway which suddenly breaks off and shoots a man, just when he fancies he has reached the goal of the eternal, unto the abyss of annihilation.

We cannot follow the famous enquirer when he attempts to trace the limits between the possible and the impossible in the development of religion. In the sultry, dreamy stillness of India, thoughts spring and grow, every surmise and every sensation grows, otherwise than in the cool air of the West. Perhaps if any thing here appears beyond the comprehensible and if we reach a point which is to us a limit of the comprehensible, we shall permit much to pass and stand as incomprehensible and await the future which may bring us nearer the solution of the enigma.

Max Muller's researches, which were under the then circumstances of the case, based on only a portion of the authentic texts bearing on this branch of the subject, did not fail to attract the attention of the native literate of Ceylon, the country which has preserved to the present day Buddhist temperament and knowledge in its purest form. And by the joint labours of eminent Singhalese students of Buddhist literature such as the late James d'Alwis and European enquirers among whom we may mention specially Childers, Rhys Davids and Trenckner, literary materials for the elucidation of the dogma of the Nirvana have been amply unearthed and ably treated. I have endeavoured to complete the collection for which we have to thank these learned scholars, and in that attempt I have submitted all the testimony of the sacred Pali Canon, that contained the discourses of Buddha as well as that in the writings upon the rights of the Order, to a detailed examination, so that I believe I am in a position to hope that no essential expression of the ancien dogmatic and doctrinal poets has been omitted. Before I undertook this task, it was my conviction that there is in the ancient Buddhist literature no passage which directly decides the alternative whether the Nirvana is eternal felicity or annihilation. So much the greater therefore was my surprise, when in the course of these researches I hit not upon one passage, but upon very numerous passages which speak as expressly as possible upon the point regarding which the controversy is waged, and determine it with a clearness which leaves nothing to be desired. And it was no less a cause of astonishment to me when I found that in that alternative which appeared to have been laid down with all possible cogency viz., that the Nirvana must have been understood in the ancient Order to be either the Nothing or a supreme felicity, there was finally neither on the one side nor on the other perfect accuracy.

We shall now endeavour to state the question as it must have presented itself to the dogmatic Buddhist on its own premises and then the answer which the question has received.

A doctrine, which contemplates a future of eternal perfection behind transitory being, cannot possibly admit of the kingdom of the eternal first beginning only at the point where the world of the transient ends, cannot conjure it up immediately as it were out of the Nothing. In the kingdom of the transient itself there must be contained, vieled perhaps like a latent germ, but still present, an element which bears in itself the pledge of everlasting being stretching out beyond origination and decease. It is possible that, where the claims of strict dialectic sequence are opposed by motives of another kind, thought pauses before accepting this so obvious a conclusion; but it is important before we examine these deviations from the logical sequence which we may possibly expect to find, to obtain a view of the form in which the logical consequences must have presented themselves to the Buddhist thought.

The finite would appear in the dogmas of Buddhism to rest wholly upon itself. Whatever we see, whatever we hear, our senses as well as the objects which are presented to them, every thing is drawn within the cycle of origination and decease, everything is only a Dhamma, a Sankhara, and all Dhammas and Sankharas are transitory. Whence this cycle? No matter whence; it is there from a past beyond ken. The existence of the conditional is accepted as a given fact; thought shrinks from going back to the unconditional.

We see, the finite world bears in itself no traces which point to its connection with a world of the eternal. How could it possibly be otherwise? Where the opposition of the transient and eternal is carried to the point which Indian thought has ever reached, there can in fact be no union conceived between the two extremes. Had the eternal any share whatsover in the occurences of the world of the changeable, a shadow of the changeable would fall in its own unchangeability. The conditional can only be thought of as conditioned through another conditional. If we follow the dialectic consequence solely, it is impossible on the basis of this theory of life to conceive how, where a series of conditions have run out, annihilating itself, anything else is to be recognized as remaining but a vacuam.

This is the view that the oriental scholars of Europe have formed of the Nirvana of the great Buddha. Now let us see what the Great Master himself and his immediate followers and his great disciples said about Nirvana. They say:—

" He whose senses have become tranquil like a horse well broken in by the driver, who is free from pride and the lust of the flesh and the lust of existence and defilement of ignorance—him even the gods envy. Such a one whose conduct is right remains like the broad earth unvexed; like the pillar of the city gate unmoved, like a pellucid lake unruffled. For such there are no more births, tranquil is the mind, tranquil are the words and deeds of him who is thus tranquillized and made free by wisdom."

"The disciple who has put off lust and desire, rich in wisdom has here on earth attained the deliverance from death, the rest, the Nirvana, the eternal state."

"He who has escaped from the trackless, hard mazes of the Sansara, who has crossed over and reached the shore, self-absorved without stumbling and without doubt, who has delivered himself from the earthly and attained Nirvana, him I call as true Nirvana."

"Nirvana, Nirvana, so they say, friend Sariputra," said a Brahman monk, "but what is Nirvana, friend?" "The subjugation of desire," replied Sariputra," the subjugation of hatred, the subjugation of perplexity; this, O friend, is called Nirvana."

"The body of the Perfect One, O disciples, subsists, cut off from the stream of becoming. As long as his body subsists, so long will gods and men see him. If his body be dissolved, his life runs out, gods and men shall no more behold him.

"Dissolved is his body," said Buddha at the death of one of his disciples, "extinct is perception, the sensations have all vanished away. The confirmations have found their repose, the consciousness has sunk to its rest."

"That mendicant conducts himself well who has conquered error by means of insight; from whose eyes the evil of error has been removed, who is well trained in religion and who is free from yearnings and skilled in the knowledge has attained unto Nirvana.

"They who by steadfast mind have become exempt from evil desire and well-trained in the teachings of Goutama, they having obtained the fruit of the fourth path and immersed themselves in that ambrosia have received without price and are in the enjoyment of Nirvana. Their old Karma is exhausted, no new Karma is being produced, their hearts are free from the longing after future life, the cause of their existence being destroyed and no new yearning springing up within them, they the wise are extinguished like this lamp."

"They plunged into meditation, the immovable one who valiantly struggles ever more, the wise grasp the Nirvana, the gain which no other gain surpasses."

"Hunger is the most gredious illnesss, the Sankharas are the most grevious sorrow; recognizing this of a truth, man attains the Nirvana, the supreme happiness."

"The wise who cause no suffering to any being, who keep their body in check, they walk to the everlasting state; he who reached that knows no sorrow."

"He who is permeated by goodness, the monk who adheres to Buddha's teachings, let him turn to the land of peace, where transientness finds an end to happiness."

"There is no fire like lust, there is no sin like hate, there is no misery like the Skandhas, there is no happiness like peace. Hunger is the worst disease, the Sankharas the worst suffering. Knowing this as it really is, Nirvana is the best Bliss."

The colloque between king Malinda and Nagasena gives a clear idea of Nirvana as understood by the immediate followers of the Great Master. We give below the translation of this celebrated conversation.*

King Malinda said:—"There are some things in the world that are called *Karmaja*, as they come into existence because of Karma; others that are called *Rituja* as they come into existence because of the season of time; and others that are called *Hetuja*, as they come into existence because of *Hetu* (cause). Now is there anything that is neither Karmaja, Rituja or Hetuja?"

---

* See Malinda-Prasna.

Nagasena replied:—"Space and Nirvana are neither Karmaja, Rituja or Hetuja."

Malinda said:—"Do not say that which is contrary to the teachings of Buddha, nor reply without thought."

Nagasena asked:—"Why do you speak to me thus?"

King Malinda replied:—"You say that Nirvana is neither Karmaja, Rituja or Hetuja. But has not Buddha in hundred thousand different ways declared to the Bhikshus that an entrance into the path of Arhats secures the attainment of Nirvana? Then how is it you say that Nirvana is neither Karmaja, Rituja, nor Hetuja?"

Nagasena replied:—"Budha has said this. But he has not said that for the production of Nirvana there is any Hetu."

King Malinda said:—"Venerable Sir, you say that the Buddha has declared that the path of Arahatship is the cause, Hetu, of the attainment of Nirvana, and yet you say also that Nirvana is without cause, Hetu. I am confounded; I go from darkness to deeper darkness. If there is a cause for the attributes or accompaniments of Nirvana, there must also be a cause for the production of Nirvana. The son must have a father, the father must have had another father. The pupil must have a teacher; that teacher must have had another teacher. In like manner, if there is a cause for the attainment of Nirvana, there must also be a cause for its production."

Nagasena said:—"Nirvana is not a thing that can be produced, and therefore it has not been said by Buddha that it has a cause."

Malinda said:—"This may be true, but explain to me how it is."

Nagasena replied:—"Then lend you ear in a proper manner and pay attention. Can a man, by his natural strength, go from this city of Sagal to the forest of Himalaya?"

Malinda replied:—"Yes."

Nagasena said:—"In like manner though the fruition of

the paths may cause the attainment of Nirvana; no cause by which Nirvana is produced can be declared. A man may, by his material strength, go in a ship to the other side of the sea, but he cannot in the same manner bring the sea to the shore. In like manner the path that leads to Nirvana may be pointed out, but not any cause for its production. Why? Because that which constitutes Nirvana is beyond all computation;—it is a mystery not to be understood."

King Malinda asked:—"Is it because Nirvana is produced by neither merit nor demerit that it is beyond comprehension?"

Nagasena said:—"Yes, as Nirvana is not produced by either merit or demerit, as it is not produced from any *Hetu* like trees and other similar things, as it is not caused by *Ritu* (season) like the rocks &c, it is called *asankhyata* (a mystery). As it is entirely free from evil desire, it is called Nirvana. It is not caused by Sakra, Maha Brahma or any other being. It cannot be said it is produced, nor that it is not produced; that it is past or future, or present; nor cannot be said that it is the seeing of the eye, or the hearing of the ear, or the smelling of the nose, or the tasting of the tongue, or the feeling of the body."

Malinda said:—"Then you speak of a thing that is not. You merely say that Nirvana is Nirvana; therefore there is no Nirvana."

Nagasena replied:—"Great king, Nirvana *is*. It is a *perception* of the mind. The pure, delightful Nirvana, free from *avidya* (ignorance) and *trishna* (desire), is *perceived* by the Rahats who enjoy the fruition of the Paths."

King Malinda said:—"If there be any comparison by which the nature or properties of Nirvana can be apparent, be pleased thus to explain them."

Nagasena replied:—"There is the wind, but can its color be told? Can it be said that it is blue, or any other colour?

Can it be said that it is in such a place, or that it is small, or great, or long, or short?

Malinda said:—"We cannot say that the wind is thus; it cannot be taken into the hand and squeezed. Yet the wind *is*, we know it, because it pervades the heart, strikes the body and bends the trees of the forest, but we cannot explain its nature or tell what it is."

Nagasena said:—"Even so Nirvana is destroying the infinite sorrow of the world and presenting itself as the chief happiness of the world, but its attributes and properties cannot be described."

King Malinda asked:—"Will all who obey the precepts attain Nirvana, or are there some who are not able?

Nagasena replied:—"The following cannot attain Nirvana.

(1) Quadrupeds, pretas and sceptics.

(2) Those who commit five great sins.

(3) Who do not follow the doctrines of the Buddhas.

(4) Those who force a priestess.

(5) Those who do not hear *bana*, having opportunities to hear it.

(6) Those who are carried away by the objects of sense.

(7) Children under seven years.

King Malinda asked:—"Why cannot children attain Nirvana? Are they not free from the three evils,—Raga, Dwesa and Moha as well as from pride, scepticism, passion and evil reasoning? Then why are they excluded?"

Nagasena replied:—"If the child were able to understand that which is right and reject that which is wrong, he might attain Nirvana; but his faculties of thought are weak; he cannot with a mind so limited comprehend that which is vast and endless. In like manner, no man, by his natural strength, can root up Maha-meru; nor can the whole of the extended earth be irrigated by a few drops of water, nor the whole world be illuminated by a fire-fly."

Malinda asked :—" Is the joy of Nirvana unmixed, or is it associated with sorrow ?"

Nagasena replied :—" It is unmixed satisfaction, entirely free from sorrow."

Malinda replied :—" The dangers of the warfare are not an enjoyment, but its trials are ended in seeking the kingdom or in defending it. Princes seek the kingdom in sorrow and when it is attained receive the enjoyment of royalty; on this account it is that the enjoyment of royalty is mixed satisfaction. The toil of the warfare is one, the enjoyment of its result another."

Nagasena said :—" In the same way, the happiness of Nirvana is unmixed though those who seek it are subject to sorrow; the sorrow is one, the happiness another, the two states are entirely distinct. Or you may receive another comparison to the same effect. A disciple sets himself to the attainment of knowledge, and for this purpose places himself under the care of a preceptor; the knowledge he acquires is an unmixed good, but he has great pain and sorrow in acquiring it; it is the same with those who seek the happiness of Nirvana."

The King said :—" You speak of Nirvana, but can you show it to one, or explain it to me by colour, whether it be blue, yellow, red or any other colour; or by sign, locality, length, manner, metaphor, cause or order; in any of these ways, or by any of these ways, or by any of these means, can you declare it to me ?

Nagasena said :—" I cannot declare it by any of these attributes or qualities."

Malinda said :—" This I cannot believe."

Nagasena said :—" There is the great ocean; were any one to ask you how many measures of water there are in it or how many living creatures it contains, what would you say ?"

Malinda said:—"I should tell him that it was not a proper question to ask as it is one that no one can answer."

Nagasena said:—"In the same way, no one can tell the size or shape, a colour or other attributes of Nirvana; it has its own proper and essential character. A Rishi might answer the question to which I have referred, but he could not declare the attributes of Nirvana, neither a deva could do it."

The King said:—"It may be true that Nirvana is happiness and that its outward attributes cannot be described, but cannot its excellence or advantages be set forth by some mode of comparison?"

Nagasena said:—"It is like the lotus as it is free from *Klesha*, as the lotus is separated from the mud out of which it springs. It is like water as it quenches the fire of Klesha, as water cools the body; it also overcomes the thirst for that which is evil as water overcomes the natural thirst. It is like a medicine as it assists those who are suffering from the passion *Klesha*, as medicine assists those who are suffering from sickness; it also destroys the sorrow of renewed existence."

Malinda said:—"This declaration I cannot believe and for this reason. He who seeks Nirvana is subject to pain, both of body and mind; in all situations he is pursued by sorrow; pain is communicated by every organ of sense, and he sees that he has to leave much wealth and many relatives and friends. Those who possess the advantage of this world are thereby rendered joyful; there are things pleasant to the sight and other senses; and in this way regret is caused when they have to be left; on which account I think that the joy of Nirvana cannot be unmixed."

Nagasena said:—"It is nevertheless true that the joy of Nirvana is unmixed. Is there not such a thing as the enjoyment of royalty and is it not unmixed with sorrow?"

Malinda replied, "Yes, there is."

Nagasena said:—"But a king is displeased with his people who live on the limit of his domains; he persues them; whilst thus engaged he suffers much from flies, mosquitos, cold, wind, sun and air; he must fight; his life will be exposed to danger. How then is it you say that the enjoyment of royalty is as medicine destroys disease; and it is immortal, as medicine wards off death. It is like the sea, as it is free from every kind of defilement; it is vast, infinite so that countless beings do not fill it, as the sea is unfathomable, and is not filled by all the waters of all the rivers; it is filled with the perfume of emancipation from existence as the surface of the sea is covered with the flowers resembling waves. It is like food as it promotes age, as food increases the length of life; it increases the power of the Rishis as food increases the strength of men; it increases the virtues of those who receive it, as the reception of food adds beauty to the body; it overcomes the weariness produced by Klesha, as food destroys the weariness of the body and it drives away sorrow and pain as food destroys hunger. It is like space as it is not produced by any exterior cause; it has no living existence, it does not die, it does not pass away, it is not reproduced; it cannot be collapsed, it has no locality, it is the abode of the Rahats and Buddhas as the space is the habitation of birds; it cannot be hidden and its extent is boundless. It is like the magical jewel as it gives whatever is desired; it also imparts joy and by the light it gives is a benefit and assistance. It is like red sandal wood, as it is difficult to be procured; its perfume is also peerless and it is admired by the wise. It is like *ghee* as it increases the beauty of the colour; its perfume is universally diffused and its taste is delightful. It is like Mahameru, as it is higher than the three worlds; it it also firm; its summit is difficult to approach; and as seeds will not vegetate on the surface of the rock so *Klesha* can never flourish in Nirvana, and it is free from enmity and wrath."

King Malinda said:—"You declare that Nirvana is neither past, nor future, nor present, and that it cannot be said that it is produced, then does the being who acquires it attain something that has previously existed, or is it his own product, a formation peculiar to himself?"

Nagasena said:—"Nirvana does not exist previously to its reception, nor is it that which was not brought into existence; still to the being who attains it there is Nirvana."

Malinda said:—"There is much doubt about Nirvana in the world. Therefore I trust you will answer my questions in a clear and decisive manner that my mind may be no longer agitated respecting it-"

Nagasena said;—"It is free from danger, without fear, happy, peaceful, the source of enjoyment, refreshing, pure, delightful. When a man who has been boiled before a heap of fire is released therefrom and goes quickly into some open space, he feels the most agreeable sensation; it is the same with the man who, released from ignorance, hatered and other coils, attains Nirvana. The fire is ignorance, hatred etc. The man exposed to the fire is he who seeks to attain Nirvana, and the open space is Nirvana. Again, when a man who has been confined in a filthy place where there are the dead bodies of snakes and dogs is released therefrom and goes without delay to some open space, he also feels the most agreeable sensation. The filth is *Pancha karma*; the man confined in the filthy place is he who is seeking Nirvana and the open space is Nirvana. And again when a man is in danger from a band of enemies armed with swords, he is in great fear and struggles violently to release himself, and then goes to some place where he can be free from fear and at rest. The place that is free from fear is Nirvana."

Malinda said:—"How does the monk who seeks Nirvana obtain it? How is it effected or brought about?"

Nagasena said:—"The man who seeks Nirvana carefully investigates the properties of Sanskaras; by this he sees that they are connected with decay, sorrow and death. Thus he discovers that there is no satisfaction attached to successive existence; that there is no such thing as permanent happiness. The man who sees a bar of iron that has been heated to the highest possible degree can discover no way whatever in which it will be desirable to hold it, and it is the same with him who contemplates the evils of successive existence, he can see no form whatever in which it is to be desired. Like a fish cob in a net, like a frog when attracted to the mouth of a serpent, like a bird in the claws of a cat, like a Naya in the beak of Jarenda, like the moon in the mouth of Rahu, he struggles to obtain release from existence. As the man who has gone to a distant country, when he sees the road that leads to his native land, thinks it will be well if he returns by that road, so the wise monk tries to gain entrance unto the Fourth Path, that he attains Nirvana."

The king asked :—" Is Nirvana in the East, South, West or North, above or below? Is there such a place as Nirvana? If so, where is it?"

Nagasena replied :—" Neither in the East, West, North, or South, above or below, nor in the infinite *Sakwalas* is such a place as Nirvana."

Malinda said :—" Then if Nirvana has no locality, there can be no such thing. When it is said that any one attains Nirvana, that declaration is false. For the production of grain there is the field, for the production of perfume there is the flower, for the production of the flower there is the forest, for the production of fruit there is the tree, for the production of gold there is the mine. If any one wishes for flowers or fruits, he goes to the place where they be procured, and there meets with them; therefore if there were such a thing as Nirvana it would have a locality; and if there be no such place, there can be no Nirvana. The devas and men who are expecting it will be deceived."

Nagasena replied :—" There is no such place as Nirvana,

yet it exists. The monk who seeks it in a right manner will attain it. Fire may be produced by rubbing two pieces of sticks, though previously it had no locality and it is the same with Nirvana,"

The king said :—" Be it so ; but when Nirvana is attained, is there such a place ?"

Nagasena :—" When a monk attains Nirvana, there is such a place."

Malinda asked :—" Where is that place ?"

Nagasena replied :—" It may be any where."

The king asked :—" Does the all-wise Buddha still exist ?"

Nagasena replied :—" Yes, Bhagavata still exists."

Malinda asked :—" Can you point me out the place where he exists ?"

Nagasena said :—" Our Lord has attained Nirvana, where there is no repetition of birth. We cannot say, he is here, he is there. When a fire is extinguished, can it be said that it is here and it is there ?"*

Thus we find Nirvana is not annihilation ; it is the door to enter a *State* which a man can attain both when alive and when dead. " But this is a matter hard to understand ;" as says the Mahavagga, "the suppression of all the Sanskaras, the forsaking of all sins, the destruction of yearning, the absence of desire, the extinction—the Nirvana."

Buddha said " the Life is mortal ; where there is life there is death, there is suffering, &c. The fire of life can be extinguished ; thus a man can go beyond life, beyond death, old age, sufferings &c. This extinguishing the fire of life, the great Buddha called the Nirvana. Beyond Nirvana is a *state,*—a *state* where there is no life and no death, no sufferings, and no sorrows. But Buddha intentionally

---

* See Molindaprasna. Nagasena, without admitting the existence of the Supreme Source of the universe, says virtually the same thing. Nirvana is the State which is in fact the state of the Supreme One according to the Brahmana Philosophy.

and deliberately avoided the discussion about this state. He never attempted to describe it, for he said it is beyond all human descriptions. But he firmly believed that such an indescribable state exists, and that man can attain to (Nirvana.)

Then Nirvana is extinguishing the fire of this life by which Buddha does not mean death or annihilation,—he means the achievment of a state which no man can describe. He said also that the original cause of this life is Ignorance. As a man *does not know* the means by which this Nirvana is achieved, he goes on taking births after births. This Ignorance is the cause of all his miseries. The knowledge of the means to achieve Nirvana leads him to a state in which there are no more births.

Is this atheism? Could there be any grander idea of Theism? The great Buddha believed in the existence of a *Supreme State* which is beyond all description or conception possible by man. Therefore he did not name it, nor did he make an attempt to describe it. It is the indescribable State beyond Nirvana,—that is all. Man can attain to it,—man can rise beyond the reach of life and death, pleasure and pain. Buddha pointed out the Great Path to it to the entire human race. No body in the world is or even was a greater Theist than Siddhartha Goutama, the great Buddha of the world. No body preached a higher religion than He.

——:o:——

CHAPTER IV.

THE PATH OF NIRVANA.

Now how is this Nirvana to be attained, and by whom? There are four Stages or Paths (Sans—Marga, Pali—Magga) to it,—namely:—

1. Sowan.
2. Sakradagami.
3. Anagami.
4. Arya.

Each Path is divided into two grades, namely:—

(1). The Perception of the Path.

(2). Its Fruition (Margaphala).

An entrance into any of these four Paths secures, either immediately or more remotely, the attainment of Nirvana.

1. The Path *Sowan* or *Srotapatti* is so called, because it is the first stream that is entered before Nirvana. It is divided into twenty four sections. After one enters in this Path, there can be to him only seven births in any world but the four hells.

2. The Path *Sakradgami* is so called, because he who enters it will receive only one more birth. It is divided into twelve sections and one may enter this path from the world of men and have one birth in Devaloka, or he may enter it from Devaloka taking afterwards one birth in the world of men.

3. The Path *Anagami* is so called, because he who enters it will not be born again in a Karmaloka, *i. e.* either in the world of men or devas. But he may be born in Brahmaloka whence he will enter Nirvana. This Path is divided into forty eight sections.

4. The Path *Arya* or *Arahat* is so called, because he who enters it has overcome all *Kleshas* or miseries. He has gone

beyond all births. This Path is divided into twelve sections. When the fruit tree is cut down, the latent fruit that is in it, which has not yet appeared, but which would appear in due time if it were permitted to remain, is destroyed. In like manner by this path all miseries are destroyed that otherwise would continue to exist and would have brought forth births.

The following are the five gradations of beings.*

1. There is the unwise being, who is under the influence of Kleshas or evil desire and of anxiety, ignorance and impurity, who has not attained to the fruition of the Path. He has not attended to the precepts, by which he might overcome inpurity; his mind is not disciplined to the exercise of the tranquility of *Samadhi*; he has not secured the wisdom produced by abstract meditation. The mind of such a being is gross and slow, because he is not accustomed to the more profound exercises of abstraction. Thus there is a clump of bamboos;which as they grow embrace each other and become entangled; they have many knots, and thin branches are twisted together into one mass. Now if one of these trees be cut down at the root, the process of felling it away will be slow. Why? Because the leaves, knots and branches are all entangled together in such a confusion that they cannot be extricated. In the same way when any one is under the influence of the errors that characterise the unwise man, his mind is heavy and slow. Why? Because it is entangled in the meshes of evil desire. This is the first gradation.

2. There is the being who has entered the First Path, to whom the doors of the four hells are shut. He has maintained the true profession and entirely approves the doctrines of the Great Master. He has thus arrived at the frontier of the First of the Paths. He has rejected the error called *Sakkya dristiti* which teaches "I am, this is mine." He has

* See Malinda Prasna.

no doubts as to the reality of Buddhas. He sees clearly that if he desires to obtain Nirvana, he must follow the practices enjoined by the Buddhas. As for these then his mind is free, not bound, but light and quick, but as to the other Paths, it is stale, slow, gross and entangled. Thus in these degrees it is pure, in all others, it is still under the influence of impurity. How? When the bamboo that has been cut down is cleared for the space of three knots, it might be felled away to this distance with ease, were it not that it is entangled by the upper branches that yet remain. In the same way, the being that has entered the First Path is free as to the three doctrines, but he is slow, heavy and entangled as to the rest which he has not yet embraced. This is the second gradation.

3. There is the being who has entered the Second Path. He has rejected the three errors overcome by the man who has entered the First Path; he is also saved from *Kama-raga* and the wish for doing evil to others. Thus in five degrees his mind is pure, but as to the rest his mind is slow and entangled. How? When five knots of the bamboo have been cleared, it might easily be drawn thus far, were it not held by the upper bamboos that are yet entangled. In the same way the man who has entered the Second Path is free as to the five particulars, but as to the rest he is still bound, heavy and dull. This is the third gradation.

4. There is the being who has entered the Third Path. He is free from the five errors overcome by the man who has attained to the Second Path. He is also free from the five *Sanyajanas*, evil desire, ignorance, doubts, the precepts of the sceptics and hatred. Thus in ten degrees his mind is pure, but as to the Path he has not yet entered, namely Rahatship, it is still slow, heavy, dull and entangled. How? It is like the tree that has ten knots cleared, but the rest remain entangled. This is the fourth gradation.

5. There is the being who has entered the Fourth Path

and has become a *Rahat*. He has destroyed the four *asrayas* namely *Kama*, *Bhava*, *Dristi* and *Avidya*. He is free from the impurity of *Klesha* and has arrived at the fruition of the Four Paths. He has vomitted up Klesha, as if it were an undigested mass. He has cast it away, as if it were a burden. He has arrived at the happiness which is obtained from the sight of Nirvana. He is no longer subject to the repetition of existence; he is endowed with the four supernatural powers of the Rahats; he has arrived at the most exalted state of *Srawakas*, and in consequence of these attainments, his mind is light, free, quick towards Rahatship, and all that precedes it, but heavy, bound, dull, as to that which is peculiar to the Pratakya Buddhas. This is the fifth gradation.

6. There is the being called Pratakya-Buddhas. He has attained the high state of privilege that he enjoys, by his own unaided exertions, as he has had no teacher, no one to instruct him. He is called Pratakya, severed, or separated, and is solitary, alone, like the unicorn. Thus his mind is light, pure, free towards the Pratakya Buddhaship, but dull, heavy, bound towards the state of the Supreme Buddhas. He has learnt that which belongs to his own, but he understands not the five kinds of knowledge that are perceived by the Supreme Buddhas, and by no other being. He knows not the thoughts of others, he has not the power to see all things nor to know all things. In these respects his mind is heavy. Thus a man whether by day or night arrives at the bank of a small stream into which he descends without fear in order that he may pass to the other bank. But at another time he comes to a river which is deep and broad; there is no bridge by which he can cross, he cannot see the opposite bank. In consequence of these obstacles he is afraid to venture into the water; he cannot cross the stream. In the same way, the Pratakya Buddha is free as to that which is connected with his own order, but bound as to all that is peculiar to the Supreme Buddhas. This is the sixth gradation.

7. There is the being who knows all things, he is endowed with the ten powers. He has attained to the Supreme Buddhaship, he has entirely overcome evil desire; he has ascertained all the hinderances to the reception of Nirvana, but he knows fully all that is excellent and good; he has the eighteen properties of the Buddhas, he has destroyed the infinite Klesha, he can perform the wonderful *Pratiharyas*. This is the seventh gradation.*

Entering into the Paths brings in innumerable supernatural powers. They who have entered into any of the Paths can fathom the thoughts of all in the same or the preceding Paths. Thus he who has entered the first Path can know the thoughts of any being in the same Path, but not of those of any other Paths, and so forth.

There are five great powers (*abhijnanas*) which a Rahat obtains. Namely:—

(1) Idhividyajnana (power of idhi.)

(2) Dewyasrotajnana (the power of hearing all sounds, whether distant or near, whether of men or of Devas.)

(3) Chitopariyajnana (the power to know the thoughts of other beings.)

(4) Purweniwasunusmertijnana (power to know the previous births.)

(5) Satwayangechatuppatijnana (the power to know the future births.)

---

* About Pacceka Buddhas and the Supreme Buddhas Oldenberg thus remarks:—" High above these four stages (the 1st four of the above) stand these perfect Ones who have of themselves alone become partakers of the Buddhahood (have become Pacceka or Pratakya Buddhas); they have won the knowledge that brings deliverence not as disciples of one of the holy, universal Buddhas, but of their own power, yet their perfection does not extend so far that they could preach it to the world."

" Above the four grades of believers and saints, there stand, last of all, embodying in themselves the essence of every supreme perfection, the exalted, holy, universal Buddhas." See Buddha pp. 321—322.

The divine eye of the Rahat can see that which cannot be perceived by the eye of flesh, as it can see any beings whatever, whether in hell, upon earth, or in Devaloka. It is not possessed to the same extent by all the Rahats, but differs in degree and proportion to the attainments of its possessors. There are many things that are too subtle to be perceived by one with this power but may be seen by another who is endowed with it in a superior degree. The lowest power is to be able to see things that are in existence at the time when it is exercised; but one who is endowed with this power may not be able to see that which has only existed at some previous period and has passed away or been destroyed, or he may not be able to discern objects at the very instant of their formation from their being so exceedingly minute.

The following conversation, between king Malinda and the monk Nagasena will give an idea what Buddhists meant by a Rahat.

King Malinda said :—" You have declared, reverend Sir, that when a layman becomes a Rahat, he must on the same day either become a monk or attain Nirvana. Now we shall suppose that a layman becomes a Rahat, but there is no one qualified present to ordain him as a monk, could such a one admit himself as a monk, or would he remain as a layman, or would he attain Nirvana; how would it be ?"

Nagasena replied :—" He could not ordain himself, as this would be contrary to the rule, nor could he remain a layman, so that either some one must come to admit him to the boon or he must attain Nirvana."

King asked :—" Why is it so ?"

Nagasena said :—" There are many evils connected with the state of a layman; it is therefore a state of weakness, and on this account a Rahat must at once either become a monk or attain Nirvana."

King Malinda asked :—" Can any one who has this body go to Utterkuru or to the Develokas and Brahmalokas ?"

Nagasena replied :—"It is possible for one who has a body composed of the four elements to visit the places you have named."

King Malinda asked :—" In what way can this be done ?"

Nagasena said :—"Can you at your will leap from the ground, say to the height of a space of a cubit ?"

Malinda said :—" With ease I can leap eight cubits high."

Nagasena said :—"How do you do this ?"

Molinda said :—I determine to leap, through this determination my body becomes as it were buoyant, and I rise from the ground."

Nagasena said :—" Just so the monk who has the power of idhi determines to go to such a place ; by the determination of his mind his body becomes as it were imponderous, and he is enabled thereby to pass through the air."

Malinda said :—"You have declared that the Rahats feel no pain of mind, though they are still subject to pain of body, but does not the mind subsist, because of the body? Is the Rahat without authority, mastery, or supremacy over the body ?"

Nagasena replied :—" It is even so."

Malinda said :—This does not appear to be right. Even a bird has authority over its nest."

Nagasena said :—"There are ten things that in every birth accompany the body, namely,—

1. Varna (colour.)
2. Tapa (heat.)
3. Khuda (hunger.)
4. Thrisna (thirst.)
5. Mala (facæs.)
6. Mutra (urine.)
7. Nidra (sleep.)
8. Vadi (disease.)
9. Khaya (decay.)

10. Mrityu (death.)

Over these ten a Rahat exercises no power."

Malinda said :—" Will you kindly explain to me how it is that this occurs ?"

Nagasena said :—"Because of the earth all beings exist, the earth cannot be commanded by all these beings. In like manner, because of the body the mind exists, the mind cannot command or control the body."

Malinda said :—" How is it then that others have pain both of body and mind ?"

Nagasena said :—" Because there has been no accomplishment of *Vidarsana* and other exercises by which the mind is brought into subjection. There is a hungry bull that is tied only by a small withe which it breaks in its anger and then runs away. In the same way, when the mind is not under discipline, it becomes irritated, breaks away from restraint and disturbs the body, and then there is crying, fear and the voice of sorrow; thus there is pain both of body and mind. But the mind of the Rahat is under proper discipline ; it does not disturb the body ; it is bound as to a pillar by Samadhi and other exercises ; it is filled with the pleasure of Nirvana, and the Rahat is therefore free from the pain of mind, whilst he is still subject to the pain of body."

Malinda said :—But would it not be a thing to be esteemed as a wonder if when the body is quieted or agitated, the mind were to remain tranquil ? Kindly explain to me how this can be."

Nagasena said :—"The branches of a tree are shaken by the wind but the trunk remains unmoved. In like manner as the mind of the Rahat is bound to the firm pillar of Samadhi by the cord of the Four Paths, it remains unmoved even when the body is suffering pain."*

---

* See Malinda Prasna.

CHAPTER V.

HOW TO ATTAIN RAHATSHIP.

THE means of attaining Rahatship is *Bhavana* (meditation) and *Samadhi*. There is hardly any difference between Brahmanic Dhyana, Dharana and Samadhi with the Buddhistic Bhavana, Dhyana and Samadhi.

There are five principal modes of Bhavana (meditation), namely :—

(1) Maitri.
(2) Mudita.
(3) Karana.
(4) Upakesha.
(5) Asubha.

No one can enter properly upon the exercise of the *Bhavana* who has not previously kept the Precepts.*

If there be such a man, let him at the close of the day or at the dawn of day sit in such a place where he will be free from interruption with his body in a suitable posture.† Let him meditate on the glory of the Buddhas, the excellence of *bana*‡ and the virtues of the monks.

1. *Maitri-Bhavana* :—When the monk has arrived at a convenient spot and placed himself in a proper position, let him exercise this wish :—May all the superior orders of beings be happy. May they all be free from sorrow, disease, and evil desire. May all men, whether they be monks or

* Moral disciplines as mentioned in the Sutras. They are equivalent to the *Yama* and *Niyama* of the Yoga of the Brahmans. It is in short the acquirement of the complete control over one's own mind. As in the case of an adept of Yoga, so no Bhiskhu can enter upon the exercise of Bhavana without first being a moral hero.

† This almost corresponds with the *Asana* of the Hindu Yoga.

‡ *Bana* is the Sermons that Buddha used to deliver to his disciples.

laymen, all the Devas, all who are suffering the pains of hell, be happy. May they be free from sorrow, disease and evil desire." Then the same wish must be exercised relative to all sentient beings in the four cardinal points, all the four-half-points, all above and all below, taking each of these four directions separately and in order, or if they cannot be taken separately, it will suffice if the wish be exercised to all sentient beings.

1. Maitri Bhavana:—In the exercise of this mode of meditation, the thoughts must not at first be fixed upon one whom the monk dislikes, nor on any particular friend, nor on any one that is indifferent to him neither liked and disliked, nor on any enemy. The thoughts must not at this time be fixed upon any individual in particular, nor on any one that is dead.*

2. Karuna Bhavana:—In the practice of this mode of meditations the priest must exercise the wish "May the poor be relieved from their indigence and receive abundance," Karuna is thus produced. When we see any objects in distress, we feel agitation in the mind, and from this arises *karuna* (conpassion). It is said that when we see distress of any kind, we feel the wish to relieve it, and this feeling is *karuna*.

3. Mudita Bhavana:—In the exercise of this mode of meditation the priest must express the wish "May the good fortune of the prosperous never pass away, may each one receive his own appointed reward." The principal meaning of *mudita* is joy, but it is not the joy arising from earthly possessions. It feels indifferent to individuals.

As the husbandman first portions out a certain plot of ground and then ploughs it, so the priest who exercises any of the above three modes of meditation may first direct his attention to a certain number of persons, then to the inhabitants of a street and so on in order to the whole village, the kingdom, the Sakwalas and the Out-Sakwalas.

* Maitri is Sneha (affection, love). It is opposite of *Kroda* (anger.)

4. *Asubha Bhavana*:—The principal meaning of the word *asubha* is inauspicious, that which is the opposite of good fortune or that which produces dissatisfaction, aversion and disgust. In this exercise the priest must reflect that the body is composed of thirty-two impurities, that as the worm is bred in the dunghill, so it is composed, conceived in the womb, that is the receptacle of filth, that disgusting secretions are continually proceeding from its nine apertures, that, it sends forth an offensive smell.

The ascetic who would practise *Asubha Bhavana* must apply to some one who is able to instruct him, who must take him to the cemetry and point out to him the offensive parts of a dead body, but if he hears that there is a body in the forest, he must not go there, as he may be in danger from the wild beasts that are attracted to the same spot, nor must he go to any place that is very public, as in such a spot his mind would be distracted by the various scenes that he would witness and he would meet with women.

5. *Upeksha Bhavana*:—In the exercise of this mode of meditation all sentient beings are regarded alike, one is not loved more than another; towards all there is indifference. This exercise is superior to all the other and is practised by the Rahats.

The four modes of meditation, Maitri, Karuna, Mudita, Upeksha are called Brahma Vehara Bhavana.

The three reflections in the impermanency, suffering, and unreality of the body are as the gates leading to the city of Nirvana.*

Dhyana means that which burns up evil desire or the cleaving to existence. It is sometimes used in the sense of meditation and at other times is allied to *Samadhi*.*

There are five principles connected with the Dhyanas; with these five they are perfect as when we speak of the four

* The above is quoted from the two celebrated Buddhist Sacred works, namely, Salugya Sutra and Visudha Marga Sutra.

divisions of the army or five kinds of musical instruments or eight directions, they are—

1. Vitarka (attention).
2. Vichara (reasonings).
3. Priti (joy).
4. Sepa (comfort).
5. Chitta Ekagrata (mental restraint).

Dhyanas are divided into five sections, namely :—

1. Pratamadhyana.
2. Dwitayadhyana.
3. Thritiya Dhyane.
4. Chaturtaobyanà.
5. Panchamadhyana.

(*a*) To the First Dhyana belongs Vitarka (attention.)

(*b*) To the Second Dhyana belong Priti (joy), Sepa (comfort) and Chitta Ekagrata (mental restraint.)

(*c*) When the Third Dhyana is accomplished, Upeksha is attained.

(*d*) When the Fourth Dhyana is accomplished, there is an entire destruction of the cleaving to existence.

In the exercise of the first Dhyana the mind is like the waves upon the water, when there is some large and some small, there is no clearness, that which is the subject of contemplation is like a fish seen in the water and the Samadhi that is attained is of an inferior order.

In the Second Dhyana the Samadhi becomes more pure as the mind recedes further and further from Vitarka and Vichara. There is a degree of Upeksha possessed in the 1st and 2nd Dhyanas, but it is not perfect. They are like a man who walks in a place covered with sharp stones, whilst the 2nd Dhyana is like a man who walks in a plain and even road.

When the Third Dhyana is entered, the mind, if not properly controlled, goes out after the pritā it has abandoned and as the calf that is tied at a distance from the cow continually seeks to break away from its confinement that it may reach the udder it has been accustomed to draw milk.

With the Fourth Dhyana this is connected with *Vedana.* When the husbandman wants to catch a refractory bull, he drives the whole herd into the fold, and then letting the animals out one by one, he catches the bull. In like manner in order to discover this form of Vedana, all the sensations must be collected together and examined one by one, when it will be perceived. It is exceedingly small and scarcely to be discerned, as it is not connected with either pleasure or pain. When the mind is thus cleansed by Upeksha, it becomes exceedingly pure.*

The state of mind that is produced by Dhyanas is called *Parikrama.* According to its character will be the power of the divine eyes that will be received as they will be more or less clear, strong, extensive in the circle of their vision and parmanent in their existence.

There are two kinds of Samadhi, namely *Upachari* and *Arppana.* They cause the destruction of those things that act as an enemy to the Dhyanas.

1. In Upachari Samadhi the mind is not rightly firm, not entirely at rest or calm. It is like a child that is unable to walk properly and is continually falling, as the *nimitta* is sometimes received and sometimes lost.

---

* There is some difference between the Buddhistic and Brahmanic Dhyanas. According to the latter the 5th Dhyana is entered but according to the former the 5th is avoided.

After the accomplishment of the Dhyanas, the Buddhists seek to enter the Paths.

At the life-time of Buddha, there were strict rules of life—but hardly any rites, worship or ceremonies. The only ceremony or festival was *bana* and his invitations in the houses of rich men when he used to deliver his grand sermons. But now Buddhism is full of rites and ritualism. See the history and developement of Buddhism as narrated in Part IV. of this work. Its justification will be found in the arguments of the monk Nagasena as put forward by him before the king Malinda.

2. Arpana Samadhi is more powerful. It is like a man who rises from his seat and walks steadily for the space of whole day, as when it is received, the mind continues in one even frame undisturbed and unshaken. He who would receive Arpana Samadhi must be careful in the following matters.

1. Residence—must be free from all disagreeables.
2. Road—must be within 750 bows.
3. Conversation—must not treat of the thirty-two forbidden topies.
4. Company—he must not keep company with improper persons.
5. Food—must be agreeable.
6. Season—must also be agreeable.
7. The position of the body—the posture must be pleasant.

Samadhi is that which keeps the thoughts together. Samadhi is the principal root of all the other virtues. All others are inferior to it, come after it and bind towards it.*

---

* Oldenberg thus remarks on the Buddhistic ideas of Dhyana and Samadhi :—" Budddhism, following a common feature of all Indian religious life which preceded it, regards as stages prepatory to the victory is won, certain exercises of spiritual abstraction, in which the *religiux* withdraws his thoughts from the external world with its motley crowd of changing forms, to anticipate in the stillness of his own Ego, afar from pain and pleasure, the cessation of the impermanent. The devotion of abstraction is to Buddhism what prayer is to other religions." See Buddha, pp. 314—315.

——:o:——

CHAPTER VI.

BUDDHIST MORALITY—*Beatitude*.

THE disciples of the Buddha were divided into two chief classes, namely ordained monks who were called *Bhikshus* and lay members who were called *Upashakas*.

But who were the *Upasakas*? They were Buddha's lay-followers. Oldenberg says:—" While there was framed from the beginning for the monastic church an organization, clothed with the strict forms of spiritual procedure, there was no attempt made of creations of a similar kind for the quasi church of lay-brothers and lay-sisters. Certain custom of spiritual life and practical beneficience must obviously have arisen; even here definite institutions have not followed. There was not so much as any sharply drawn line between the laity who were to be regarded as adherents of the Order of Buddha and those who stood aloof therefrom. Entry into the circle of votaries was dependent on no qualification and followed regularly upon a form fixed by custom, but not determined by rule, namely upon the person taking the step diclaring in the presence of a monk, either on his own behalf alone or jointly with wife, children and servants, that he takes his refuge in Buddha, Dharma and the Order."

There were very hard and fast rules for the members of the Order,—there were no such hard rules for the lay-members. As we shall separately deal with the Buddha's Great Order, we shall here mention the moral precepts that the Great Masters enjoined on all.

The Religion of Buddha pre-eminently stands at a very high altar in respect of moral teachings. We quote a few

* See Oldenberg's Buddha, pp. 382—383.

passages from various Buddhist works to give an idea of the high ideal in which the Buddhist morals were always held.

In Mangulla Sutta a Deva asks Buddha thus :—

Many Gods and Men
Have held various things blessings
When they were yearning for happiness.
Do thou declare to us the chief good.

The Buddha replies :—

1

Not to serve the foolish,
But to serve the wise,
To honour those worthy of honour,
This is the greatest blessing.

2

To dwell in a pleasant land,
Good works done in a former birth,
Right desires in the heart,
This is the greatest blessing.

3

Much insight and education,
Self-content and pleasant speech,
And whatever word be well-spoken,
This is the greatest blessing.

4

To support father and mother,
To cherish wife and child,
To follow a peaceful calling,
This is the greatest blessing.

5

To bestow alms and live righteously,
To give help to kindred,
Deeds which cannot be blamed,
These are the greatest blessings.

6

To abhor and cease from sin,
Abstinence from strong drink,
Not to be weary in well-doings,
These are the greatest blessings.

7

Reverence and lowliness,
Contentment and gratitude,
The hearing of the Law in due seasons,
This is the greatest blessing.

8

To be long-suffering and meek,
To associate with the tranquil,
Religious talk at due seasons,
This is the greatest blessing.

9

Self-restraint and purity,
The knowledge of the Noble Truths,
The realization of Nirvana,
This is the greatest blessing.

10

Beneath the stroke of life's changes,
The mind that shaketh not,
Without grief or passion,
This is the greatest blessing.

11

On every side are invincible,
They who act like these,
On every side they walk in safety,
And these are the greatest blessings.

We shall now quote a few general precepts from various Buddhist Sutras.

1

As the bee injuring not
The flower, its color or scent,
Flies away taking the nectar,
So let the wise man dwell upon earth.

2

One may conquer a thousand men in battle.
But he who conquers himself alone is the greatest victor.

3

It is good to tame the mind,
Difficult to hold in and flighty,
Rushing whereon it listeth;
A tamed mind is the origin of bliss.

4

For never in this world hatred ceases by hatred.
Hatred ceases by love. This is always its nature.

5

Let a man overcome anger by kindness, evil by good.
Let him conquer the stingy by gifts, the liar by truth.

6

Not by birth one becomes low caste,
Not by birth one becomes a Brahman,
By his actions alone one becomes low caste.
By his actions alone he becomes a Brahman.

7

Anger, drunkenness, obstinacy, bigotry, deception, envy, self-praise, disparaging others, evil communications, these constitute uncleanliness, not verily the eating of flesh.

8

Neither abstinence from fish or flesh, nor going naked, nor shaving the head, nor matted hair, nor a rough garment, nor sacrifices to Agni, will cleanse a man, not free from delusions.

9

Regarding the Vedas, making offering to priests, or sacrifices to gods, self-mortifications by heat or cold and many such penances performed for the sake of immortality, these do not cleanse the man, not free from delusions.

10.

Mind precedes action. The motive is chief; actions proceed from mind. If any one speak or act from a corrupt mind, suffering will follow the action, as the wheel follows the lifted foot of the ox.

11.

Their anger is not subdued who recall to mind—he abused me, he struck me, he plundered me. Anger will never be appeased by anger, but by gentleness. This is the doctrine of the ancients.

12.

Persons do not reflect, we shall speedily die; if any do thus reflect, their quarrels speedily terminate.

13.

He who lives regarding the pleasures of existence, with unrestrained passions, immoderate in food, indolent, unpreserving *Maraya* (lust) will certainly subdue him, as the feeble tree is overturned by the blast. He who lives meditating on the evils of existence with restrained passions, temperate in food, religious and preserving, *Maraya* will certainly not overpower him, as the solid rock stands unmoved by the storm.

14.

Those who regard evil as good, or good as evil, will never attain to excellence; but are nurtured in errors. Those who know good to be good and evil to be evil will attain to excellence; being nourished by truth.

15.

As the rain completely penetrates the ill-thatched roof,

so will lust completely subdue the unmeditative mind. As the rain cannot penetrate the well-covered roof, so lust cannot overcome the contemplative mind.

16.

The sinner mourns in this world, and he will mourn in the next world. In both worlds, he has sorrow; he grieves, he is tormented, perceiving his own impure actions. The virtuous man rejoices in this world, and he will rejoice in the next world. In both worlds he has joy. He rejoices, he exalts, perceiving his own virtuous deeds.

17.

The sinner suffers in this world, and he will suffer in the next world. In both worlds he suffers,—knowing sin has been counted by him and dreadfully will he suffer in the regions of torment. The virtuous man is happy in this world, and he will be happy in the next world. In both worlds he is happy—knowing he has acted virtuously and greatly will he rejoice in heaven.

18.

The worldly minded man who understands much of religion and talks much concerning it without keeping its precepts is like a herdsman of other man's cattle who is not a partaker of the flock he tends. The pious man, who though he understands but little and talks but little of religion, is an observer of its precepts, who removes lust, wrath, and folly far from him, who is considerate, possessed of a mind free from evil and without attachments, he in this world and that to come is a partaker of the fruits of piety.

19.

Earnestness is the path of Nirvana; thoughtlessness the path of death. Those who are in earnest do not die, those who are thoughtless are as if dead already.

20.

Those who are advanced in earnestness, having understood this clearly, delight in earnestness and rejoice in the knowledge of the Aryas.

21.

Follow not after vanity, nor after the enjoyment of love and lust. He, who is earnest and meditative, obtains ample joy.

22.

It is good to tame the mind which is difficult to hold in, flighty, rushing wherever it listeth; a tamed mind brings happiness.

23.

Let the wise man guard his thoughts, for they are difficult to perceive, very artful, and they rush wherever they list; thought well-guarded brings happiness.

24.

Before long, alas, this body will lie on the earth, despised without nnderstanding like a useless log. Not a mother, not a father will do so much, nor any other relative. A well-directed mind will do us great service.

25.

The fool who knows his folishness is wise at least so far. But a fool who thinks himself wise is called a fool indeed. If a fool is associated with a wiseman all his life, he will perceive the truth as little as a spoon perceives the taste of soup.

26.

If a man would hasten towards the good, he should keep his thoughts away from evil. If a man does what is good slothfully, his mind delights in evil. If a man commits a sin, let him not do it again. Let him not delight in sin; pain is the outcome of evil. If a man does what is good, let him do it again; let him delight in it; happiness is the outcome of good.

An evil-doer sees happiness as long as his evil deed has not ripened, but when his evil deed has ripened, then does the evil-door see evil. A good man sees evil deeds as long as his good deed has not ripened, but when his good deed has ripened, then does the good man see happy days. Let no man think lightly of evil, saying in his heart,—It will not come nigh unto me. Even by the falling of water-drops, a water-pot is filled; the fool becomes full of evil even if he gathers it little by little. Let no man think lightly of good, saying in his heart,—'It will not come nigh unto me.' Even by the falling of water-drops a water-pot is filled, the wise man becomes full of good, even if he gathers it little by little.

27.

All men tremble at punishment; all men love life; remember that thou art like unto them and do not kill nor cause slaughter. Do not speak harshly to any body; those who are spoken to, will answer thee in the same way. Angry speech is painful; blows for blows will touch thee.

28.

How is there laughter, how is there joy, as this world is always burning? Why do you not seek light, ye who are surrounded by darkness? This body is wasted of sickness; frail; this heap of corruption breaks to pieces; life indeed ends in death.

29.

Self is the Lord of Self;—who else could be the Lord? With self-will subdued, a man finds a lord, such as few can find.

30.

Let us live happily then, not hating those who hate us. Among men who hate us, let us dwell free from hatred. Let us liwe happily then, free from ailments among the ailing. Among men who are ailing, let us dwell free from ailments! Let us live happily then, free from greed among the greedy?

Among men who are greedy, let us dwell free from greed. Let us live happily then, though, we call nothing our own. We shall be bright gods feeding on happiness.

31.

Let no man ever look for what is pleasant, or what is unpleasant. Not to see what is pleasant is pain, and it is pain to see what is unpleasant. From pleasure comes grief, from pleasure comes fear. He who is free from pleasure, knows neither grief nor fear. From affection, from lust, from love, from greed, comes grief and fear. He who is free from affection, lust, love or greed knows neither grief nor fear.

32.

Let a man overcome anger by love, let him overcome evil by good, let him overcome the greedy by liberality, the liar by truth. Beware of bodily anger and control thy body. Beware of the anger of the tongue and control thy tongue. Beware of the anger of the mind and control thy mind. Being of a pious mind, one should observe Upastha* on the 14th, 15th and the day of the lunar fort-night and Pati Haraka Pakkha† should also be duly observed.

In the next place a wise man who has kept the fast day should in the morning, being of a pious mind and taking constant delight in doing so, provide the members of the Order with food and drink according to his ability.

---

* Upastha means fasting. Rhys Davids thus explains it. The Upastha days are the four days in the lunar month; when the moon is full or new or half way between the two. Upastha is therefore a weekly festival.

† The Patihara Pakkha or Extra Fort-night is an epithet of three distinct periods:—(1) the three months of *Was* or rain, (2) the month succeeding *Was* called Chivara month or robe month, because it is then customary to provide mendicants who require them with new sets of robes, (3) the first half of the robe month. See Rhys David's Buddhism page 141.

He should maintain his father and mother in a just manner and should practice a just trade; the householder, observing all this with diligence, reaches the self-shining gods.

The thirst of a thoughtless man grows like a creeper; he runs from life to life, like a monkey seeking fruit in the forest. Whomsoever this fierce thirst overcomes, full of poison, in this world, his sufferings increase like *Buana* grass. He who overcomes this fierce thirst, difficult to be conquered in this world, sufferings fall from him, like water drops from a lotus leaf.*

—:o:—

CHAPTER VII.

PRECEPTS—TEN SINS.

Ten Sins are :—

(*a*) Three of the body namely—

(1) One should not destroy life.

(2) One should not take what is not given.

(3) One should not commit adultery.

---

* In chapters I. to V., we have briefly sketched the Buddhist metaphysics and written all that is worth knowing of the Buddhist philosophy. In the following chapters we have spoken of the Buddhist Ethics and morals to be followed both by the monks as well as by the lay-members. The precepts have been culled from the various Suttras; the latter a few from the Dhammapada. We quote these verses from the Buddhistic Book Dhammapada as translated by Professor Max Muller in the Sacred Books of the East, Vol. X. The Professor says :—"I cannot therefore see any reason why we should not treat the verses of the Dhammapada, if not as the utterances of Buddha, at least as what were believed by the members of the Council under Asoka in 242 B.C., to have been the utterances of the founder of their religion."

(*b*) Four of the speech namely—
(1) One should not tell lies.
(2) One should not slander others.
(3) One should not abuse another.
(4) One should not hold vain conversations.

(*c*) Three of the mind namely—
(1) Coveteousness.
(2) Malice.
(3) Scepticism.

THE TAKING OF LIFE.

There are five things necessary to constitute the crime of taking life. (1) There must be the knowledge that there is life. (2) There must be the assurance that a living being is present. (3) There must be the intention to take life. (4) With this intention there must be something done as the placing of a bow or spear or the setting of a mace, and there must be same movement towards it as walking, running or or jumping. (5) Life must actually be taken.

There are six ways in which life may be taken. (1) By the person himself with a sword or lance. (2) By giving the command to another. (3) By the use of projectiles such as a spear, an arrow, or stone. (4) By treachery as the digging of pits and covering them slightly over, setting spring or poisoning ponds. (5) By magical rules. (6) By the instrumentality of demons.

There are eight causes of the destruction of life,—(1) evil desire, (2) anger, (3) ignorance, (4) pride, (5) coveteousness, (6) poverty, (7) wantonness, (8) Law.

THEFTS.

There are five things necessary to constitute the crime of theft,—(1) the article taken must belong to another, (2) there must be something taken that belongs to another, (3) there must be intention to steal, (4) there must be some acts done or efforts to obtain possession, (5 there must be actual acquirement.

ADULTERY.

There are twenty-one descriptions of women whom it is forbidden to approach. Among them is a woman protected by her relatives, or bought with money, or who is cohabiting with another of her own will, or works for another person for wages though she is not a slave, or who is betrothed, or a slave living with her owner, or working in her own house, or taken as a spoil in war. All these are to be regarded as the property of another and are therefore not to be approached.

Four things are necessary to constitute this crime. (1) There must be some one that it is unlawful to approach. (2) There must be the evil intention. (3) There must be some act or effort to carry the intention into effect. (4) There must be the accomplishment of the intention.

LYING.

Four things are necessary to constitute a lie. (1) There must be the utterance of the thing that is not. (2) There must be the knowledge that it is not. (3) There must be some endeavour to prevent the person addressed from learning the truth. (4) There must be the discovery by the person deceived that what has been told to him is not true.

SLANDER.

When any one attempts to put friends at enmity, or to sow dissension between men, says here what he heard there, or there what he heard here, it is slander. If he speaks evil of persons and places that are esteemed by others, or if by insinuation he leads to question the sincerity of each other's profession, it is also slander.

UNPROFITALBE CONVERSATION.

When things are said out of the proper time, or things,

that cannot in any way tend to profit, are spoken, the precept that forbids unprofitable conversation is broken.

COVETOUSNESS.

When any one sees that which belongs to another and desires to possess it, or thinks it would be good were this to belong to him, he transgresses the precept that forbids covetousness.

SCEPTICISM.

One who does not believe the Law and has no faith in any thing, and one who is always questioning all religious matters, induces others to be like him and prevents others to be devotional is a sceptic.

GENERAL.

Intoxication :—When any intoxicating liquor has been taken with the intention that it shall be drunk and something is actually done to procure the liquor, and it has passed down the throat, the precept is broken that forbids the use of toddy and other intoxicating drinks.

Gambling :—There are six evil consequences that result from frequenting the places of gambling (1) The man who loses is angry with him who wins. (2) He is sorrowful, because another has seized his substance. (3) His property is wasted. (4) When the gambler gives evidence in a Court of Justice, his testimony is not believed even though he should speak the truth. (5) He is not trusted either by his friends or superiors. (6) He cannot procure a wife from being unable to provide the proper ornaments and jewels.

Idleness :—He who says it is too hot or too cold or too early, and on this account refuses to work is an idle man and will be deprived of the means of existence.

Bad company :—The man who has sinful friends, unwise associates, and frequents the company of those who follow evil practices will come to destruction both in this world and in the next.

Places of amusement :—There are six evil consequences that arise from frequenting places of amusement: The mind is ensnared by the following practices :—(1) dancing, (2) singing, 3) the beating of drums, (4) gambling, (5) the clapping of hands, (6) The game of water jars.*

——:o:——

CHAPTER VIII.

MUTUAL RELATIONS.

The most favourite Sutra on the duties of every-day-life common both to the Northern and Southern Schools of Buddhism is the Sigalowada Sutra. We give a summary of it.

The teacher was residing in the Jastivana Vihara near Rajgriha, and one day going out as usual to collect alms, he saw a house-holder named Sigala bowing down with streaming hair and wet-clothes and clapsed hands to the four quarters of heaven and the Nadir and the Zenith. "Why," asked the Holy One, "Sigala, are you doing all this?" "Good monk," replied Sigala, "I am honouring, reverencing and holding sacred the words of my father, and to avert evil from the six directions."

"Sigala," said the Buddha, "the best way to guard the six quarters is by good deeds to men round him, to his parents as the east, his teachers as the south, his wife and children as the west, his friends and relations as the north, men devoted to the religious life, Brahmanas and Sramans, as the Zenith, and his slaves and dependents as the Nadir.

"How this could be done, sire?" asked Sigala.

The Buddha replied.

---

* The above summary is made following the way of Hardy & Rhys Davids. See Buddhism and Manual of Buddhism.

PARENTS AND CHILDREN.

Parents should,—

1. Restrain their children from vice.
2. Train them in virtue.
3. Have them taught arts or sciences.
4. Provide them with suitable wives or husbands.
5. Give them their inheritance.

The children should say:—

1. I will support them who supported me.
2. I will perform family duties incumbent on them.
3. I will guard their property.
4. I will make myself worthy to be their heirs.
5. When they are gone, I will honour their memory.

PUPILS AND TEACHERS.

The pupil should honour his teachers,—

1. By rising in their presence.
2. By ministering to them.
3. By obeying them.
4. By supplying their wants.
5. By attention to instruction.

The teacher should show his affection to his pupils.

1. By training them in all that is good.
2. By teaching them to hold knowledge fast.
3. By instruction in science and lore.
4. By speaking well of them to their friends and companies.
5. By guarding them from danger.

HUSBAND AND WIFE.

The husband should cherish his wife,—

1. By treating her with respect.
2. By treating her with kindness.
3. By being faithful to her.
4. By causing her to be honoured by others.

5. By giving her suitable ornaments and clothes.

The wife shows her affection for her husband,—

1. When she orders her household aright.
2. When she is hospitable to kinsmen and friends.
3. When she is a chaste wife.
4. When she is a thrifty house-keeper.
5. When she shows skill and diligence in all she has to do.

FRIENDS AND COMPANIONS.

The honourable man should minister to his friends,—

1. By giving presents.
2. By courteous speech.
3. By promoting their interest.
4. By treating them as his equals.
5. By sharing with them his prosperity.

They should show his attachment to him,—

1. By watching over him when he is off his guard.
2. By guarding his property when he is careless.
3. By offering him a refuge in danger.
4. By adhering to him in misfortune.
5. By showing kndness to his family.

MASTERS AND SERVANTS.

The master should provide for the welfare of his servants and dependants,—

1. By apportioning work to them according to their stength.
2. By supplying suitable food and wages.
3. By tending them in sickness.
4. By sharing with them delicacies.
5. By now and then granting them holidays.

They should show their attachment to him,

1. By rising before him.
2. By retiring later to rest.

3. By working cheerfully and thoroughly.
4. By being content with what is given them.
5. By speaking well of him.

LAYMEN AND MONKS.

The honourable man ministers to mendicants and Brahmans,—

1. By affection in acts.
2. By affection in words.
3. By affection in thoughts.
4. By giving them a ready welcome.
5. By supplying their temporal wants.

They should show their affection to him,—

1. By dissuading him from vice.
2. By exhorting him to virtue.
3. By feeling kindly towards him.
4. By instructing him in religion.
5. By clearing up his doubts.
6. By pointing the way to heaven.

"By thus acting," said Buddha, "the six quarters are each preserved in peace and free from danger. He who worships these six quarters will be competent to the duties of a house-holder and shall be exalted."

Sigala then acknowledged himself converted and became a Upasaka.

—:o:—

CHAPTER IX.

THE BUDDHIST RITES AND CEREMONIES.

DURING the lifetime of Buddha there were no prayers, no worship, rites, ceremonies and festivals amongst the Buddhist monks or lay-disciples. Buddha was dead against all this. His religion was based on self-development and self-culture and had nothing to do with external ceremonies. If there was anything like a religious meeting, it was *bana*, which was sermons delivered by him or by any other prominent Bhikshu to a congregation of monks and lay-Buddhists.

After his death, the Bo-tree under which he attained Nirvana grew to be a great place of pilgrimage. Hundreds of thousands of men from all parts of the country came and paid respects to the Bo-tree at Gya by throwing at its foot flowers and all sorts of offerings. Thus in time Gaya became a great pilgrimage and a big city.

His remains were originally buried in ten places, and mounds were erected over them. They were called Dagobas. Along with the secred Bo-tree, these ten Dagobas were also considered to be great places of pilgrimage.

But in a few years Buddha was diefied; his statues or idols were made and worshipped as gods. Temples were raised over them. Buddha became a god,—a god of gods that he drove away from the tenet of his great religion. This is not all. Many others of his great followers were also diefied and worshipped as gods; many more imaginary geds were created, and temples were built in their honour. Thus Buddism became full of idolatry and ceremonies*

How is it possible for Buddhism to tolerate this? This subject was argued at length between Nagasena and king Malinda.†

King Malinda:—" Unbelievers argue in this manner:— If Buddha now receives the offerings of men, he has not attained Nirvana, as in that state all cleaving to existing objects is destroyed. He is then still connected with the world, he is yet existent, he is in the world and has the same attributes as other beings; therefore the assistance that he can

---

* See Part IV.

† See Malinda Prasna.

render is imperfect, vain and worthless. But if he has attained Nirvana, he is not connected with the world, he is not existent, he cannot receive the offerings that are made to him; there is therefore no benefit from presenting them, as he has no life, no being, no *prana*. None but a Rahat can answer this argument of the Thirtakas; therefore be pleased, venerable Sir, to set aside this difficulty.

Nagasena replied:—"Buddha has attained Nirvana in which there is no cleaving to existence; he does not receive the offerings that are presented at the foot of the Bo-tree. When he became a Supreme Buddha, all evil desire was destroyed; he has attained Nirvana. Who is it that affirms that Buddha now recieves the offerings? Buddha receives the offerings without any earthly cleaving towards them.

Malinda said:—"The father magnifies the son and the son the father; therefore this is not an argument that we can bring before the unbelievers. Each one praises his own. Be pleased, therefore, to bring forward some other argument that will convince the sceptics."

Nagasena said:—"Buddha has attained Nirvana; he does not receive the offerings that are made to him by the people of the world; neverthless those who make offerings to the relics of the Buddhas, or listen to their *Bana* will receive the three great favours, *viz.*

1. The happiness of the world.
2. That of the Devalokas.
3. That of Nirvana.

Thus when grass or fuel has been thrown into a fire that has been kindled, is there any desire to receive them on the part of fire?"

King Malinda said:—"The fire has no mind, and therefore cannot receive them on account of desire."

Nagasena said:—"When that fire, although it has no mind, receives the grass, and fuel is extenguished, is the world without fire?"

Malinda said :—"No, any one who wishes to have fire, can produce it by the friction of two pieces of wood".

Nagasena said :—"Therefore those who say that no benefit can be received from the making of offerings to Buddha, utter that which has no foundation in truth. Whilst Buddha was in the world, the glory that he possessed may be compared to a brilliant flame; now that he has attained Nirvana, his passing away is like the extinguishing of that flame; but as the flame receives the grass and the fuel that are thrown in it, though without desire on its part, or although Buddha does not receive the offerings of the faithful, the rewards of those offerings are certain; for as a man may procure a flame by rubbing together two pieces of wood, by the light of which he will be able to carry on whatever work he has in hand, so the faithful, by making offerings to Buddha and reflecting on the excellences of Dharma will reap the reward for which these exercises are practised. There is another comparison which you may listen to. There is a high wind, it shakes the trees and causes them to fall and then dies away. After thus passing away, is it from desire that it again returns."

King replied :—"This cannot be, because it has got no mind."

Nagasena said :—"Does the wind that passes away make some sign to the wind that is to come ?"

Malinda said :—No, any one may cause wind by means of a fan. When he is warm, he can cool himself in this way."

Nagasena said :—"Therefore the unbelievers that say there is no benefit from the making of offerings to Buddha speak falsely. As the wind spreads itself in every direction, so is the virtue of Buddha everywhere diffused; as the wind that passed away is not again produced, so there is no reception of the offerings in the part of Buddha. As men are subject to be annoyed by heat, so are Devas and men afflicted by the three-fold fire of evil desire, enmity and ignorance; and as men when thus annoyed cause a wind to refresh their persons by means of some other instrument, so are they assisted who seek the protection of Buddha; and the three-fold fire is extinguished, although Buddha has attained Nirvana and does not receive the offerings that are presented. Another comparison may be given. A man strikes the drum and causes a sound to be produced; the sound dies away. Is it afterwards again produced?"

Malinda said:—"No, the sound has passed away, but the same man can cause a repetition of the sound by again striking the drum."

Nagasena said:—"In like manner though Buddha has attained Nirvana, the benefit to be received from the making of offerings and meditating on the *bana* is still certain. This benefit is gained, though Buddha does not receive the offerings. Buddha foresaw the things that would happen in the future and he said to Ananda:—"Ananda, when I am gone, you must not think there is no Buddha; the discourses I have delivered and the precepts I have enjoined, must be very successors and representatives and be to you as Buddha." Therefore the declaration of the Thirthakas that there is now no benefit from the presenting of offerings to Buddha is utterly false. Though he does not receive them, the benefit to the giver is the same as if he did."

PART III.

SANGHA.

CHAPTER I.

THE most important of Buddha's works was his SANGHA, the ORDER of BHIKSHUS. He preached a religion which was based on the religious and philosophical belief then extant. He believed in the Transmigration and Karma, the two most important foundations on which the religion of the Hindus stood. He avoided the discussion of the existence or non-existence of God, which was done by Kapila in his Sankhya long before him. In fact, in his philosophical, ethical and moral teachings, there was very little which was new, or which was not believed or known amongst the people of India. If there was anything new that he did it was his *Sangha*, his great Order of Monks.

What is then this Sangha? Long before the birth of Buddha, there were innumerable monks and ascetics, believing in various philosophical theories and observing many hard austerities, but each was independent of the other. At best they followed a particular leader, but each leader, with his followers and pupils, was perfectly independent, having nothing to do with any other leader, philosopher or teacher. Such was the scattered state of the monkhood in India.

Buddha promulgated a new idea. He formed a Society, an Order, the member of which became a Bhikshu,—a monk, renouncing home and hearth, and giving up *Kamini* and *Kanchana*, *i.e.*, woman and wealth. They gave up the world in order to work out their own salvation. But they were not independent of each other,—they were each a part of a whole,—member of an organised body. None can follow the great religion of Buddha unless he takes refuge in BUDDHA, DHARMA, and SANGHA. He must be the member of the Order. Buddha created a Society, a new race of men, a race of moral heroes,—a race of salvation-workers,—a race of Buddhas, the Enlightened.

Thus did Buddha's great SANGHA exist in the world,—the SANGHA containing a race of holy men, a race of moral heroes, a race of the Enlightened. It stood before man as a light-house which guided the mariners to lead their ship to the port of salvation. It stood before the world as a great bonfire that lighted the benighted men to their home of peace. As there arose from day to day the great luminary that lightened the world and gladdened the heart of men, so stood the great *Sangha* of Buddha, the Enlightened.

If there was any thing new that Buddha did, it was this. Dr. Oldenberg says :—" It appears from the very beginning to have been a society governed by law. The completion of procedure prescribed by law was necessary to the reception of a postulant into the Society. The law of the Order pointed out to him his course of action and omission. The society itself as a court of discipline seemed conformly to the ecclesiastical rules by keeping up a regular judicial procedure."

Thus the *Sangha* was guided by strict laws. But who made the laws which the members of the *Sangha* were bound to obey? On this point Dr. Oldenberg thus remarks :—" Although the Order of Buddha's disciples or members thereof specially called on and qualified to do so, have virtually acted as law makers, yet in theory the community has distinctly disclaimed all legislative functions. The authority to frame a law for the community belongs to Buddha alone according to Buddhist theory. All commands and prohibitions received their character as binding rules from the fact that Buddha has enunciated or is supposed to have enunciated them. With his death both the possibility and the necessity for creating new laws has become extinct."

All these laws were collected into the great book PATIMOKHA. Were they all enunciated and promulgated by Buddha in one day? Or did he write a book on them and place them before his disciples? No. They were promulgated as the occasion arose. The following is an outline of the way in which these laws were made.

"When the Exalted Buddha was staying in such and such a place, this and that irregularity occured. The people who came to know of this were irritated, murmured and complained. How can monks, who follow the son of the Sakhya house, commit such offences like wanton worldlings or like unbelieving heretics as the case in point has occurred. The spiritual brothers hear the whisperings of the people, they too are irritated, murmer and complain. How can the venerable so and so be guilty of the like? They mention the matter to Buddha. He calls his disciples together, delivers to them an admonitary address, and then issues the order. "I order, O disciples, that this or that shall or shall not be done. Who so does this is liable to such and such a punishment."

Thus the Order was formed and thus the laws were promulgated. The Order began its eventful career with sixty monks and expanded into thousands. Its members scattered over the earth preaching the noble gospel of Buddha to innumerable races. At last three fourths of the human race followed the noble path to which the great Buddha led.

The *Sangha* was a power. The power did not lay in Buddha or in any of the Bhikshus, prominent or insignificant, but it lay in the *Sangha* as a body-corporate. The Sangha was a great Republic. The united voice of the members, and the unnanimously passed laws were all supreme. It was in fact the ruling voice—the supreme controlling power,—the great moral force of Buddha's great religion. He who took refuge in *Sangha,* became a superior being;—he was on his way to the Eternal Peace.

—:o:—

CHAPTER II.

ADMISSION INTO THE ORDER.

Entry into the SANGHA was open to every one. Buddha at the commencement of the Order thus spoke:—

"Open thou, O wise one, the door of Eternity;

Let be heard what thou, O sinless one, hast discovered."

Though every one could enter into the Order, yet as a necessity some restrictions were imposed. The following were debarred.

(1). Men afflicted with serious bodily deformities and sickness.

(2). Confirmed criminals.

(3). Persons in the royal service,—specially soldiers.

(4). Debtors and slaves.

(5). Sons having no consent of their parents.

(6). Children under twelve years. Above twelve years, boys boys admitted as "novice," but unless he was twenty years of age, he could not be taken into the Order.

ORDINATION.

The ceremony of initiation was completed in two grades:—namely (1) Prababjja and (2) Upasampada.

The Prabbajja is the going away from a prior state, *i.e.* from the lay-life, or from a monastic sect holding another faith.

The Upasampada is the entry into the circle of the Bhikshus, the fully accredited member of the Buddhist Order.*

The Prabajja was a very simple ceremony. The candidate put on the yellow garment, had his hair and beard shaved off and uttered three times in reverential attitude to the monk or monks present the three great Buddhist Formula namely,—

"I take my refuge in Buddha."
"I take my refuge in Dharma."
"I take my refuge in Sangha."

Then he repeated the Ten Precepts, namely—

(1) I take the vow not to destroy life.
(2) I take the vow not to steal.
(3) I take the vow to abstain from impurity.
(4) I take the vow not to lie.
(5) I take the vow not to take intoxicating drinks.
(6) I take the vow not to eat at forbidden times.
(7) I take the vow to abstain from dancing, singing, music and stage plays.
(8) I take the vow not to use garlands, scents, unguents or ornaments.
(9) I take the vow not to take high or broad bed.
(10) I take the vow not to take gold or silver.

From that day he became an *attachee* to the Buddhist Order, but not a full member. That he became after the Upasampada ceremony.

THE NOVICIATE.

At the life-time of Buddha,—almost every body, if he liked, could at once become a Sramenara or noviciate for the

* See Malinda Prasna, page 76; Mahavasna Vol. I, page 3, Mahavagga I, 38, Maha Pariniban Sutta page 59. Prabbajja is equivalent to Brahmacharyea and Upasampada to Sanyasa.

Buddhistic Order. But after his death, the rules were made stricter.

The principal duties that were to be attended to by a Sramenara are set forth in a work named *Dinacharya* or the daily observances. We quote it below:—

"He who, with a firm faith, believes in the religion of truth, rising before day-light, shall clean his teeth and shall then sweep all the places that are proper to be swept, such as the court-yard, approaches to the Vihara, &c. When this is done, he shall retire to a solitary place and for the space of three *Dandas* meditate on the Obligations. When the bell will ring, he will go to the Dagoba and offer flowers, just as if Buddha was present in person. He will, before it, meditate on the nine virtues of Buddha with a fixed and determined mind.

The next act that he is required to perform, is to look at his *lita* or calendar, in order that he may learn *Avachwa*.*

It will now be time for him to take the alms-bowl, and when going his round, he is to bear in mind the four *Karmasthanas*, not to go too near, nor to keep at too great a distance from his preceptor. At a convenient distance from the village, having swept a small clean space, he is to adjust his robe properly. If going with the preceptor, he is to give the book into his hands and accompany him to the villages, carefully avoiding the sight of women.

According to the rules contained in the Sikhya, he is to proceed along the road, and after the alms have been received, he is to retire from the village in a manner previously declared. Taking the bowl and outer robe of his superior, he shall then proceed to his Vihara.

If there be a place appointed for the robe, he shall put it there after folding it; then place a seat, wash his feet,

---

* The length of the shadow by which the age of the moon may be known.

enquire if he is thirsty, place before him the tooth-cleaner and bring the alms-bowl. The *Gathas* must be repeated before eating and after eating, and the food is to be taken in the manner laid down in the *Sikhya*. Then taking the bowl of his superior, he will wash it,.put it in the sun to dry and then keep it in its proper place. This done, he is to wash his own face, and putting his robe, he is first to worship his superiors and then Buddha.

The next act is to go again to a solitary place, and there repeat the *Gathas*, considering whether he has omitted the practice of any Obligations or in any way acted contrary to them. After which he must practice *Maitri Bhavana*.*

About an hour afterwards, when his weariness is gone, he is to read one of the sacred books, or write out a portion of one; and if he has any thing to ask from his preceptor, or any thing to tell him, this is the time at which it should be done. In some convenient place, the *bana* is to be read, one by one each day in regular order. The Samenara Novices shall kindle a fire, light a lamp, make all arrangements for the reading of the *bana*, call the Bhikshu who is to recite it, wash his feet and sit down in an orderly manner and listen to the *bana*.

With the four articles that he has received as a novice of whatsoever kind they may be, whether good or bad, he must rest contented; nor must he covet to have any thing more than the allowed requisites of the priesthood. Maintaining a course of good behaviour, he must keep under control the five senses, with matured wisdom and without any haughtiness of either body, speech or mind. He must associate with those who are not ascetics, nor follow their customs, and he must be careful to avoid the commission of the least crime."*

The following ten precepts should be observed by the Sramenara.

---

* See Devachara Sutra.

1. The speaking disrespectfully of Buddha.
2. The speaking disrespectfully of the Truth.
3. The speaking disrespectfully of Sangha.
4. The entertaining heritical notions.
5. Sexual intercourse with a nun.
6. The eating of food after midday.
7. Seeing of dances or the hearing of music or singing.
8. The use of ornaments and perfumes.
9. The use of a seat or couch more than a cubit high.
10. The receiving of gold, silver, or money.
11. Practising some deception to prevent another monk from receiving that to which he is entitled.
12. Practising some deception to injure another monk.
13. Pratising some deception in order to cause expulsion of a monk from the Sangha.
14. Speaking evil of another monk.
15. Uttering slanders.

The Sramenaras are enjoined to read the following works.

1. Sramana-Sikhya.
2. Dina-achariya.
3. Chutura-kamastahana (four meditations).
4. Dhammapada.
5. Piruvana pota (Manual of Exorcism).
6. Sikhya (containing 70 rules).
7. Pilillul Bhavana.
8. Chatura Sangwara Sila.

The Sramenara is taught that there are eight benefits to be derived from becoming a recluse.

(1). Deliverance from the love of wealth and the love of pleasure.

(2). The reception of food in a proper manner.

(3). The custom of eating any food that comes to hand of what kind soever it may be.

(4). Deliverance from the oppression of wicked men and kings.

(5). Freedom from all anxiety about such things as gardens, fields and cattle.

(6). Deliverance from the dread of theives.

(7). Deliverance from the dread of persons in authority.

(8). Deliverance from fear in whatever place.*

There are also ten things that tempt the Sramenaras to cast the yellow robe off after it has been assumed.

1. The mother.
2. The father.
3. The wife.
4. The Children.
5. The Poor relations.

That is,—the thought will come that these relatives ought to be provided for which cannot be done by the recluse.

6. The Friends.
7. The Property.
8. The desire of obtaining wealth.
9. The desire of worldly honour.
10. The love of pleasure.†

After a month, and in many cases after years,—the candidate for the full membership of the Order, he who desired to be the Bhikshu, made a formal application, on which, if the monks thought that he was fit to be taken into the Order,—they assembled in a meeting and ordered the applicant to appear before them. Bowing reverently on the ground before the assembled monks and raising his joined hands to his forehead, the applicant thus spoke:—"I entreat the Order, reverned Sirs, for initiation. May the Order, reverend Sirs, raise me up to Itself. May it have pity on me. And for the second and for the third time I entreat the Order, reverend Sirs, for initiation. May the Order,—reverend Sirs, raise me up to Itself. May it have pity me." Then one of the

* See Pujuwalia.

† See Malinda Parsna.

monks thus questioned him :—" Hearst thou, so and so, now is the time come for thee to speak truly and to speak honestly. I ask thee, how things are. What is thou must say thereof,—It is. What is not, thou must say there of,—It is not. Art thou afflicted with any of the following diseases, namely leprosy, white leprosy, consumption, epilepsy? Art thou a human being, or something else (demon, ghosts &c) in human shape? Art thou a man? Art thou thine own master? Hast thou no debts? Art thou not in the royal service? Hast thou the permission of thy father and mother? Art thou full twenty years of age? Hast thou alms-bowl and the garments? What is thy name? What is thy Teacher's name?"

When the applicant had given answers to all these questions satisfactorily, then the monk thus addressed the Order :—"Reverend Sirs, let the Order hear me. So and so here present desires as the pupil of the venerable so and so to receive ordination. He is free from the obstacles to ordination. He has the alms-bowl and garments; so and so entreats the Order for ordination. Whoever of the venerable monks is for granting so and so ordination, let him remain silent, whoever is against it, let him speak out."

This was told thrice, and if no one spoke against the proposal, then it was declared,—So and so has from the Order received ordination. The Order is in favour of this, therefore, it is silent.

Then the Four Rules of Buddhistic austerity were repeated, namely.

(1) The food of him who has gone from home into homelessness shall be the morsels which he receives by begging.

(2) His clothing shall be made out of the rags which he collects.

(3) His resting place shall be under the trees of the forest.

(4) His medicine shall be the urine of cattle.

Then the four great Prohibitions were administered to him.

(1) An ordained monk may not have sexual intercourse,—not even with an animal. The monk who has sexual intercourse is no longer a monk,—he is no disciple of the son of the Sakya house. As a man, whose head is cut off, cannot live with the trunk, so also a monk who practises sexual intercourse is no longer a monk, he is no disciple of the son of the Sakhya house. Thou must abstain therefrom all thy life.

(2) An ordained monk may not take what has not been given to him, what is called a theft—not even a blade of grass. The monk who takes ungiven a *pada* or a *pada's* worth, or more than a *pada*, commits what is called a theft, he is no longer a monk: he is no disciple of the son of the Sakya house. As a dry leaf which has separated itself from the stalk cannot again become green, so also a monk, who takes ungiven a *pada* or a *pada's* worth, or more than a *pada*, what is called a theft is no longer a monk; he is no disciple of the son of the Sakya house. Thou must abstain thereform all thy life.

(3) An ordained monk may not knowingly deprive any creature of life, not even a worm or an ant. The monk, who knowingly deprives a human being of life, even by the destruction of a fœtus, is no longer a monk; he is no disciple of the son of the Sakya house. As a great stone, which has been split into two parts, cannot again be made into one, so also a monk, and so on.

(4) An ordained monk may not boast of any superhuman perfection, be it a condition of abstraction, or of rupture, or of concentration, or of elevation, or of the path of deliverance, or of the fruit of deliverance, he is no longer a monk; he is no disciple of the son of the Sakya house. As a palm tree, the top of which has been destroyed, cannot again grow, so also a monk and so on.

THE ORDER OF MONKS.

From that day, he is an ordained *Bhikshu* of the Buddhist *Sangha*.* There was nothing however to prevent the ordained monk or the Order to break off from their mutual relation. A Bhikshu could give up his alms-bowl and his yellow robe and returned to worldly life whenever he liked it.†

THE ORDER OF NUNS.

The Order of the Buddhist Nuns (*Bhikshuni Sangha*)‡ was under the guardianship of the Order of the monks (*Bhikshu Sangha*).§ If a maiden or a woman wishes to be

---

* The assertion often made that the person entering the Order changes his family name for a cloister name (as was the custom with the Brahmanic monks) is erroneous, or at any rate supported only by solitary cases. Ananda, as a member of the brotherhood, is called "the Venerable Ananda," Kassapa of Uruvila is called "the Venerable Kassapa of Urruvila." See Buddha, pages 352—353.

† Dr. Oldenberg says:—"If the monk be guilty of any serious transgression, specially if he infringes the four great prohibitions, imposed on him at Ordination, it becomes the right and the duty of the Order to renounce him."

And again:—"The monk who has a lingering fondness for a worldly life, the exit from the Order is always open. The Order makes no effort to detain him. He can do so silently, but the proper way for him is to declare before a witness (not necessarily a Bhikshu) that he renounces Buddha, Dharma and Sangha."

Koppen (in page 338) says:—It happens every day that monks who have entered the cloister under the compulsion of parents or to avoid the service of the king, or from poverty, from laziness, from a love of solicitude or of study, or from any other worldly motive, again quit the cloister to succeed to an inheritance, to marry &c."

‡ The two Orders of Monks and Nuns were called Ubhato Sangha. The two Orders had equal shares in all Gifts. Mahavagga, VIII, 32 says:—"Even if there be many monks and only one nun, she obtains the half."

§ See Oldenberg's Buddha, page 377.

ordained as a *Bhikshukini*, she will have to keep the vows of six rules for two years, namely—

(1) Not to kill any living creatures.
(2) Not to steal.
(3) Not to commit unchastity.
(4) Not to tell a lie.
(5) Not to drink any intoxicating beverages.
(6) Not to eat at the forbidden hours.

If she could pass two years strictly sticking to these six vows, she is then "ordained on one side" before the Order of Nuns.* But even then she is not a full *Bhikshukini*; she would have to appear before the Chapter of Monks and in its presence go through the whole ceremony of Ordination. The Chapter then administered upon her the following "Eight High Ordination."†

1. "A nun, if she have been ordained even a hundred years ago, must bow most reverentially before every monk, even though he be ordained even on this day, rise in his presence, raise her clasped hands and duly honour him. This rule shall she observe, esteem sacred, keep, respect and through her whole life not transgress.

2. A nun is not permitted to pass the rainy season in any district in which monks are not residing. This rule also shall she observe, esteem sacred, keep, respect and through her whole life not transgress.

3. The nuns are to go once in the half month to the monks for two things;—they are to ask for the confessional ceremony and to apply to the monks for the preaching of the Sacred Word. This rule also shall she observe, esteem sacred, keep, respect, and through her whole life not trangress.

4. At the end of the rainy season, the nuns are to give the threefold invitation to both sides of the Order. This rule

* The procedure was the same as that of the monks.

† See Cullavagga X. 1. 4.

also shall she observe, esteem sacred, keep, respect and through her whole life not transgress.

5. A nun who has been guilty of a grave offence must submit herself to a half monthly discipline of penance before both sides of the Order. This rule also shall she observe, esteem sacred, keep, respect, and through her whole life not transgress.

6. Ordination is to be applied for from both sides of the Order only when the applicant has lived for a probationary period of two years in the six rules. This rule also shall she observe, esteem sacred, keep, respect and through her whole life not transgress.

7. Under no circumstances is a nun to revile or scold a monk. This rule also shall she observe, esteem sacred, keep, respect and through her whole life not transgress.

8. From this day forward is the path of speech against the monks closed to the nuns. Yet is not the path of speech against the nuns closed to the monks. This rule also shall she observe, esteem sacred, keep, respect and through her whole life not transgress."

From the day of Ordination the following were the rules they had always to observe strictly.

1. Every half month the nuns were to betake themselves to the monks who had been named to them by the resolution of the Order to receive spiritual instruction and admonition.*

2. A nun was never allowed to associate with a monk who was also not allowed to set foot to a nunnery. He was

---

* Dr. Oldenberg remarks:—In the presence of another monk, this monk sits waiting the nuns ; and when they have made their appearance, bowed themselves to the ground and sat down before him, he speaks to them of the Eight High Ordinances and expounds to them, either by way of sermon or by question and answer, what he deems profitable of the teachings and maxims of Buddha.

Dipavansa, Chapter XVIII and also Cullavagga X. 8.

allowed to see a nun only when she fell ill and required his consolation.

3. To make a journey with a monk, to go abroad in the same boat with him, to sit with him alone, and without witnesses, was strictly forbidden.

4. To live in the forest hermitages was forbidden to the nuns. They were to live within the walls of the village or in huts or nunneries; but never alone. They were to live by two or in greater numbers.

5. The daily life and religious exercise of the nuns were the same as those of the monks.

—:0:—

CHAPTER III.

CELEBACY AND AUSTERITIES.

The life of a Buddhist Bhikshu is a life of strict celebacy and severe austerities.* The following practices are forbidden and transgressing any of them means severe penances.

---

* The rules and practices that a Bhikshu is to observe are laid down in the celebrated Pali work, called Patimokha, translated in the Sacred Books of the East. We have mainly followed this work in the following Chapters. Patimokha or the Book of Penances is the chief part of Vinaya Pitaka,—a Pitaka which contains the rules that are to be observed by the members of the Sangha. (See Introduction, chap iii.)

This is the story told how Vinaya Pitaka was recited and promulgated by the immediate followers of Buddha. Soon after his death, a Council was held under the presidency of Kasyapa who said :—"Which shall we repeat first—the Vinaya, Sutra or Abhidharma?"

The Bhikshus replied :—"The Vinaya is the life of Buddhism. If Vinaya is properly defined, the religion of our Great Master will continue to exist. Let us therefore first define the Vinaya Pitaka."

Mahakassyapa said :—"Whom shall we appoint as the principal person to recite and define this Pitaka?"

(1) Sexual intercourse with any being of whatever kind or form.

(2) Wilful pollution.

(3) Contact with the person of a woman.

(4) Commendation of acts of impurity before a woman.

(5) Acting the part of a procurer.

(6) Sitting with a man in any private place.

(7) Giving the robe to a nun to smoothe or wash it.

(8) Receiving a robe from a nun.

(9) Sleeping with one who is not a priest for more than three times.

(10) Preaching more than five or six sentences to a nun or a woman in private.

(11) Preaching to a nun after sunset or without the sanction of the Sangha.

The Bhikshus replied :—"When Buddha was alive, he declared that Upali was most perfectly acquainted with the Vinaya, and that no one has clearer understanding of the Divine Words than he; therefore let it be Upali."

Accordingly with the permission of the Sangha, Upali rose with reverence from his seat, made obeisance to the assembly, rose on the Vedi (altar) in the midst of the hall and remained with his face towards the East.

Mahakassyapa then asked :—"What is the first section of the Vinaya? When was it spoken? On whose behalf? On account of what transgression?"

Upali replied :—"The first section was spoken by Buddha in Vesali on account of Sudidema who had transgressed the precept of chastity."

In this manner, the investigation was carried on regarding all the other sections of the Vinaya and the cause, the person, the fault, the rule or ordinance established in consequence and the additional rule were declared. The enquiry in all cases was made by Mahakassyapa and answered by Upali who repeated all things to the assembly in a full and perfect manner, so that not a single letter or the least particle of the Vinaya Pitaka was lost. When the whole was recited, Upali did obeisance to the assembly and retired to his own seat. (See Hardy's Eastern Monachism.)

(12) Except in case of illness to go to see a nun.
(13) Except in a caravan or in danger to travel with a nun.
(14) To mix with any woman in any place.
(15) To converse with a woman without special cause.

Every Bhikshu is enjoined at his Ordination that when the head is taken off, it is impossible that life can be retained in the body and that in like manner the monk who holds sexual intercourse with any one is thereby incapacitated from continuing to be a son of Sakya.*

A Bhikshu is directed to live in a state of entire abstraction from the world, so that when in the midst of temptations all impurity may be avoided. The door of the eye is to be kept shut. It is better to have a red hot piece of iron run through the eye, than for the eye to wander, as by this means evil desire will be produced.

The true Bhikshu is enjoined to renounce all carnal indulgences, but this is but an inferior mode of celebacy. There must be a complete annihilation of all affections. He must forget that he has now or ever has had any connection with the world of men.

The Bhikshu is forbidden to dig the ground or to cause it to be dug, he is not to cut grass or trees, he is not to sprinkle water in that in which there are insects, or cause it to be sprinkled: he is not to go to view an army.

The Bhikshu is to remain as clean as possible. He is to use a tooth-cleaner every morning.

The Bhikshu may not enter the village or sit down in it laughing loudly, but speaking in a low tone with a steady gait, not swinging the arms about or turning the head or with his arms placed on his hips or with his head covered. He may not sit on his heels in the village and sit lolling. And he is not to perform the offices of nature standing, nor upon any growing vegetable substance or in water.

---

* See Kamachana.

It is forbidden for a Bhikshu to attend dancing, singing music or drama, nor to take part in them.

He is forbidden the use of high, honourable, rich or luxurious seats or couches. He is not allowed to take even as little as a blade of grass, when it is not given. If he takes a sandal or any thing of the same value or above that value, he ceases to be a Sramana.

He is not allowed knowingly to deprive any animal of life though it be even so insignificant as an ant. And if he deprives any human being of life, he ceases to be a Sramana.

No monk is allowed to make pretensions to the possession of Rahatship; and if any Bhikshu acts contrary to this precept, he ceases to be a son of Sakya.

There are thirty-two subjects in which the Bhikshus are forbidden to talk:—

(1) About kings, (2) robbers, (3) royal guards, (4) armies, (5) narrations that cause fear, (6) wars, (7) harrangues, (8) food, (9) drinks, (10) garments, (11) vehicles, (12) couches, (13) garlands, (14) perfumes, (15) music, (16) villages, (17) towns, (18) cities, (19) provinces, (20) relatives, (21) women, (22) intoxicating liquors, (23) streets, (24) ghosts, (25) deceased relatives, (26) wealth, (27) origin of the earth, (28) the origin of the seer, (29) the sayings of sceptics, (30) mental error (31) sexual enjoyments, (32) their imaginations.

How a Bhikshu is to be known how far he is advanced in the path of Nirvana? *Visudhi Marga Sutra* answers:— There are sixty-three *Charitas* (states of mind) of which the principal are *Raga*, *Dwesa* and *Moha*.

1. Raga is complaccency, pride or evil desire.
2. Dwesa is anger of which hatred is a component part.
3. Moha is the ignorance of truth.

The manifestation of these principles is diversified as seen in the conduct of different priests, according to—

1. The position of the body.
2. The work that is performed.

3. The manner of eating.
4. The objects that are seen.
5. The general conduct.

(*a*) *The position of the body*:—The Bhikshu, who is under the influence of the first principle, when he walks, puts his foot down gently; both his feet are put down and lifted up in an uniform manner and they are peacefully bent when moved. The monk, under the influence of the second, seems to plough the ground under his feet or to dig it; he walks hurriedly and lights his foot with violence. The Bhikshu, under the influence of the third, has no uniformity in his gait; he puts his foot down as if he were doubtful or afraid and walks as if fatigued.*

In like manner when the first sits down or reclines, it is done gently; his feet and hands are placed in the proper place and he rises in a quiet manner. The second sits down quickly and rises as if in displeasure. The third sits himself down in any way, puts his hands and feet in any posture; and when he rises he does so as if with reluctance.

(*b*) *The work that is performed*:—The first, when he prepares to sweep any place, takes hold of the broom in a proper way, neither too firmly nor too loosely and sweeps evenly. The second seizes the broom with violence, sends the dust here and there and sweeps without any uniformity. The third holds the broom loosely, throws the dust away carelessly and does not sweep clean. It is with all other things. The first does them in the best manner, the second indifferently, and the third negligently.

(*c*) *The food that is eaten*:—The first likes food with delicious flavour; he makes the rice into neat round balls and throws it into his mouth gently. The second likes sour things or those that are highly seasoned; he fills his mouth and eats in haste. The third has no partiality for any particular

---

* Magandhiya Sutra.

kind of food; he lets it fall whilst he is eating and throws it into his mouth without care.

(*d*) *The objects that are seen*:—The first, when he sees any common thing, looks at it as if it were something wonderful. If it is only good in a trifling degree, his attention is arrested. He looks over any faults that there may be and is loth to leave that which pleases him. The second, when he sees any thing that is not pleasing, turns away from it at once. If there be only a trifling fault, he is angry, he does not acknowledge the good that there may be, and he turns away as if it were unworthy of regard. The third looks at all things without manifesting any emotion. If any thing is depreciated, he commends it, or if it is praised, he commends that also.

(*e*) *The general conduct*:—The first does not see his own fault; he boasts to others of things, he does not possess; he is deceptive, proud and covetous; he likes his bowl, robe and person to appear to the best advantage. The second cannot endure the faults of another; he seeks to destroy the good name of the other Bhikshus, envies their prosperity and goes about to injure their possessions. The third goes on without diligence or care; his mind is in doubt, he is never settled, without discrimination and does not perceive errors.

There are three other states namely:—

(1) Sraddha (confidence.)

(2) Buddhi (wisdom.)

(3) Vitarka (reasonings.)

The Bhikshu who is under the influence of the first may be known by his being always cheerful. He delights in hearing *Bana*; he does not associate with the world, he does not hide his own faults and he seeks the assistance of the Three Gems, Buddha, Dharma, Sangha.

The second is kind and tractable; he eats his food slowly and is thoughtful; he avoids much sleep and does not procrastinate, he reflects on impermanency and death.

The third talks much; he delights in being where there are many people; his mind is never settled; at night he thinks he will do this and that, but he does not attempt to do in the day what he has resolved in the night.

—:o:—

CHAPTER IV.

POVERTY AND MENDICANCY.

Poverty is the glory of every Buddhist Bhikshu. Previous to his Ordination, he must possess eight articles called *At-Pirikara.* (1, 2, 3) Robes of different descriptions, (4) a girdle for the loins, (5) an alms-bowl. (6) a razor, (7) a needle, (8) a water stainer. The last is to be used whenever a Bhikshu is to drink water, lest he destroys any insects.

These are the only properties that a monk can possess or receive as alms. But the Buddhistic Order or Sangha can accept every kind of property, from land, buildings, Viharas to chairs and couches.* A Bhikshu, however, is to renounce

* Dr. Oldenberg remarks :—"That the Order was allowed to have any kind of possession whatever, which was forbidden to the individual brethren has been often asserted, but as far as I can see quite groundlessly. The more important items of property which belonged to the Order could not indeed by gift or division pass into the possession of individual monks. (See Cullavagga vi. 15—16). But it was not unallowable for a monk to possess things of this description (See Mahavagga viii. 27—5). Then after his death they fell into the property of the Order of monks of the four quarters of the world, present or absent, while smaller articles of a deceased monk were divided among the brethren with a special regard for those who had attended to him during his sickness. Whether any other heirs but the Order of the monks or nuns could be nominated is not known."

evèry kind of property and stick to the severest poverty. Money, wealth and property are his greatest enemies.

A Bhikshu is not allowded to eat any food not given in alms unless it be water. When in health, the food must be procured by his own exertions by carrying his alms-bowl from house to house in the village or city, near which for the time being he resides. When going to receive alms, the bowl is slung across his shoulder and is covered by the outer robe. It may be made of either iron or clay, but of no other material. It must first be received by the Order, and then formally presented to the Bhikshu, when it is found that his old alms-bowl could not be used any longer. No monk gets a new bowl so long as his old one has not been bound by five legatures to prevent it from falling to pieces.

When passing from place to place, a Bhikshu must not look to a greater distance before him than the length of a yoke, nor must he look on one side or upwards, nor bend his body to look at any thing on the ground. He is not to look at elephants, chariots, horses, soldiers, and women.

He must not call a woman by name, nor for what kind of food there is in the house and what kind is to be given.

It is forbidden to proclaim his purity or attainments to the house-holders, male or female, in order that he may gain honour and gifts. He must not do any thing to induce others to present him with anything or honour him.

There are some places where a Bhikshu is allowded to go when seeking alms and where he is not. To the following places he is forbidden to go.

(1) Houses of ill fame.

(2) Houses of widows.

(3) Houses of women whose husbands have gone to a distant place.

(4) Houses where there are unmarried young girls.

(5) Houses or shops where there is intoxicating liquor.

(6) Palaces of kings.

(7) Houses of noblemen.

(8) Dwellings of unbelievers.

(9) Places where the unbelievers frequent.

A Bhikshu is allowed to go to those places only where he will be well received.

There are two ways of seeking alms,—one is called *Kaya-Vinapati*, that which belongs to the body, and the other *Vachi-Vinapati*, that which belongs to the speech. Of each of these two modes of seeking alms, there are two kinds,—the one proper and the other improper. Thus when the priest approaches a house with the alms-bowl in hand, he must remain as if unseen, he must not hear, nor must he make any other sign indicating his presence. He must not go too near to a house. If he does any thing contrary to these rules,—he transgresses the precepts. The proper way is to take the alms-bowl in a becoming manner. If any thing is given, he stands in silence to receive it; if not, he quietly passes on.

Buddha said :—"A Bhikshu should never ask for any thing, he disdains to beg. He carries the alms-bowl,—that indicates that he solicits food. He should never speak a word asking any thing."

A Bhikshu must go from house to house without passing over even the meanest one. He is not required to go more than three times to a house. If he does not get any thing there, but if he perseveres, it is considered a merit. The monk who keeps the superior rule receives food as he passes on, standing for a moment only before each house. He, who keeps the middle rule, may remain before the house for a short time and must then pass on. He, who keeps the inferior rule, waits until the food is given, though there is delay.

When the members of the Order of Buddha had to maintain their life on the gifts of laymen, it was necessary to promulgate some rules for alms-giving (*dana*). The lay-followers of Buddha were required to give in alms only what they had honestly earned, and that too with a willing mind. There must be no regret for what had been given. It was necessary that the thing given, the intention of the giver, and the receiver of the gift all must be pure.

There are four divisions of alms-giving, namely :—

(1) *Chira dana* (gifts of robes.)

(2) *Ahara-dana* (gifts of food.)

(3) *Sayanasana dana* (gifts of bed.)

(4) *Gilanapatya dana* (gifts of medicines and sick-diet.)

There is another sort of *dana*, called *Sanghika*. It is divided into seven kinds, namely :—

1. The gifts of robes, food, &c., to a supreme Buddha or his immediate disciples.

2. The gifts of the above to the monks and nuns assembled together.

3. The above gifts to a monk when alone.

4. The above gifts to a nun when alone.

5. The gifts of above to a monk or nun when permission has been asked before.

6. The giving of any thing to a monk when permission has been received from the Sangha.

7. The giving of any thing to a nun under similar circumstances.

The Buddhistic Scriptures say :—Of all the modes of acquiring merit, that of alms-giving is the highest. It is the principal virtue of all virtues that is necessary to acquire Buddhahood. It is the first of the four great virtues, namely—

(1) Alms-giving.

(2) Affability.

(3) Promoting the prosperity of others.

(4) Loving others like his own-self.

When the gift-givers and the receivers are all pure, the reward is proportionately great.

When the giver possesses that which is good, but presents in alms that which is bad, it is called *dana dasee.*

When he gives according to that which he has, whether it be good or bad, it is called *dana sahaya.*

When he himself retains that which is bad, but presents that which is good, it is *danapati.*

The following are the rewards of *Dana* :—

1. When any one gives that which has been procured by his own labour, he will get wealth, but no retinue.

2. When he gives what he has received from others, he will have attendants, but no wealth.

3. When he gives both kinds, he will get both the above rewards.

4. *Kala Dana* (proper gifts) is the giving of alms to strangers, travellers, and sick persons, and in times of famine and the giving of the first fruit of the garden or field. This *Dana* brings in immense rewards.

5. When alms are given without thought or affection, or by the hand of others, and when they are thrown to the receiver disdainfully, or given after long intervals, it is called *Asat purusha dana.* There is no reward for him who gives intoxicating liquor, or alms to musicians, dancers, songsters &c.

He who gives alms in a proper manner will have continued joy; he will be admitted to the society of the wise; his fame will spread on all sides and reach as high as Brahmaloka, and after death he will be born in one of the Devalokas. Alms given in the proper manner promotes long life, personal beauty, agreeable sensations, strength and knowledge. Buddha said :—" There is no reward, either in this world or the next that may not be recieved by the alms-giving. By means of it the glories of Sakra and Maha Brahma, of the Chakravarti, the Rahats, Pasi-Buddhas and the Supreme Buddha are received."

CHAPTER V.

THE DIET.

The following regulations are enjoined regarding the diet of a Bhikshu.

1. A monk is never to drink intoxicating liquor.

2. He is not prevented to avoid animal food altogether, but there are many regulations to guard against the abuse of this previlege.

3. A monk must not take food after the sun has passed the meridian.

4. When ghee, butter, oil, honey, sugar or other articles used as sick-diet are received, they must not be kept in store more than seven days.

5. Except in case of sickness, he must not take food more than one day in a place where food is made for many.

6. Except on authorised occasions, he must not take food expressly provided for a number of monks.

7. Except on authorised occasions, he must not take his ordinary meal before going by invitation to any place to receive an offering of food.

8. Except where he will share with other monks, he must not accept more than one bowl of food.

9. When a meal is given in a house, he must not take any food from any one else.

10. A monk must not take food of the previous day.

11. Except in sickness, he must not take ghee, butter, oil, honey, sugar, fish, fresh, milk or curds.

12. The food given in alms must be received by him meditatively. It is not to be recieved carelessly, so that when receiving, a portion may not fall to the ground.

13. The liquor and the solid food are to be taken

together; they must not be taken separately. The alms-bowl must not be taken to the mouth.

14. The food is to be eaten meditatively, with care, so that it is not scattered about. That which will come first to the hand must be taken.

15. The liquor and the solid food must be eaten together.

16. Except in sickness, a monk must not ask for rice and curry.

17. He must not look at another's food.

18. He must not eat mouthful, larger than a pigeon's eggs, but in small round balls.

19. He must not fill his mouth, nor put his hand into his mouth when taking food.

20. He must not talk when his mouth is full, nor allow particles to drop from his mouth, nor swallow his food without being properly musticated. He must swallow one mouthful before another is taken.

21. He must not shake his hand to free it from the food. He must not put out the tongue, nor smack his lips, nor suck or eat with noise.

22. He must take up a vessel of water when his hand is soiled from eating.

23. He must sit to eat his meal.

Sadharmaratnakara says:—"The hours in which food is forbidden to be eaten are called *Vikala*. The appointed hours are from sun-rise to the end of the fifteenth hour, *i.e.*, until the sun has passed the meridian. The food that is taken in any other hour of the day or night is called *Vikala-bhojana*.

The Bhikshus were commanded by the Great Master to be contented with as much as is necessary to appease his hunger."

Visudhi Marga Sutra says:—"The priest is not to eat as a pastime, nor for pleasure, nor to make the body strong, nor to render it beautiful. As the hunger is the most powerful of all appetites, he may eat to ward it off. As a man and woman, when crossing a vast desert with a child, if their food fails them, eat the flesh of their own child in their anxiety to escape from the desert,—with similar disgust must the priest eat his food, that he may escape from the evils of existence."

It is said in the *Visudhi Marga* that there are ten modes of defilement produced by food, namely,—

(1) In going to the place where it is to be received.
(2) Its reception.
(3) The act of eating.
(4) The ingredients in which it is made.
(5) Its place of deposit.
(6) Before it is digested.
(7) After it is digested.
(8) The fruit it produces.
(9) Its discharge.
(10) The pollution from its touch.

(*a*) As regards the first:—In the journey that the monk must go to procure his food, he will have to pass along roads that are difficult, dangerous, dirty; he will be exposed to wind and cold, and he will see many disagreeable objects, such as filths of all kinds.

(*b*) As regards the second:—As he waits in different places to receive food, insects will come from dirty places and settle on his robes, and in his bowl. Some persons will tell him to go away, while others will take no notice of him, and in passing from place to place, he will have to encounter foul smell and tread on many kinds of refuge.

(*c*) As regards the third:—In eating the food, there will be many things to cause shame. The tongue must do the work of the hand, and before the food is swallowed it must be made of the consistence of the vomit thrown up by a dog.

(*d*) As regards the fourth :—When the food has passed into the stomach, it becomes foul and corrupt. Even in the bodies of the Buddhas, there are bile, phlegm and blood. If the bile be too abundant, the food that has been eaten will become like oil. If the phlegm be too abundant, it will be like the juice of a fruit. And if the blood be too abundant it will become like red dye.

(*e*) As regards the fifth :—The place to which the food descends is not a vessel of gold. In a child, ten years of age, it is like a privy that has been used for many years without being cleaned, increasing in loathsomeness with the age of the individual.

(*f*) As regards the sixth :—When a shower in the hot season falls upon a village inhabited by low people, it runs into the cess at the extremity of the place, abounding with all kinds of filth, and when the sun arises froth and bubbles are formed upon the surface of this compass. In like manner when food is taken into the body, in a little time it is mixed with all kinds of impure secretions, and the digestive fire, working upon the man, causes it to appear with a surface like that of the compass.

(*g*) As regards the seventh :—When the food is digested, it does not become gold or gem, but is changed into excreta and urine.

(*h*) As regards the eighth :—The food passes away from the body by nine apertures, but principally by the intestinal passage, and a part of it is ejected by pores of the skin.

(*i*) As regards the ninth :—When the food is eaten, it soils the fingers, teeth and tongue; and even by continual washing, it is not possible to take away the defilement and smell.

There were a few strict regulations which superior Bhikshus used to observe. A Bhikshu who kept these Ordinances never received food given under any of the following circumstances.

(1) For the sake of an assembly of monks.

(2) That which has been given at an appointed time.

(3) That which is given to a certain number of priests.

(4) Food given on a certain number of days.

(5) Food given on the day of pooja.

(6) Food prepared for monks who are strangers.

(7) For priests who are going on a journey.

(8) For sick monks.

(9) For those Bhikshus who minister to their sick companions.

(10) Food given to a temple.

—:o:—

CHAPTER VI.

DRESS AND DWELLING.

The following regulations were enjoined for the dress of the Bhikshu.

1. He is permitted to wear three robes, called (*a*) *Sanghatiya*, *(b) Uttarasanggaya* and *(c) Anatara-Vasakaya*.

2. He is not allowed to keep an extra robe for more than ten days.

3. The whole of all the three robes he must always keep with him.

4. When cloth is received for a new robe, it must be made up without delay.

5. Except in case a robe has been stolen or accidently destroyed, he is not to ask robe from another.

6. No Bhikshu is to induce any one to collect or to pay money for the purchase of his robes.

7. The monk must not accept money from the messenger of a king or other noble personages for the purchase of a robe.

8. When the Bhikshu wants a robe, he may go thrice to a person and remind him of his want, but it is preferable to try to get it in silence.

9. A monk must not seek the extra robe allowed for the rainy season before the last month of the hot season.

10. When a monk has given a robe to another, he must not afterwards try to regain it or have it taken away.

11. He must not ask for cotton thread, and then give it to a weaver to be made into cloth.

12. The time for offering a robe being at the end of the rainy season, the monk must not receive a robe more than ten days before that period.

13. When a monk receives a new robe, he must not disfigure it.

14. He must not give his robe to another.

15. No cloth shall be used as a covering for a sore that is more than two spans in breadth and four in length.

16. The monk must not use in the rainy season a robe larger than six spans in length and two and half in breadth.

17. He is never to use a robe as large or larger than the robe of Buddha.

18. He must wear the under-garment in such a way as it covers the body completely from the navel to the knee. With the upper-robe the body is to be covered from the shoulder to the heels.

19. When a monk has forfitted a robe on account of having kept it beyond the prescribed period, he is to deliver it up to a Sangha.

The following are the nine objections to the dress of the aymen that the great master thought of in his mind.*

---

* See Pujawaliya Sutta.

1. It is too magnificent.
2. It must be got from others.
3. It soon becomes soiled.
4. It is soon worn away.
5. It cannot be procured at will.
6. It is a thing of value.
7. It may be stolen.
8. It enervates the body of the wearer.
9. It gives rise to evil desire.

The following are the twelve advantages in wearing the ascetic yellow robe.

1. It is plain.
2. It can be got without applying to others.
3. It can be made by a monk with his own hands.
4. It does not soon become soiled.
5. Thieves will not notice it.
6. It can be easily procured in any place.
7. It becomes the wearer.
8. It does not give rise to evil desire.
9. It does not cause covetousness.
10. It can be easily put on.
11. It requires no trouble to procure it.
12. When evil desire has been destroyed, it does not cause its reproduction.

Visudhi Marga Sutra says :—"The robe is to be put on by the priest as if it were a bandage to cover a sore, or a cloth to cover a skeleton, and he must carry the alms-bowl as if it were viand of medicines. There are some priests who put on the robe as young men or even as lewd women to attract attention, but this is contrary to the precepts. It may be put on to keep off the snow, as by extreme cold disease is produced and the mind is prevented from exercising continued thought. Its principal advantage, however, is to cover the shame of the priest; other benefits are occasional, but this is without intermission."

So much for the dress of a Bhikshu. For the dwelling, residence in a forest was never insisted upon by Buddha, and his Bhikshus lived in Viharas, and when on tour in camps in great numbers together. In fact, it was rather insisted that Buddhist Bhikshus should never live alone.

The apparent contradiction between the command given to the people to build Viharas and the advice given to the priests to dwell in solitude struck king Malinda, and he asked Nagasena to explain it.* The great monk said:—"The beast of the forest has no settled dwelling; he eats his food here and there, and lies down to sleep in whatever place he may happen to be, and the faithful priests must in these respects be like him. But still from the building of Viharas, there are two advantages, namely, (1) It is an act that has been praised by all the Buddhas, and they who perform it will be released from sorrow and attain Nirvana; (2) when Viharas are built, the priestesses have an opportunity of seeing the priests for receiving instructions. Thus there is a reward for those who build dwellings for the Bhikshus, but the faithful monk will not prefer such a place for his residence.

It is said in the Pujawaliya Sutta that Buddha once reflected that there were the following eight objections to reside in a house:—

1. It causes much trouble in its creation.
2. It requires continual repair.
3. Some more exalted personages may require it.
4. The persons living in it may be numerous.
5. It causes the body to become tender.
6. It affords opportunity for the commission of evil deeds.
7. It brings in the coveteous thought, namely "This is mine."
8. It hurbours lice, bugs and other vermin.

He then reflected that there were the following ten advantages in residing under a tree:

1. Such a place can be found with ease.

2. It can be found in any locality.

3. On seeing the decay of the leaves, the Bhikshu is reminded of other impermanences.

4. It does not cause any covetous thought.

5. It does not afford any opportunity for evil deeds.

6. It is not received from another.

7. It is the residence of the Devas.

8. It requires no fence around it.

9. It promotes health.

10. As the Bhikshu can meet with it any where, it is not necessary for him to think that he will have to return to the place he previously occupied.

Patimokkha lays down the following regulations for the dwelling of the members of the Sangha :—

1. That the residence of the Bhikshu, if it be built for himself alone, shall be of twelve spaces in length and seven in breadth.

2. The site must be chosen in a place that is free from vermin, snakes, insects, wild beasts, &c.

3. There must be a path around it wide enough for the passage of a cart.

4. Before possession is taken, a Chapter of monks must see that it is not larger than the prescribed limits.

Oldenbergh thus summarises the regulations that were enjoined to the Bhikshus as regards their diet, dress and dwelling* :—

"The dwelling, food, and clothing of the monks are laid down in detailed regulations. The character of these rules is very decided : the abstaining from every thing which implies comfortable enjoyment, being at one's ease in worldly possessions, is just as urgently demanded as on the other side excesses of ascetic practice are wholly eschewed. Here

* Buddha, p. 358—360.

we find none of those strange features with which a fanciful enquirer has recently made up the picture of what he calls original Buddhism; a society of ascetics who were allowed to live under no roof, but to pass their whole life under the open heavens sitting in cremationy rounds or under trees, whose whole appearance bears upon it the stamp of deformity, impurity,—* in truth all negligence in outer appearance, specially in clothing, is most strictly tabooed. In the case of younger monks, who are placed under the superintendance of an elder brother, the latter has to pay attention to those committed to his care; he is required to see that they make their clothes right, dye them, and wash them properly. The sanitation and ventilation of the quarters occupied by the monks, the cleaning of furniture, the washing of all articles that require it are prescribed with the greatest minuteness in the works on the rules of the Order. Touching the greater or lesser degree of abstinence from the necessities and comforts of regular life, a certain freedom is allowed to the individual to allow scope for his individual likes and dislikes. Whoever wished might take a vow to live on the food which he might obtain on his begging-expedition from house to house, but no one was forbidden to accept the invitations of pious laymen to dine, and we read that Buddha himself accepted such invitations on numberless occasions. Whoever wished might patch together rags, which he had collected, to make himself a monk's yellow garment; wondering monks who happened to come to a cremation ground used perhaps to gather there the shreds from which they made their clothes. But no one was forbidden to dress himself in the garments which laymen presented to the monks. Buddha said, "I grant you, O monks, that he who wears clothes given by the laity may also wear clothes made up from gathered rags. If you have a fancy for both, O monks, I have no objection to it."

* See Wassiljew page 15.

Whoever wished might dwell in a forest or in the caves of the mountains, but no one was forbidden to take up his abode near a village or a town. With sticks and grass, gathered in a forest, every monk could easily construct a hut for himself, and laymen not unfrequently even lent assistance or caused building operations to be carried on at their expense for the Order, so that monks' houses *i.e.*, Viharas, detached dwellings or a complex whole with assembly rooms, council-chambers, dining halls, structures for worm-baths and ablutions, as well for the Order in its entirety as for the members individually, were at their disposal. On the whole we have undoubtedly to picture to ourselves monks, those even who had chosen a life in the forests,* dwelling rather in huts or houses than under the open sky, perchance under the shade of a tree. Even wanderer had as a rule a shelter at their disposal. Novices and scholars used generally to go on ahead and see that quarters were prepared for their teachers among the communities whose places of residence they passed through."

* Cullavaga VIII. 6. Describes the poor dwellings of the monks living in the forest. In Suttavivanga II. I. we read the description of the stately Vihara that the monk Udayi built in the forest. There were monks in rags living under the canopy of heaven, as well as handsomely robed monks living in palatial Viharas even during the life time of Buddha.

CHAPTER VII.

THE THIRTEEN ORDINANCES.

Every Bhikshu, every Sramana, every member of the Sangha, was expected to obey strictly the observances laid down in the celetrated Thirteen Ordinances. They are as follows :—

The FIRST ORDINANCE :—It is called *Pansukulikanga. Pansu* means earth, *kula* means heap, *anga* means body, that is one who wears clothes picked up from earth. A Bhikshu who keeps this Ordinance must resolve, " I will not receive the garment given by a house-holder. I will receive it only according to Precepts." The Precepts forbid using clothes that are not found under any of the following circumstances :—

1. The cloth that has been thrown into a burial ground, or thrown away in the bazar, or thrown out of a window.

2. The cloth used for the purification of woman at child birth.

3. The cloth thrown away by a person after bathing.

4. The cloth thrown away by persons who have carried a corpse.

5. The cloth eaten by cattle, white ants or rats.

6. The cloth that has been partially burnt and thrown away.

7. The cloth that is torn at the end.

8. The shred and remnant of a cloth.

9. The cloth that has been put up as flags by persons who have sailed away in a vessel.

10. The flag tied in a battle-field after the fight is over.

11. The cloth put on an ant-hill with an offering to a demon.

12. The cloth that once belonged to a monk, or that has been used at the anointing of a king.

13. The cloth that has been left on a wayside, the claimant being no where.

14. The cloth cast on shore by the waves.

15. The cloth given by the Devas.

All the Thirteen Ordinances can be kept in three ways, namely (1) superior, (2) middle and (3) inferior.

The superior way of the first Ordinance allows the cloth placed in any place by another monk. The inferior allows the cloth placed at his feet by another monk. The cloth given by a house-holder makes a Bhikshu transgress this Ordinance.

The SECOND ORDINANCE:—It is called *Techiwarakanga*, meaning one who uses three robes. The three robes are the one under-cloth, one upper-cloth, one that covers whole of the body. He who observes this Ordinance connot possess more than three robes at one time. If he possesses a fourth, this Ordinance is broken.

He who keeps the superior Ordinance may put on one robe when the other two are being dyed if he be in a village, but if he be in a forest, he must remain naked. The middle Ordinance allows one robe to be worn when the other two are being dyed; the inferior allows the robe of another to be put on when his robe is being dyed.

The THIRD ORDINANCE:—It is called *Pindapatikanga* meaning one who supports himself by morsels of food. He who keeps this Ordinance cannot receive food which has been given under any of the following circumstances:—For the sake of an assembly of monks, that which has been given at an appointed time or by invitation, that which has been given to a certain number of monks, food given on a certain number of days in each half-moon, food prepared for monks who are strangers.

The FOURTH ORDINANCE ;—It is called *Sapandanacharikanga*, meaning one who does not pass over any house at his begging excursions. He who keeps this Ordinance is forbidden to pass by any house however mean or poor when he goes out with his alms-bowl in hand.

The FIFTH ORDINANCE :—It is called *Eakasanakanga*, meaning one who eats at one place. He who keeps this Ordinance must not eat food in two three different places; he must remain on one seat till he finishes his meal. It is not proper to rise until the meal is finished. If the monk has sat down, but not begun to eat, he may rise; but if he has begun to eat, he must not rise; and if he rises, he must not sit down to eat again. He who keeps its superior Ordinance cannot receive more food than what he had when he first sat down, whatever be the quantity. He who keeps the middle Ordinance may receive any thing given to him as long as he eats. The inferior Ordinance allows one to receive more food, even when he has finished, provided he has not risen.

The SIXTH ORDINANCE :—It is called *Pattapindikanga*, meaning one of one vessel. He who keeps this Ordinance must eat from one vessel only. If he has liquid and solid food, he must take first the one and then the other, but he must not put two in two separate vessels. He, who keeps the superior Ordinance, may throw away the refuse of sugar-cane when he has sucked the juice, but all other things that are in the bowl he must eat. He must not break flesh, cakes or any other eatables either with his teeth, hands, or an instrument in order to divide it. He, who keeps the middle Ordinance, may break his food with one hand whilst holding the bowl with the other. He who keeps the inferior Ordinance may break any thing put into his alms-bowl.

The SEVENTH ORDINANCE :—It is called *Khalapachhabhattikanga*, meaning one who does not eat after a fixed time. He, who keeps this Ordinance, cannot eat any more after he has met with that which is *Akapa*, *i.e.*, if he has any reason to refuse that which is brought to him, when he is eating; or if he be presented with that which is improper to be eaten from its loathsomeness or otherwise. He who keeps the superior Ordinance may only eat that which is in his mouth and nothing more, although even the first handful of food that he takes is *Akapa*. He who keeps the middle Ordinance may eat that which is *Akapa* and nothing more. He who keeps the inferior Ordinance may eat as long as he remains on the seat.

The EIGHTH ORDINANCE:—It is called *Aranyakanga*, meaning one living in the forest. He, who keeps this Ordinance, must not live near a village, but must remain in the forest. If there be a boundary to the village or a wall, he must remain as far from it as a strong man can throw a stone. And if there be no boundary, he must reckon from the place where the women of the last house are in the habit of throwing water. If there be a single waggon or a single house, that must be considered as a village. If there be men or men who are intending to come, all the same it is the village. If a superior monk be ill and what is necessary for him cannot be procured in the forest, he may be taken to a village, but the monk, who accompanies him, must return before the sun rises next morning, even if his superior be dangerously ill. He who keeps the superior Ordinance must always live in the forest. He who keeps the middle Ordinance may remain in a village during the *was*. He who keeps the inferior Ordinance may live four months of the hot and four months of the rainy season in a village.

The NINTH ORDINANCE:—It is called *Rukhamulikanga*, meaning living under a tree. He who keeps this Ordinance must not live under a roof, but always at the root of a tree. But he must not live under the following trees:—

1. A tree at the limit of a country.

2. A tree in which a Deva resides and who receives fferings from the people.

3. A tree from which gum is taken or eatable fruits are gathered.

4. A tree in which there are owls.

5. A hollow tree.

6. A tree in the midst of a Vihara.

He, who keeps its superior Ordinance, must not live in a place that is pleasant or agreeable. He, who keeps the middle Ordinance, may live in a place prepared by others. He who keeps the inferior Ordinance may call a Sramanera to help him in preparing the place. None of these can live in a house.

The TENTH ORDINANCE:—It is called *Abhokasikanga*, meaning living in an open space. He, who keeps this Ordinance, must live under the canopy of heaven; he must not live under a house or even a tree. He may enter a Vihara to hear *bana* or to say *bana*; he must not live there. He who keeps its superior Ordinance must not live near a tree or rock or a house, but in the open space; he can put up his robe as a screen. He, who keeps the middle Ordinance, may live under an overhanging rock. He who keeps the inferior Ordinance may live in a cave.

The ELEVENTH ORDINANCE:—It is called *Sesanikanga*, meaning leaving in a cemetery. He who keeps this Ordinance must always live in a cemetery, and it must not be near a village. He must not construct there a dwelling place. He must not stay away from the place even for a single night. He must always be there at mid-night. He must not enter a village or a house. He who keeps its superior Ordinance must always live in a place where there is the burning of corpses, the stench, the weeping for the dead. He who keeps the middle must remain in the place where there is any of the above three. He who keeps the inferior may live in a place which was a cemetery for sometime.

The TWELFTH ORDINANCE:—It is almost the same as the above.

THE THIRTEENTH ORDINANCE :—It is called *Nesajjakanga*, meaning one who always remains in a sitting posture. He who keeps this Ordinance must not lie down to sleep. He must not recline at full length, but may walk, stand or sit. He who keeps the superior Ordinance may not lean on any place or make his robe into a seat or take hold of a piece of cloth fastened to a tree. He who keeps the middle Ordinance may take recourse to any of the above. He who keeps the inferior Ordinance may sit to his convenience. But none is allowed to lie.

The above will clearly indicate how austere was the life of a Buddhist Sramana,—but none was compelled to do any of the above. All were free.

—:o:—

CHAPTER VIII.

REGULATIONS AND THEIR ORIGIN.

The life of a Bhikshu,—the life of a Buddhist Sramana is a life of long discipline. The great Order of Buddha is full of Regulations. They were too numerous to mention here. In fact the minutest detail about the way how a Bhikshu should lead his life has been elaborately laid down. We have mentioned in the previous chapters only a few of the important and will conclude by mentioning a few more in this chapter. How they were originated would be dwelt with later on.

Sleep :—According to *Dinachariya*, a Bhikshu is to arise before day-light. Every monk is enjoined to follow the example of the great Master. Buddha slept during one-third of the third watch. In the first watch he preached or talked with his followers on religious topics. In the second watch he answered the questions put to him by the Devas; in the first division of the third he slept, in the second he used to be in meditation, and in the third he looked abroad with his divine eye to find out whom to preach the Truth.

Tonsure:—A Bikshu from the commencement of his Sramana life must shave his head. He is provided with a razor as one of the eight articles he can possess, so that he can regularly keep his head shaved. According to the Precepts he cannot allow his hair to grow to a greater length than two inches, but the custom is to shave once a week.

Obeidience:—The following rules have been laid down in the Patimokha.

1. A monk must not bring a groundless charge against another monk.

2. He must not charge another monk for trifling matter.

3. He is charged not to create dissensions or to perpetuate dissensions amongst the monks.

4. He is not to assist any other in any dissension.

5. He must not refuse admonitions.

6. If spoken to on account of any evil conduct, he must not quarrel and impute personality.

7. He must not use contemptuous speech, or slander any monk.

8. Unless empowered by the Sangha, he must not declare to others the crimes of any monk.

9. He is not to go to a place to annoy a monk and for him to leave that place.

10. He must not from anger expel a monk or cause him to be expelled.

11. He must not act unkindly or do any thing that would give the least pain or cause the least displeasure to any monk.

12. He must not hide or cause to be hidden even in sport any article belonging to any monk.

13. He is not to bring forward a matter already decided.

14. He must implicitly obey the Laws binding on all the monks.

15. He is not to be angry with another monk and push him away.

16. He is not to suggest doubts against another monk.

17. He must not listen to other's conversations or quarellings.

18. A young monk in company with an elder one must always show him proper respect.

19. He must not jostle him or go in front of him.

20. He must not sit on a higher seat, or talk when near him, or move his hands and feet when talking with him.

20. He must not walk before him with his sandals on, or to walk in the same place at the sametime.

21. The Superiors must not be harsh with the youngers. None should interfere in any way with any others.

Discipline :—No Sangha could be formed if the monks present are all under censure for the same crime. In that case they must be absolved by some one who is not guilty. But if they are guilty of different faults, they can absolve each other and then form the *Sangha*.

When a monk has been guilty of any of the thirteen crimes that involve suspension and penance and shall conceal the fact, upon its discovery he is placed under restraint as many days as he has concealed it ; then for six nights he is subjected to a kind of penance; and after this period he may be absolved by a Sangha in which at last twenty monks must be present.

The matters brought before a Sangha must be deliberately investigated and the sentence is to be determined by the majority. The punishments are reprimand, forfeiture, penance, suspension and exclusion.

Such was the grand way in which the Great Order of the Greatest Man of the world was conducted. But were all these Regulations made by Buddha in a day or in a month? How did they originate?

King Malinda asked the celebrated monk Nagasena thus:—"Sire, if the Rishis, by their own intuitive knowledge, could tell at once the nature of all diseases and to prescribe remedies for them, why did not Buddha, who by his divine eyes must have seen beforehand the faults of his disciples, forbid the commission of such and such things previous to their occurence."

In fact when Buddha first preached his great religion in Benares, he had not established any thing about the Sangha. It was formed and established long afterwards, and at its first inception all these rules and regulations were not laid down. The reason thus explains the great monk Nagasena:—"It was foreseen by Buddha at the commencement that there were 150 Precepts it would be proper to enforce. But he reflected thus:—"If I at once enforce the observance of all these Precepts, the people will say—In this religion there are a great number of things that it is necessary to observe. It is indeed a most difficult thing to be a Bhikshu;—thus they would be afraid. Those who would think of becoming a monk would hesitate,—they will not accept the Truth. Thus will they be born in a place of torment. It will therefore be better to issue a Precept forbidding an act when that fault has been committed."

And the Great Master thus, when a fault came to his notice, forbade it. Thus were laid down one after the other all the rules and regulations of the great Order. Each particular incident brought about a Precept. We shall give a few examples.

1. There was a Bhikshu named Sudina. He, at the earnest solicitation of his mother-in-law, lay with the woman who was his wife before he became a monk in order to give birth to a child. There was at that time no Precepts prohibiting such an act. When this came to the notice of Buddha, he reproached the monk and enacted the following law, declaring it to be universally binding upon those who would renounce the world.

" What priest soever shall have intercourse with a woman is overcome and excluded."

2. Under the impression that intercourse with a woman is prohibited, a Bhikshu named Amita acted improperly in a forest infested with monkeys. He was removed from the Order and Buddha declared :—

" Intercourse of any and every sort is prohibited."

3. At one time some Bhikshus without formally cutting their connection with the Order lived as house-holders. Afterwards on account of many afflictions and domestic bereavements, they desired to be re-admitted. Buddha thus enacted :—

"Any Bhikshu who has engaged to live according to the Laws given to the Sangha, if he shall without having made confession of his weakness, become a lay, hold intercourse with females of what kind so ever, is overcome and excluded."

Except such, all others if they again desired were permitted to rejoin.

4. On one occasion when Goutama Buddha and his monks were in Viranja, a famine prevailed so extensively that the Bhikshus were not able to procure any food when going from house to house. The monk Maggalayana asked

permission to exert his supernatural powers in order to obtain food, but Buddha declared :—

"Supernatural powers should never be attempted or exhibited by any Bhikshu."

5. At one time Jivaka, the physician of the king of Magadha, presented to Buddha two magnificent robes, but Buddha thought of thieves and so told Ananda, who cut them into thirty pieces and then sewed them together in five divisions. On seeing this Buddha made the following Law.

"Bhikshus should have only three robes at a time and they should always be made of thirty pieces of cloth."

6. Once a Bhikshu lived at a place called Isigilla near Rajgriha. Having his hut thrice broken down by the people, he made a house entirely of clay, he originally being a potter. Collecting grass, &c., he burnt it thoroughly. But when Buddha saw it, he reproved him and declared :—

"Burnt houses are never to be made by a Bhikshu."

7. A certain monk wishing to ruin another Bhikshu named Dabo was unable to accomplish his object without resorting to a mean trick, for Dabo's conduct was blameless. He one day saw a flock of goat and named a he-goat Dabo and a she-goat Nittya, who was excluded from the Order. Then he declared that he saw Dabo and Nittya engaged in an improper act. An enquiry was made, and his meanness was found out. Whereupon Buddha enacted :—

"No Bhikshu should take hold of trifles and found a direct or indirect charge against any monk."

8. At one time there was a monk who was under the influence of passion. As he was unable to maintain his purity, he thought it better to die than to continue his life. He therefore threw himself from the precepice near the rock Gyakuta. But it so happened that he fell upon a man who

was cutting bamboos at the foot of the hill. The monk escaped but the man was killed. He then went and told Buddha what had happened. Buddha reproved him, but declared that he had not transgressed by killing the man, as his act was unintentional. But he enacted this Law:—

"*No Bhikshu should ever think of committing suicide, for it is a great sin.*"

9. In the city of Vesali, there was a monk who one day, on going to beg, sat down upon a chair that was covered with a cloth underneath which there was a child who was killed. About the sametime there was a Bhikshu who received food mixed with poison which he gave to another monk not knowing that it was poisoned. That monk died. Both of these two Bhikshus went to Buddha, and in much sorrow informed him what had happened. The Great Teacher declared that the monk who gave poisoned food to another monk was innocent, as he knew not it was poisoned, but he who sat on the chair and killed the child was excluded from the Order, because he did not take proper care to know what was on the chair underneath the cloth and also because he sat down without being asked by the house-holder.

Thus were laid down the Laws one after the other as each incident came to the notice of Buddha. They were multipled till they grew numerous during his long life and forty years of his mission. All these rules and regulations,—all these Laws and Precepts,—were collected and recited by Upali in the first Council of the monks which was held immediately after the death of the Great Master. They became known by the name of Vinaya, one of the *Three Pitakas.* Of the five sections into which the Vinaya Pitaka is divided, the first and second, namely *Parajika* and *Pachita* contain a code of Ordinances relative to crimes and misdemeanors for the members of the Order. The third and the fourth, namely *Mahavagga* and *Kulavagga*, contain miscellaneous rules and regulations relative to Ordination, Was &c. The fifth *Parivanapata* contains a summary of the whole.*

—:o:—

CHAPTER IX.

THE CULTS.

Cults in its proper sense Buddhism has none. Oldenberg says:—" For a faith which looks upon man's own heart as the sole place in which decision between happiness and ruin can be caried into effect, what the lip utters and what the hand does can have a value only in so far as it is concomitant of a symbol corresponding to that internal process."

* The Precepts and Prohibitions contained in the Parajika and Pachitta 227 in number are collected together in a work called Patimokha. The subjects of investigation are arranged in the book in the following Order.

1. *Parajika,* 4 in number referring to crimes that are punished by permanent expulsion.

2. *Sanghadisesa,* thirteen in number that require suspension and penance, but not permanent expulsion.

3. *Aniyata-dhamma,* two in number that require expulsion, suspension, or penance according to circumstances.

4. *Nirsagiva-Pachittiya Dhamma,* thirty in number requiring forfeiture of such articles as the monks are permitted to possess.

5. *Pachittiya Dhamma,* ninety-two in number requiring confession and absolution.

6. *Patidesani Dhamma,* four in number involving reprimand.

7. *Sikhya Dhamma,* seventy five in number, containing various prohibition s, inculcating certain observances and proprieties.

8. *Adhikarana Samata Dhamma,* seven in number, the rules to be observed in conducting judicial investigations relative to the conduct of monks. See Gogerlys' Essays.

Rites and Ritualism therefore Buddhism has none. Buddhism is a religion without prayer. What then were their religious acts? If there were any, they were extremely few. The most prominent being the "Fast Day." Twice in the month, at Full-moon and at New-moon day, the monks of each district, wherever they might happen to be, came together to celebrate the "Fast Day."

The eldest Sramana among the monks of a district called the meeting, and every monk residing within its jurisdiction was bound to be present. Under no circumstances, the Fast Day could be celebrated in the absence of even one monk.

Only in the case of insanity, a monk can be excused. If a Bhikshu was ill and he could not send a monk to give an assurance of his purity from the transgressions, the Sangha *i. e.* all the monks assembled, must go to his bed-side.

By the light of a torch, the monks took their seats, no lay man, no novice, no women could be present on any pretence. When all were seated, the oldest of the monks recited in a loud voice :—

"Reverend Sirs, let the Sangha hear me. To day is the Fast Day, the fifteenth of the half month. If the Sangha is ready, let the Sangha keep Fast Day and have the formula of confession recited. What must the Sangha do first? Report the declaration of purity, reverend Sirs, I shall recite the formula of Confession."

All the members of the Sangha present replied :—"We all who are here present, hear and consider it well."

The oldest of the monks said :—"Whoever has commited a transgression, let him confess it. Where there is no transgression, let him be silent. From your silence I shall infer that you are clear, reverend Sirs. As an individual man, to whom a question is put, is supposed to answer, so is it in the case of an assembly like the present, when a question has been put three times. A Bhikshu, who on the question being put three times, does not confess a fault which he has committed and which he remembers is guilty of an intentional lie. But intentional lying, reverend Sirs, brings in annihilation, thus has the Exalted One said. Therefore, a Bhikshu, who has committed a fault, remembers it, and seeks to be pure therefrom, is to confess his fault. For what he confesses will be light in him."

If every body remained silent, the leader said again, "If a monk who has chosen the exercises and the fellowship of the Bhikshus, has carnal intercourse with any creature whatever, down even to a beast, without renouncing these exercies and without admitting his weakness, then this involves a defeat and expulsion from the Order."

After a silence, he turned thrice towards all the monks present and said :—

"Here now I ask the venerable so and so :—Are you free from this transgression? And for the second time I ask, are you free? And for the third time, I ask, are you free?"

If all remained silent, he said :—"Free are the venerables from this,—therefore they are silent. So I take it."

Next in similar terms he mentioned of the three other gravest sins, namely theft, murder, and false assumption of Rahatship and asked the same questions.

Then in similar terms he went on enumerating other minor transgressions, for example :—

"The monk who lowers himself to touch a woman's person with corrupt thoughts while he clasps her hand or clasps her hair or touches one part or other of her body, the Sangha inflicts upon him degradation."

"The monk who in any house belonging to the Sangha, knowingly so arranges his quarters that he thereby incommodes a monk who has come before him and says within himself, who finds it too narrow, may go out,—having just this and nothing else in view, he is guilty of sin."

Thus the Elder went on asking guilty or not guilty on every precept and regulation of Patimokha, and each monk had to confess if he was guilty. These Fast Days were held twice every month.

Beside these Fast Days,—there was another annual ceremony called *Pavarana* (invitations). When the three months of the rainy seasons (*was*) were over, the monks of each district who had passed this time in common retirement assembled one day all in a meeting in which every one from the oldest to the youngest sitting in a reverential posture, raising his clasped hands, asked his fellow monks:—

"Reverend Sirs, I invite the Order, if ye have seen any thing on my part or have heard any thing or have any suspicion about me, have pity on me, Reverend Sirs, and speak. If I see it I shall atone for it."

These are all the public ceremonies that the Buddhist Bhikshus knew. Whatever went beyond this,—the keeping up of instructive meditation and religious concentration is left wholly an unfettered action of the individual monk.

But for the lay disciples,—visiting holy places, worshipping the Bo-tree and adoring the relics of Buddha with flowers and other offerings were allowed. In fact, a lay-Buddhist had no Buddhist Religion to follow. He was asked to lead a good life, that is all. For religious ceremonies, or festivals, he had the entertainments of Buddha and his Sangha; for his religious acts, he had the alms-giving to the monks. Buddha's religion was not for lay-men; but lay-men found in it some thing that they never found any where and flocked in thousands to become Buddhists. What was the mystery? It was nothing else but that the simple teaching of great Buddha made all men good.

Four places are mentioned in the Maha-Pari-Nibban Sutta as deserving of honour and worship by the believing lay-men, namely, (1) the place where Buddha was born, (2) the place where he attained Nirvana, (3) the place where he set in motion the Wheel of Law, and (4) the place in which he breathed his last.

Buddha said :—"For he, O Ananda, who dies in the Faith on the pilgrimage to such holy places, when his body dissolves, is beyond death, walks the good road, and is born again in the heavenly place."

How these pilgrimages were honoured and worshipped, we got a glimpse from the Sacred Suttas. "At the great Tree of Knowledge (Bo-tree at Buddha Gaya) of the Buddha, there was a festival celebrated. Then I took vessels of many kinds and offered sweet-smelling water. When the Tree of Knowledge was to be bathed, a great rainfall began. At the supremely holy foot of the Tree of Knowledge of the Buddha, I planted carefully with a cheerful heart a banner."

Even the body of the Great Master he did not leave as a burden or a relic to his monks. On his death-bed he said :—"Let not the honours due to the body of Tathagatha trouble you, O Ananda. There are wise men among the nobles, the Brahmans and the citizens who believe in Tathagatha; they will do honours to the body of the Tathagatha."

——:o:——

CHAPTER X.

SRAMANAS, PAST AND PRESENT.

We have briefly sketched the great Order of Buddha; we have given an idea what it was like; we have mentioned some of its precepts and laws, rules and regulations; but what sort of men were its members, and how did they live and work? What sort of men were the Sramanas of old, and again what sort of men are they now?

During the lifetime of the great Master and many years after his death, the Sramanas, the Bhikshus of the Buddhist

Order,—the followers of Buddha,—diligently attempted to follow the foot-steps of their illustrious Teacher. They lived as he lived, they worked as he worked; in fact the best and the greatest of them were but the prototypes of Buddha.

Theragatha thus graphcally describes the life of a Sramana who adhered to the stricter Ordinances:—"In solitude and quiet where the wild beasts have their dwelling there let the abode of the monk be, that he may be able to dwell in retirement and seclusion. On dung-hills, on cremation grounds, and on the streets, let him seek wherewith he may prepare for himself clothing; rough let the garment be which he wears. With submissive air let him move, watching the doors of his senses and keeping himself in check, from house to house in order to beg for food. Let him be content also with poor food, let him not desire any thing else,—many savoury things. He who is fond of savoury things,—his spirit is not fond of abstraction. Needing content, apart from the world, let the wise man live; lay men and anchorites both let him avoid. Like a dumb or a deaf man let him not speak, who is wise, at an unseasonable moment in the Order."

But this Law was for those only who lived an austere life. Their number was a few, and Buddha never asked any body to lead such a strict and severe life. His life was simple, and not austere and severely ascetic. The majority of his followers also like him lived a simple, honest, pure and virtuous life.

This was the life of the great Master:—"From year to year the change from a period of wandering to a period of rest and retirement repeated itself for Buddha and his disciples. In the month of June, when after the dry scorching heat, of the Indian summer, clouds came up in towering masses, and the rolling thunders heralded the approach of the rain-bearing monsoon, Buddha and his disciples prepared for retirement and passed the *was* in solitude and meditation."

The rains being over, the itinerant began. Buddha went from town to town and village to village, always attended by a great concourse of disciples. In the main streets through which the religious pilgrims passed, the believers, who dwelt near, had taken ample care to provide shelter to which Buddha and his disciples might resort, or where monks who professed the doctrine dwelt. There was sure to be found lodging for the night in their abodes, and even if no other cover was to be had, there was no want of mango or banyan trees at the foot of which the band might halt for the night.

The most important head-quarters during these wanderings in which Buddha's pilgrim life was passed, are the Capital cities of the kings of Kosala and Magadha,—Sravasti, and Rajgriha. In the immediate neighbourhood of these towns, the community possessed numerous pleasant gardens in which Viharas have been built. Here the masses of the population,—lay as well as monastic,—flocked together to see him and to hear him preach. Here were held the combats of the dialecticians, and theological disputants,—here were given the *bans*.

If the day be not filled up by an invitation, Buddha undertook his circuit of the vIllage or town in quest of alms. He as well as his disciples rose early, when the light of dawn appeared in the sky, and spent the early moments in spiritual exercises or in conversation with the disciples. He then proceeded with his companions towards the town.

When he had returned from his begging excursions and had eaten his meal, there followed,—if not sleep, at any rate peaceful retirement. Resting in a quiet chamber, or better still in the cool shades of dense foliage, he passed the sultry close hours of the afternoon in solitary contemplation, until the evening came on and drew him once more from holy silence to the bustling concourse of friend and foe."*

* Oldenberg's Buddha, pages 141—150.

Such was the life of the great Master and such was the life of his great followers who carried his religion across mountains and seas and made his name adored and worshipped in the distant Tibet and Tartary, China, and Japan, in Ceylon, Siam and Burma.

Do they still exist? The time was when the religion of Buddha spread over the major portion of the earth,—but in course of time, his religion either disappeared or was merged in other religions, such as those of Persia, Afganistan, Palestine and India. But still he is adored in Nepal, Bhutan, Tartary, Mongolia, Manchuria, China, Japan, Siam, Burma, Ceylon, and many other countries. Still he is adored and worshipped by no less than one-third of the human race. But do his Bhikshus, the Sramanas of his great Order, still exist?

CEYLON:—Spence Hardy writes:—"In nearly all the villages and towns of Ceylon that are inhabited by the Singhalese or Kandians, the priests of Buddha are frequently seen, as they have to receive their food by taking the alms-bowl from house to house. They usually walk along the road at a measured space, without taking much notice of that which passes around. They have no covering for the head and are generally bare-footed. In the right hand they carry a fan, which they hold up before the face when in the presence of women so that the existence of evil thoughts into the mind may be prevented. The bowl is slung from the neck and is covered by the robe, except at the time when alms are received. When not carrying the bowl, they are usually followed by an attendant with a book or a small bundle.

The explanation of the Sacred Texts to the pupils occupies a considerable portion of the superior priests. In some parts of the island medicine is practised by the priests to a considerable extent, and they are much in repute for their skill. Under the native monarchies the priests possessed many privileges and received the most distinguished honours. There are many of the Viharas that have no lands attached, but in many instances, the temples are rich in lands, and some of the most productive valleys in the interior belong to the Vihara in Kandi called Malagawa.

The priests cannot possess lands as their own personal property, nor can they make over to others the property of the temples, but in many cases the revenues of the temples are scattered,—the sacred buildings are allowed to fall into ruins."*

This is how a Sramana is burnt after death in Ceylon. The body is placed in a planquin and then carried to the spot where it is to be burnt, preceded by banners and tomtoms. About twenty priests follow in procession. It marches once round the pile which is composed of a great heap of wood, laid in regular lairs. The body, divested of its robes, is placed with its face downwards in the centre of the pile to which the head priest applies the torch and the whole is soon in a blaze. Pieces of cloth are distributed to the poor, but no form is read, nor is any address delivered to the people. A rude monument is generally made over the ashes of the priests on the summit of which a Bo-tree is generally planted.†

BURMAH:—Throughout Burmah, monasteries are seen near every village, and generally in situations that are beautiful and romantic in their character. These secluded sites may have been chosen by the monks for study and meditation. The Buddhisms of Ceylon and Burma are almost identical,—for Burmah was converted to Buddhism by Ceylon missionaries.

In Burmah there is a large number of monks who maintain that there is an Eternal God. They deny the doctrine of transmigration and affirm that at death the future state of

* See Hardy's Eastern Monarchisms, pages 310—322.

† As for this ceremony amongst the Burmese Bhikshus called Pungees, see below.

every human being is eternally fixed. They worship the images of Buddha and conform to Ceylon usages. But they are rejected as heretics by their other countrymen.*

About one hundred years ago, a class of metaphysicians arose in Ava called Paramats who respected only the Abhidharmana and rejected the other books that the Buddhists consider sacred, saying that they were only a compilation of fables and allegories. The founder of the sect, Keran, with about fifty of his followers, was put to death by the order of the king.

NEPAL:—Hodgson says:—"All Buddhas (of Nepal) are properly ascetics,—some solitary,—mostly house-holders. Their convents are called Viharas. The rule of these Vihara is a rule of freedom and the door of every Vihara is always open, both to the entrance of the new comers and the departure of such of the old inmates as are tired of their vows. Each Vihara has a titular superior, whose authority over his brethren depends only in their voluntary difference to his superior learning or piety. Women are held equally worthy of admission with men and each sex has its Viharas. The old Buddhist Scriptures enumerate four sorts of *Bandyas*, namely *Arhan, Bhikshu, Sravaka* and *Chailaka*, who are correctly described in the Text, and from that description it will be seen that there is no essential distinction between them. The *Arhan* being only segregated from the rest by his superior proficiency in *Bodhi-jnana.* Of the proper Institutes of Buddhism,—there remains hardly a trace in Nepal. The very names of Arhan and Chailaka have passed away—the names only of the other two exist; and out of the gradual and now total disuse of monastic Institutes, an exclusive minister of the altar, denominated *Vajra-acherjea,* has derived his name, office, and existence in Nepal not only without sanction from the Scriptures, but in direct opposition to their spirit and

* See Crawford, Sangermano, Buchanon and Judson's works; also Howard Malcolm's Travels in South East Asia.

tendency. Nepal is still covered with Viharas, but these ample and comfortable abodes have long resounded with the hum of industry and the pleasant voices of men and women. The superior ministry of religion is now solely in the hands of *Bandyas* entitled *Vajra-acherjeas* in Sanskrit and *Gubhal* in Newari. And these professions of Vajra-acherjea and of the Bhikshus have become by usage heriditary as have all other avocations and pursuits, whether civil or religious, in Nepal. And as in the modern corrupt Buddhism of Nepal there are exclusive ministers of religion or *priests*, so are many Buddhists who retain the lock on the crown of the head and are not *Bandyas*. These improper Buddhists are called *Udas*. They never dwell in the Viharas, look up to the *Bandyas* with a reverential respect and follow their trade and avocations which are disreputable."

TIBHET :—The Superior priests who are called Lamas are regarded as incarnations of Buddha and possess so large a share of political authority that they can depose the sovereign of the country and substitute another in his stead. The dress of the grand Lama is yellow; that of the other Lamas of superior rank red; they wear broad-brimmed hats.

Moorcofts says :—" Nearly two thirds of the productive lands are approprieted to the support of the priesthood." Athenæum says :—" The sacred cradle of Shamanism (the religion of the Sramanas) Tibhet is governed by a Hierearchy possessed of the most absolute sway and supported by an army, not of soldiers but of monks. In every habitable spot throughout the country, monasteries and nuneries rear up their heads in stately grandeur, while the mass of the people seem contented with the honour of contributing towards the support of this priestly system. The capital of Tibhet, Lasha, the principal residence of Dalai Lama, with a population of 30,000 souls, contains many splendid monastic establishments."

Csoma Korosi writes:—"The different systems of Buddhism derived from India and known now to the Tibetians are the following four, namely (1) *Vaibhasika*, (2) *Sautrantika*, (3) *Yogachara*, (4) *Madhyanika*. They originated with the four chief disciples of Buddha, *i. e.* Rahula, Kassyapa, Upali, and Katyana.

(*a*) The followers of Rahula were divided into four sects and wore on their religious garb from 25 to 9 narrow pieces of cloth. The distinctive mark of this class was a water-lily, jewel and tree-leaf put together in the form of a nosegay.

(*b*) The followers of Upali were divided into three sects. They wore on their religious garb from 21 to 5 pieces of narrow cloth. They carried a flower as a mark of their School and were styled 'the class which is honoured!'

(*d*) The followers of Kassyapa were divided into three sects and wore the same number of narrow pieces of cloth as the former class. They had as their mark the figure of wheel and were styled "the class that have fixed habitations."

JAPAN :—The Buddhism of Japan, in having an incarnation of Buddha, possessing unlimited power, resembles that of Tibhet. The palace of the Dairi or the Supreme Pontiff in the Spiritual Metropolis Meako, is said to form in itself a town of considerable size. The temples are built upon eminences that command the most delightful prospects. In the largest, called the temple of Dai-Bud or the great Buddha, resting on ninety-six columns, there is a great statue of the Sage of the usual form and appearance, but so immensely large that according to the Japanese, six persons can squat without inconvenience on the palm of his hand, and his shoulders reach, pillar to pillar, a space from 30 to 32 feet.

PART IV.

THE HISTORY OF BUDDHISM.

—:o:—

CHAPTER I.

THE FIRST BUDDHIST COUNCIL.

The great religion of Buddha is no longer the same religion that he preached. It has passed through innumerable changes. When Buddha died, his religion was accepted and followed by only a few thousands of men. But it is now the religion of millions of men and of innumerable races. How did all this come about ?.

Immediately after Buddha's death, his beloved followers all assembled together and held a Council at Rajgriha under the presidency of the venerable Maha Kassyapa, the oldest and the most revered of all his followers.* It was held in the Sattapanin cave and consisted of 500 members of the Order.† There did they settle the Vinaya, *i. e.*, the Rules for the Sangha and Dharma, and the general precepts and moral laws preached and ordained by their great master. It is said the whole Council chanted together the words of their

---

* We get a complete history of the development and spread of Buddhism in Mahavansa and Dipavansa. For the account of this Council, see Mahavansa p. 11 and Vinaya Texts. Vol. III. Book XI.

† The cave still exists in the Vaihara hill near Rajgriha. It is said the place was prepared for the Council by King Ajatasatru.

exalted Teacher, following Upali when the subject was Vinaya, and followlng Ananda when it was Dharma.* All these teachings were then named Thera-Veda, *i.e.* Three Vedas or knowledge. They consisted of—

1. Sutta—Discourses.
2. Geyya—Mixed Prose and Verse.
3. Vayakarana—Exposition.
4. Gatha—Verse.
5. Udana.
6. Itivrittaka.
7. Jataka.
8. Abbhuta—Mysteries.
9. Vedalla—Treatises.†

For one hundred years after the sitting of this Council, the doctrines of Buddha, as chanted by the members of the Sangha, were silently and reverently followed by hundreds of men and women all over the country. Their number daily grew larger,—races after races and tribes after tribes accepted it as a national religion. "The old Aryan civilisation had begun even at the time of Goutama to yield to changing circumstances. The influence of priesthood was becoming more exclusively spiritual, while the temporal power of the chiefs was growing. Some of the latter had even then become kings, and the oligarchies of the clans were more and more verging on despotisms. Shortly after Goutama's death, the King of Magadha, Ajatsatru, destroyed the confederation of the Wajjian clans on the opposite side of the Ganges,—and then ensued a series of struggles between Magadha and the neighhouring kingdoms of Kosambi and Sravasti. The lesser chiefs had to take sides with one or the other of the powerful combatants, while each country became the scene of intrigues for the coveted possession of the throne. These struggles gave a chance to men of the lower castes,

* See Dipavansa.

† These names are given by the Dipavansa.

which they could never have in the old system of the clans,—a system which must almost have ceased to exist when the second Buddhist Council was held at Vaisali.

The kingdom of Magadha had by that time become supreme and either just before or just after the Buddhist Council had assembled in the old capital of the Wajjians, Vaisali, a low caste Sudra by name Chandra Gupta became the king of all kings in India. When thus the old order of things had given place to new, the Buddhists began to rise rapidly in number and influence."*

But as India was then passing through a great political change, so did she pass through many social and religious changes. Buddhism was no exception; many changes had already taken place both in the rules of the Sangha and in the general percepts and morals. Some of the Buddhist monks at Vaisali maintained what were called the Ten Indulgences which were opposed by the others. These indulgences were as follows:—

1. That salt might be preserved in horns, whereas salt like other edibles might not according to the Vinaya be laid aside for use.

2. That solid food might be taken not only up till noon, but till the sun threw shadow two inches long.

3. That the rules of the Vinaya might be relaxed in the country, away from the convenience of the monastaries.

4. That ordination, confession, etc., might be performed in private houses, and not only in the *Upastha* halls attached to the monastaries.

5. That where the consent of the Order was necessary to any act, that consent might be obtained after and not only before the act.

6. That conformity to the example of others was a good excuse for relaxing rules.

---

* See Rhys Davids' Buddhism p. 219—220.

7. That whey might be taken after noon and not only liquids such as water or milk.

8. That fermented drinks, if they looked like water, were allowed to be drunk.

9. That seats covered with cloths were allowed, so long the cloths have no fringes.

10. That gold and silver might be received by the members of the Order.

Though the majority of the Buddhist monks were in favour of these indulgences, yet there was a minority which strongly condemned them. They held a Council—the second Buddhist Council—consisting of 700 monks under the presidency of Jasa, the son of Khandaha. The Council continued its sitting for eight months at Vaisali and settled and vindicated the rules of the Order and the Doctrines of the Faith. But the decisions of the Council were not accepted by the majority of the monks. They too held a Council, much more numerous than that of their stricter opponents, and hence this Council was called Maha-Sangiti or Great Council.*a

Thus we find within a hundred and fifty years after the death of the great master, his followers were divided into two great parties, one following strictly the original teachings of their preceptor, and the other becoming more liberal and adopting various new innovations. The former in latter days became known by the name of the Southern School and the former by the Northern School. The Dipavansa, the author of which belonged to the Southern School, thus speaks of the other party.

"The monks of the Great Council overturned religion.

They broke up the old Scriptures and made a new recension.

A Discourse put in one place they put in another;

---

*a On the second Council, see Mahavansa, chap. IV; Dipavansa canto IV. Vinaya Texts Vol. III. Book XII, and Taranath's History of Buddhism p. 41.

And distorted the sense and doctrine of the five Nikayas.
These monks who knew not what had been spoken at length,
And what had been spoken concisely,
What was the obvious and what the higher meaning,
Attached new meaning to new words as if spoken by the Buddha,
And destroyed much of the spirit by holding to the shadow of the letter.
They partly rejected the Sutta and Vinaya so deep,
And made a different Sutta and Vinaya and Text,
The Parivasa, the Nidesa, and a portion of the Jataka.
So much they put aside and made others in their place."

We have no records of what the more liberal monks thought of their brethern in minority. However from the records of the Southern School we find that the latter of these two great parties were again subdivided into eighteen distinct sects.*b*

But as time went on sects were added to sects ;*c many men added many things to the original grand teachings of the Buddha,—many rites and rituals, charms and incantations were introduced, and amongst the Buddhists of the Northern School inhabiting Thibet, China, Japan, and Mongolia, the religion of Buddha now exists under a mass of superstitions. Amongst the Buddhists of the Southern School, now inhabiting Ceylon, Burmah, Siam &c., the original teachings of the great Prophet are even now strictly adhered to, and much superstitions, dogmatic rites and rituals, or magical charms, and incantations have been kept away; yet even amongst them the religion of Buddha is much changed. We shall first follow the Southern School and describe the development that Buddhism met with under it, and we shall then

*b On these 18 Sects, see Burmah "Lotus" p.p. 356—359 and Koppen "Religion Des Buddha" p. p. 150—159.

c* Fa Hian mentions 96 sects.

see how the Northern School proceeded and what changes they went through and what new innovations they made.

—:o:—

CHAPTER II.

ASOKA & BUDDHISM.

Up to the time of which we are speaking, the religion of Buddha was but the religion of pious men and a few of the wise men: it never became the national religion or the State Religion. The chiefs and kings and sovereigns patronized the Buddhist monks and supported them as they did the learned Brahmanas. There was no enmity or rivalry between the Brahmans and Buddhist Sramanas. They both unobstructedly practised the different tenets of their religions under the catholic and benign protection of the kings who were generally and mostly the followers of Brahmanism.

The first king who publicly assumed the religion of the Buddha and made it the State Religion was Asoka, the grandson of the celebrated Chandragupta. The great empire founded by Chandragupta was in its zenith when Asoka ascended the throne of Magadha. Its sovereign sway extended from Assam in the East to the banks of the Indus in the West. When Asoka made Buddhism his State Religion, it became at one stroke virtually the religion of whole of Northern India.*

* The following Edict of king Asoka now discovered at Shahabazgari clearly shows that he was originally a Hindu.

"Formerly in the great Refectory and temple of the heaven-beloved king Piyadasi, daily were many hundred thousand animals sacrificed for the sake of meat (food). So even at this day while this religious edict is under promulgation from the sacrifice of animals for the sake of food, some two are killed, or one is killed, but now the joyful chorus resounds again and again that from henceforward not a single animal shall be put to death." (See Cunningham's.)

The following quotation from *Asoka Avadhana*, a Sanskrit work of Northern Buddhism, will clearly show that the Brahmanas made strenuous efforts to prevent Asoka from

---

"Beholding this (Asoka's zeal for Buddhism), these arrogant Tirthikas, oppressed by the fire of envy, collected together and said to each other : 'Should this king Asoka continue a worshipper of Buddha, all other persons encouraged by him would likewise become followers of Buddha. None among the people would be devout, none of the good Sravakas will listen to us with respect. We should therefore for the promotion of honour and fame always adopt such means as will make us fully trusted;" Excited by this speech, the arrogant Tirthikas came to the resolution of adopting immediate action. Then these Tirthikas went from house to house of well-disposed people and blessing them thus addressed them. "Hon'ble sirs, listen to us if you wish for your own good. Should you wish for a blessed life hereafter, devote yourself to true religion. Ours is the true religion, and therefore attend to it with all respect. The religion of the Buddha is not the true one, for it provides no *Moksha*." Hearing these words, some were convinced, others vacillated, and some would not believe them at all. Thus those Tirthikas, wishing for honours, daily seduced credulous people. Then those arrogant ones longing for fame and respect, proceeded to visit Vitasoka, the brother of Asoka. Appearing before Vitasoka, son of Vindusara, they blessed him and stood in front of him. Vitasoka seeing them in front of him, saluted them and enquired the object of their visit. 'Reved. Sirs, what has brought you so anxious to this place. You are always welcome to relate whatever you wish." Thus encouraged, those arrogant Tirthikas, looking at each other, thus addressed the prince ? "May success always attend you, great king, may you always prosper! May you be free from all fear. Since we have come to advice you for your good it is meet that we should tell you all. Should you wish for a blessed life hereafter, listen to our advice. Ours is the true religion, alike salutary here and hereafter. Those who know best declare it to be the best of all religions. Therefore O beloved king, believe in it, listen to our religion and follow it with ardour. Then every thing will prosper about you; and consuming all your enemies, you will become a *Chakvavarti*. The religion of the Buddha is not true, for it offers no *Moksha*. Therefore that religion should not be listened to. Since these shaven-headed, vile destroyers of their family preach a false religion overthrowing all castes and all duty, men devoid of the religion of

becoming a Buddhist. But Mr. Thomas says,—Asoka was originally not a Hindu but a Jain.

The mother of Asoka was Subhadrangi,*a the daughter of a poor Brahman of Champa.*b The astrologers told the Brahman that his daughter would be the queen of a great king. He therefore took her with him and came to Pataliputra, the capital of Magadha. With good deal of difficulty, he was successful in seeing Vindusara, the great king. He then

the Vedas, unBrahminical in their conduct and vilely passionate,—they should, O king, on no account, be respected by you. No Buddha should be revered, nor seen, nor touched, nor worshipped, nor spoken to, nor dwelt with in the same house, nor visited by any one. You should on no account eat with them nor present anything to a Buddhist Sanctuary. Even when by mistake men listen to the doctrines of the Buddha with regard, they suffer from various calamities, and at last go to hell. Hence, O king, should you wish for a blessed life hereafter, never listen to the doctrines of the Buddhas with respect. Should one by delusion, looking at the merits of their religion, accept it, fallen here, he will be translated to hell hereafter. For these reasons, O great king, accept not the doctrine of Buddha but abiding by our cannons, follow the true religion with devotion. By so doing you will here and hereafter enjoy great blessings. No evil will ever befall you, and you will proceed by the true path. Listening to our words, weigh well which is good and which is evil, and for your own advantage follow the path of duty." Vitosoka heard this address of the Tirthikas, but remained unconvinced of their truth. The Tirthikas addressed him again and again and at last brought him convinced under their control.*

* See Journal R. A. S. Vol IX p 171.

*a Amongst the Sanskrit Buddhist manuscripts found in Nepal by Mr. Hodgson are two books, one named *Divya Avadhana* and *Asoka Avadhana*, both containing the life of Asoka. Burnouf has translated *Divya Avadhana*. Dr. Rajendra Lall Mittra thus speaks of *Asoka Avadhana*. "Its author's name is not given, but it professes to have been related by one Jayasri to his desciples at the Kukkuta Vihara in a garden named *Upakanthikarana* on the right bank of the Ganges near Pataliputra. The authority quoted is that of a saint named Upa Gupta, the spiritual guide of the king." See Indo-Aryan vol. II, p. 408.

*b Champa was situated near the modern Bhagulpur.

presented him his beautiful daughter and went away to his own country.

The other queens became jealous of her and employed her in mean works. She was ordered to be a female barber. Thus did she pass her life in great misery having got no opportunity to see the king even for once.

At last her opportunity came. One day she had the good fortune to be called to shave the king. He was so pleased with her work that he asked her to pray for a boon. She told him her history and asked him to make her his queen. Her prayer was granted and soon she rose to be the chief queen.

She then gave birth to a son whom she named Asoka, for with his birth her miseries ended. She had another son who was called Vitasoka or Vigatasoka.

Asoka was ugly and unruly,—therefore the people gave him the name of Chanda (terrible). He became so wild that he was sent far off to Taxila to quell a mutiny or to be killed in the attempt. Asoka was wild, but he was a man of great parts and heroism. He was able to quell the mutiny within a very short time, and the king was so pleased that he was re-called.

Soon after king Bindusara fell ill; his eldest son Susima was away in Taxila. The ministers induced the king to appoint Asoka his Regent. But as soon as the king died, Asoka was however formally installed as the great king of Magadha. His half-brothers rebelled, but they were defeated and taken prisoners. It is said Asoka himself cut off their heads. He ruled the country with an iron hand.

A very rich merchant by name Sumudra had become a Buddhist monk. He fell into the hands of the fierce mountaineer who was Asoka's right-hand man. This bad man tried to kill the Bhikshu by various means, but failed. He then informed the king what had happened. The king ordered the Bhikshu to be brought before him. When he heard every thing from that Buddhist monk, he cut off the head of the mountaineer and declared his intention to be a follower of his great religion.

Asoka became quite a changed man. He built a *Chaitya* at Kukkut Vana, one at Ramgrama, and many others at various other places. He was then called Dharmasoka.*

"After his conversion which took place in the 10th year of his reign, he became a very zealous supporter of the new religion. He himself built many monasteries and dagobas† and provided many monks with the necessaries of life, and he encouraged those about his court to do the same. He also

---

* Asoka had 3 or 4 wives, namely, (1) Padmavati (mother of Kunala), (2) Asandhimitra, (3) Kichhigain (4) Tishyarakhita.

The 2nd and the 3rd are mentioned in the inscriptions. The *Asoka Avadhana* mentions Pavishyarakhita who tried to destroy the Bo-tre through a sorcerress, because the king spent much money for it.

The most celebrated son was Kunala. Through evil machinations of one of his step mothers, the prince became blind and adopted the life of a Bhikshu.

Asoka's brother Vitasoka also became a Buddhist monk. But he was killed by a man who wished to secure the reward proclaimed by Asoka to be given for the head of a Hindu monk of Pandravardhana who painted Buddha at his feet.

Asoka's son Mahendra and daughter Sangamitra both took the holy robe and became Bhikshu and Bhikshuni. (See Asoka Avadhana).

† This is the story told about the remains of Buddha. Just after his death the country was overrun by intercine wars. Therefore old Kassyapa collected all his remains from the ten Stupas made by the various clans and buried them in the deepest forest.

When Asoka began to search for the remains of the Great Prophet, one old venerable monk told him that when he was a boy, his preceptor one day took him in a deep forest, and showing a place, ordered him to bow there and remember well the place. He thought the remains of the Great Master might be found there.

Asoka hastened to the place, and after a search, he found what he was in search of. He then distributed the relics all over India and erected Stupas on them.

laid out gardens and constructed hospitals for men and beasts and published Edicts throughout his empire* enjoining on all his subjects morality and justice.

* Rhys Davids, says :—" Within the last 50 years a most important and interesting discovery has been made of several of these Edicts engraven in different Prakrit dailects on pillars or rocks whose wide distance from one another is sufficient to show the great extent of Asoka's empire. The pillars are at Delhi and Allahabad; the rocks at Kapada Giri near Peshwar, at Girnar in Guzrat, at Dhauli in Orrissa and at Bubra on the road running south-west from Delhi to Jayapura. They were first published and translated by James Prinsep, then republished by Wilson, and have been since then further explained by Burnouf and Professors Watergard and Kern. Their sense is not at all doubtful, but the facsimiles which have hitherto reached Europe have been imperfect and the text is by no means settled." (See Rhys David's Buddhism pp. 222-23).

The following is James Prinsep's summary of the contents of these edicts which are 14 in number.

The 1st Edict prohibits the sacrifice of animals both for food and in religious assemblies and enjoins more attention to the practice of this first of Buddhist virtues than seems to have been paid to it even by the Raja himself, at least prior to the sixteenth year of his reign.

The 2nd Edict provides a system of medical aid for men and animals throughout Piyadasi's dominions, and orders trees to be planted along the sides of the principal public roads.

The 3rd Edict enjoins the republication every 5th year of the great moral maxims, inculcated in the Buddhist creed, viz, honour to parents, charity to kinderds and neighbours, humanity to animals &c.

The 4th Edict draws a comparison between the former state of things, perhaps lawless and uncivilised and the state of regeneration of the country under the Ordinances of the beloved king.

The 5th Edict proceeds to record the appointments of ministers of religion and missionaries enumerating many of the countries to which they are to be deputed for the conversion of the young and old, the rich and the poor, the native and the foreigner.

The 6th Edict appoints in like manner *Pativedahas* (informers) who are to take cognizance of the conduct of the people in their meals, domestic life, &c.

The 7th Edict expresses not an order, but an earnest desire on the part of the king that all the diversities of religious opinion may be

He also founded an office,—that of *Dharma Mahamatra,* chief minister of Justice and Religion whose duty it was to preserve the purity of religion and to look over and care for the right treatment and the progress of the aborigines and subject races, a striking conjunction of duties. Similar officials were appointed in the dependent courts and others to promote the education of the women in the harems and elsewhere the principles of the religion of Goutama.*

obliterated, that every distinction in rank and in tastes may be harmonized into one system *Bhava-sudhi,*—that peace of mind or repose of conscience which proceeds from knowledge, from faith and entire assent.

The 8th Edict contrasts the mere sexual amusements patronised by former Rajas with the more harmless and pious enjoyments prescribed by himself.

The 9th Edict continues the thread of the same discourse by capitulating on the sources of true happiness.

The 10th Edict comments upon the glory and renown which attend merely the vain and transitory deeds of the world.

The 11th Edict upholds that the imparting of Dharma itself is the chiefest of charitable devotions, &c.

The 12th Edict is addressed to all non-believers.

The 13th Edict enjoins principal moral precepts.

The 14th Edict is a kind of summing up of the foregoing. (See Journal, Bengal Asiatic Society, vol. vii, p. 220).

To give our readers an idea what these Edicts are like, we quote below the 14th Edict.

" This Religious Edict is caused to be written by the heaven-beloved king Piyadasi. It is (partly written) with abridgment ; it is (partly) with ordinary extent ; and it is (partly) with an amplification not incoherent (or disjointed) but throughout continuous (and united), it is powerful to overcome the wise ; and it is much written and caused to be written, yet it is always but the same thing repeated over and over again.

" For the persuasive eloquence which is lavished on each separate subject shall men tender obedience thereto.

" Furthermore, at one time even unto the conclusion is this written, incomparable with the copy by Relachpu, the scriber and Pundit (See Cunningham's Corpus Inscriptionum Indicarum Vol I. Inscriptions of Asoka p 126).

* See Rhys David's Buddhism p 222 and p. 228.

In the 18th year of Asoka's reign he convened a great Council of the Buddhist monks to be held at Pataliputra. There had arisen innumerable heretics and false Bhikshus,—there had arisen much disagreements about the Buddhist Sacred Books, therefore it became absolutely necessary to hold a Council and settle all disputed points. Accordingly a Council was held of 1000 monks with Tissa as its president. The Council held its sitting for nine months, and once more the rules of the Order and the Doctrines of the Faith were solemnly rehearsed and settled. The result was thus declared by king Asoka in an Edict which has been found inscribed at a place called Babra.

"King Piyadasi of Magadha, greeting the Order, wishes it health and happiness. You know, reverend Sirs, how great is my respect and reverence for the Buddha, the Dharma and the Sangha. All these things, reverend Sirs, which were spoken by the blessed Buddha were well spoken; by looking upon them, reverend Sirs, as authority, true Law will long endure. I honour, reverend Sirs, as such the following Scriptures of the Law:—The substance of the Vinaya, the state of the guest, the fears of the Future, the Poems of the wise, the discourse on conduct befitting the wise, the questions of Upatissa, the exhortations to Rohula about falsehood, spoken by the blessed Buddha. The Scriptures of the Law, reverend Sirs, I hope that the honourable monks and nuns may constantly learn and reflect upon and so also the laity of either sex. To that end, reverend Sirs, I cause this to be written and have uttered my desire."*

At the close of the council many missionaries were sent all over the country to preach the great religion.†

---

* See Mahavansa and Dipavansa.

† See Ibid chap. 12th and chap 8th.

CHAPTER III.

SPREAD OF SOUTHERN BUDDHISM.

We know very little of the works done by the Missionaries of Buddhism sent by the great king Asoka of Magadha. But we have a continunal narrative of the introduction and spread of Buddhism in Ceylon in two most celebrated Pali works,—namely the *Mahavansa* and *Dipavansa*, in which we find it was converted to Buddhism by Mahendra, Asoka's own son, who went to Ceylon in the 18th year of his reign accompanied by a band of Buddhist monks.*

Tissa, whom the Buddhists called *Devanampiya*, beloved of the gods,—was then the king of Ceylon. He welcomed the celebrated missionary not only because he was sent by the great king Asoka of India, but because he was a man extraordinarily learned and pious. He built at the request of the venerable monk the great Buddhist Stupa called *Thaparana Dogaba* in the city of Anuradhpura, the ancient capital of Ceylon, which still stands as one of the glories of that celebrated ruined city. Under this Dagoba, it is said, the right collar bone of the Great Prophet was buried. Close by it, he erected a monastery for Mahendra and his companions on the beautiful hill of Mohintale eight miles to the east of the city.

"It was on this hill," says Rhys Davids, † "the three peaks of which, each now surmounted by a Dagoba, form so striking an object from the central trunk road which runs along its side, that the famous missionary spent most of his after years. Here on the precipitous western side of the hill, under a large mass of granite rock, at a spot which, completely shut out from

---

* Four of the names of these Monks are given in Mahavansa, p. 71, namely, Itthiya, Athiya, Sambala, and Bhaddasala. And two more, *i.e.*, Samana and Bhandu in pp. 76-77.

† See Rhys David's Buddhism pp. 230-31.

the world, affords a magnificant view of the plains below, he had his Study hollowed out, and steps cut in the rock over which alone it could be reached. There also the stone couch which was carved out of the soild rock still exists with holes either for curtain rods or for a protecting balustrade beside it. The great rock effectually protects the cave from the heat of the sun, in whose warm light the broad valley below lies basking. Not a sound reaches it from the plains,—now one far reaching forest then full of busy homesteads : there is only heard that hum of the insects which never ceases and the rusting of the leaves of the trees which cling to the side of the precipice. I shall not easily forget the day, when I first entered that lonely, cool and quiet chamber so simple and yet so beautiful, where more than 2000 years ago the great teacher had sat and thought and worked through the long years of his peaceful and useful life. On that hill he afterwards died and his ashes still rest under the Dagoba which is the principal object of reverence and care of the few monks who still reside in the Mahintale Wihaw (Mahendra Vihara)."

Only a year after, the queen and the female relations of the king—Devanam Piya Tissa—expressed a wish to be converted into Buddhism. Mahendra accordingly sent words to Magadha whence his own sister Sangamitra, already a Buddhist nun,—started for Ceylon along with a band of nuns.* She brought over with her a branch of the sacred Bo-tree from the Buddha Gya under which the great Goutama achieved Nirvana. This precious branch was planted at Anuradhpura where it still grows.†

* The names of nine of these nuns and of several of their celebrated pupils are given in *Dipavansa*, ch. 18.

† Rhys David who saw the tree in Anuradhpura thus speaks of it :— The tree could scarcely have lived so long had it not been for the constant care of the monks. As it showed the signs of decay, terraces were built up around it, so that it now grows more than twenty-feet above the surrounding soil; for the tree being of the fig species—its botanical name is *fecus religiosa*,—its living branches could then throw

Tissa reigned for 20 years and died just before the death of the great missionary Mahendra. Just after the death of king Tissa, Ceylon was overrun by the Tamils who retained the kingly power in their hands for 60 years. They were at last driven out about B.C. 164 by Dasta Gamini a grandson of Tissa's brother.

This king was a zealous supporter of Buddhism. He built two of the largest Dagobas at Anuradhpura, namely Miriswali 150 feet high and the Maha Thupa 200 feet high. He also built a huge monastery called the great Brazen Palace as it was roofed with metal. Its 1,000 granite pillars still stand just outside the sacred enclosure round the Bo-tree.

Thirty-four years after his death the Tamils again conquered Ceylon, but they were again driven out by Watta Gamini, a son of Dasta Gamini's brother in about 88 B.C. This king built the largest Dogoba in Ceylon. It is called Agni Giri Dogoba and is 290 feet high. It was in his reign 330 years after the great Nirvana that the sacred Tripitakas for the first time were reduced into writing.*

The next great event were the works of Buddha Ghosa. He was born near Buddha Gya and came to Ceylon in 430 A.D. By this great man was written *Visuddhi Marga*—a Cyclopædia of Buddhist Doctrines. He became famous and

---

out fresh roots. Where its long arms spread beyond the enclosure, wide pillars of iron or masonry have been used to prop them up, and it is carefully watered in seasons of draught. The whole aspect of the tree and its enclosure bears evident signs of extreme age; but we could not be sure of its identity were it not for the complete chain of documentary evidence which has been so well brought together by Sir Emerson Tennet.

* The *Mahavansa* relates this important event in a stanza which it quotes from the *Dipavansa*:—"The wise monks of former days handed down by words of mouth, the text of the three Pitakas and the commentary upon them. Seeing the destruction of men, the monks of this time assembled, and so that the faith might last long, they wrote them in books."

was employed by the chiefs of the Sangha in Ceylon to write in Pali the commentaries which had till then been handed over in Singhalese.*

Buddha Ghosa about 450 A. D. went to Burma and stayed there for some years. The country of the *Mugs* was converted by him and made his followers. Siam soon followed the example of its sister country and was converted in about 938 A.D. Java was visited by the Buddhist missionaries in the sixth and the seventh centuries A.D. In the thirteenth

---

* According to the dictates of their great master Mahendra wrote in Singhalese, the vernacular of the island, the doctrines of the Order and all the other sacred books. Buddha Ghosa re-wrote them in Pali, the sacred language of Buddhism. He wrote many commentaries. The following is a list of the Pali commentaries now extant.

1. Samante Pasadika on the Vinaya.
2. Kankha Vitaravi on the Patimokkha.
3. Sumangala Vilasini on the Digha Nikaya.
4. Papanca Sudani on the Majjhama Nikaya.
5. Sarattha Ppakasini on the Sannyutta Nikaya.
6. Monoratha-Suravi on the Augultara Nikaya.
7. Paramattha-Jotina on the Khuddaka Patha and Sulta Nipata.
8. Dhammapada Althakatha on the Damapada.
9. Paramattha-Dipani on the Udana, Vimana Valthu, Peta-Valthu Theragatha and Trigatha.
10. Abhidhammaltha-Dipant on the Iti-Vattaha.
11. Jataha Althakatha on the Jataha.
12. Saddhammappajotiha on the Niddesa.
13. Saddhamma-ppahasini on the Patisambhida.
14. Visuddha-Jana-Vilasini on the Apadana.
15. Madhuraltha Vilasini on the Apadana.
16. Madhuraltha-Vilasini on the Buddhavanso.
17. Cariya-pitaka-Althakatha on the Cariya Aitaka.
18. Attha-Salini on the Dhamma-Sangin.
19. Sammoha-Vinddani on the Vibhanga.
20. Panca-ppakarana Althakatha on the five last books of the Abhidhamma Pitaha.

See Childers' Pali Dictionary S. V. Atthakatha and also Rhys David's Buddhism in p. 227.

century A.D. Buddhism was the prevailing religion in Java when the great temple at Boro Badu was built. About this time Buddhism also penetrated from Java into the adjoining islands of Bali and Sumatra. All these countries adopted Buddhism of the Southern School.

CHAPTER IV.

NORTHERN BUDDHISM.

We have already said that within one hundred years of Buddha's death, his religion was split up into two distinct branches, thereafter known as the Southern and Northern Buddhism. The cause is not far to seek.

The great Buddha formulated a religion of Complete Knowledge—a Religion of Philosophy pure and simple, and he intended this for those only who would be members of his Sangha, who would live for religion and for religion only, and who would aspire to achieve the final Salvation—the cessation of more births,—the great Nirvana. For others, for the majority of people, for the house-holders and worldly men, he did not formulate any special religion,—he allowed them to remain as they were,—he never called them heretics or followers of a false religion,—he rather asked them to stick to the religion of their forefathers. Nowhere we find, he had any quarrel with the Brahmans. To the Ordained Monks of the Sangha only,—there is no God, no worship, no rituals,—not because there is no God, but because it is an unknowable mystery and therefore not necessary for the achievment of Salvation.* But the case of worldly men is separate. It is

* BUDDHA SAID :—"There is, O disciples, an unborn, unoriginated, uncreated, unformed. Were there not, O disciples, this unborn,

not for them to acquire Nirvana in this life,—they are creatures of *Karma*,—they must, and they are bound to follow the *Karma* of their previous births,—therefore they are to worship a God or gods, they must have rituals and rites,—household and social duties, and so forth,—the best that the Buddha found had already been formulated by the great Brahmans. Therefore his religion was not at all a new religion; he himself was a Hindu and his religion was but a mere development of Hinduism.* His lay-followers were Hindus in all respects,† and his monks were but Hindus

---

unoriginated, uncreated, unformed, there would be no possible exit from the world of the born, originated, created, formed." See also Dhammapada, V. 383. See also Maxmuller's Introduction, Dhammapada l. c. p. xliv. But the Great Master did not reveal this. Dr. Oldenberg asks:—"Why has Buddha not taught his disciples, whether the world is finite or infinite, whether men live on beyond death or not? Because the knowledge of these things does not conduce to progress in holiness,—because it does not contribute to peace and enlightenment." See his Buddha p. 276.

* Rhys Davids in his Buddhism p. 85 says:—"Buddhism was the child, the product of Hinduism." Sir Monier Williams in his Buddhism p. 75 says:—"We perceive again the close connection between Brahmanism and Buddhism, for clearly the Brahmacharin and Sannyasin of the one became the Sramanera or Junior monk and Sramana, or senior monk of the other."

Dr. Oldenberg in his Buddha p. p. 170--171 says:—"People are accustomed to speak of Buddhism as opposed to Brahmanism, somewhat in the way that it is allowable to speak of Lutherism as an opponent of Papacy. But if they mean, as they might be inclined from this parallel to do, to picture to themselves a kind of Brahmanical hierarchy which is assailed by Buddha, which opposed its resistance to its operations like the resistance of the party in possession to an upstart, they are mistaken."

† "But as in the history of Jesus, Lazarus and Necodemus, Mary and Martha stood side by side with Peter and John, so Buddhism also, side by side with the male and female mendicants, recognises male and female votaries (upasaka and upasika) of Buddha and his lay-believers who honour Buddha as the holy preacher of Deliverance and his word

with the Hindu Philosophical views highly developed in them.*

But after his death, as is the case with every religion and philosophy,—his disciples differred. Some strictly followed the rules formulated by the great Master for the members of the Order,—ignoring completely the liberal views entertained by their great Preceptor as regards the religion for his lay followers. By this time there arose many powerful lay-followers, who secured the co-operation of

---

as the word of Truth, but who remain in their worldy position, in wedlock, in the possession of their property, and make themselves useful to the Church as far as they can by gifts and charities of every kind." See Oldenberg's Buddha p. p. 161—162.

"Lay-brethren were always welcomed, but they were bound to Buddhism by very slender ties in regard to dogma, and were only expected to conform to the simplest possible Code of Morality. Probably the only form of admission for a layman was the repetition of the 24 syllables of the three refuge formula—"I go for refuge to the Buddha, to the Dharma and to the Sanga." It was of course understood that he was to abstain from the five gross sins, but he was already bound to do so by the rules of Hindu caste and family religion."

* Rhys Davids in his Buddhism p. 87 says:—"There was not much in the Metaphysics and Psychology of Goutama which cannot be found in one or other of the orthodox systems, and a great deal of his morality could be collected from earlier or later Hindu books. Such originality as Goutama possessed lay in the way in which he adopted, enlarged, ennobled and systematised that which had already been well said by others; in the way in which he carried out to their logical conclusion principles of equity and justice already acknowledged by some of the most prominent Hindu thinkers. The difference between him and other teachers lay chiefly in his deep earnestness and in his broad public spirit and philanthrophy. Even these differences are probably much more apparent now than they were then, and by no means deprived him of the support and sympathy of the best among the Brahmans. Many of his chief disciples, many of the most distinguished members of his Order, were Brahmans. He always classed them with the Buddhist mendicants as deserviug of respect, and he used the name Brahmans as a term of honour for the Buddhist Arhats and Saints.

many great monks. These men wanted to be more associated with the lay-followers—they publicly and openly accepted the religion of the lay-followers, *i. e.*, Hinduism then extant as a part and parcel of their religion with little variations and changes. Thus the Monks of the Southern School remained strictly the Bhikshus as were originally designed by Buddha, whereas the monks of the Northern School became more and more the priests and religious guides of the lay-followers.

It is evident the lead of the Northern School fell into the hands of the Brahmans, the old religious teachers, guides, and priests of the people. They entered into the Buddhist Sangha in order to achieve Salvation which they ever sought, but they could not, though they tried their best, to cut themselves off completely from the laymen,—they had to remain, willingly or unwillingly, the guides and priests of the people. Thus the religion of the people as a matter of course became a part and parcel of their own religion.

The schism openly took place from the time of the Second Council which took place at Vesali. The minority stuck to the strict Doctrine of the Order,—but the majority adopted new innovations, or rather openly accepted the religion of the people as a part and parcel of the Order.

The first and the most important innovation was the adoption of the sacred language Sanskrit as the medium of their religious doctrines, whereas the Southern School stuck to the Vernacular Pali. Thus all the religious books of the Northern School were written in the Sanskrit language, the Southern School writing in Pali.

The Northern School adopted the Hindu mythology almost entirely with little or no changes, whereas the Southern school gave it only a partial recognition. The following is the mythology* of the Northern Buddhists.

---

* As regards the adoption of Hindu gods and goddesses by the Buddhists, Sir M. William in his Buddhism says :—Maha-Brahma is

MYTHOLOGY OF BUDDHISM.

In the centre of the world system stands the mountain Meru. On its upper portion above the eight chief hills and the worlds of animals, ghosts, demons and men, is situated the lowest heaven of gods where abide the four Maharajas, the guardian-angels of the world who protect it from the demons. These four are represented in full armour with drawn swords, one quarter of the heavens being assigned to the guardianship of each, namely the East to Dhritarastra, king of Gandharvas, the west to Virudhaba, the king of Kavandas, the west to Virupaksa, the king of the Nagas and the North to Kuvera, the king of the Yakshas.

Above this lowest heaven and on the highest summit of Meru is the heaven of Indra and his thirty three gods, *i.e.*, eleven Rudras, eight Vasus, and twelve Aditywas.

Above this is the third heaven,—that of Yamas; then is the fourth heaven,—that of Tashitas (Boddiasatwas). The fifth is inhabited by Nirmanirati Devali. The seventh heaven is the heaven of Mara or Kamadeva (god of desire).*

Now above these six heavens the chief gods of which are on the one hand Indra, on the other hand Mara there are

---

often named, whereas Vishnu, the popular God of the Hindus is, we have seen, represented by Padmapani (Avolokitaswara) who seems to have taken his place.

Turning to God Siva, we may note that he was adopted by Buddhism in his character of Yogi or Maha Yogi. Then as the Buddhism of the North very soon became corrupted with Saivism and its accompaniments Sactism, Tantrism and Magic, so in the Northern countries various forms of Siva such as Mahakala, Bhairava, Bhima, and of his wife Parvati, Durga &c are honoured and their images are found in temples. Sometimes bloody sacrifices are offered. Amongst the Female Deities the forms of Tara are chiefly worshipped and regarded as Saktis of the Buddhas."

* This is almost a prototype of the Hindu mythology. The Hindu mythology does not speak of Mara,—But mentions Kama, who is a member of Indra's heaven.

three heavens for those who are successful in the first Dhyana, then for the second Dhyana, then for the third Dhyana, then for the fourth or the last Dhyana. All three Dhyana heavens are inhabited by Brahma gods presided over by Maha-Brahma or Brahma Sahampati, but above all these is the fourth Dhyana heaven which is the place for the Arhats and Buddhas. Thus a Buddha is greater than Indra or Mara, greater than even Maha-Brahma.*

Buddhist Trinity.

Buddha did not speak of Trinity,—but his "Buddha, Dharma and Sangha" was a sort of Trinity as that of the Hindu Triad. Soon after his death, his followers of the School made this "Buddha, Dharma and Sangha" a living Northern Triad with representations.† They went further. They brought in those great gods,—the personifications of faculties or deification of saints—whom they began to worship as did the Hindus their Brahma, Vishnu and Siva. They called these three,—Manju Sree, (He of beautiful glory), Avalokiteswara (the Lord that looks down) whom they also called Padmapani (lotus-handed) and Vajrapani (the weilder of thunderbolt.)‡ Virtually these were the Brahma, Vishnu

* Maha-Brahma is the Supreme, Infinite, unknowable One of the Hindus.

† Often two other images are associated with that of Goutama Buddha himself. And first of all, his image was joined with the other two persons of the earlier Triad, *viz* Dharma and Sangha. A sculpture, in a broken and imperfect condition, representing this earliest Triad and dating from the nineth and tenth century, was found at Buddh Gya. The image of Buddha, under an umbralla-like tree, is in the centre. That of the Sangha is on his right with a full blown lotus and having one leg hanging down, while that of Dharma (a female) is on his left with a half blown lotus. See Sir M. William's Buddhism p. p. 484—485.

‡ Manju Sree is evidently Brahma, the god of knowledge; Avalokiteswar is Vishnu, and Vajrapani is Siva. Exactly by these names these Hindu gods are sometimes mentioned in the Puranas.

and Siva, or Indra, or Rudra, of the Hindus accepted by the Buddhist monks in other names.*

DHYANI BUDDHAS.

The Northern Buddhists believed that each Dhyani heaven is presided over by a Dhyani Buddha. They gave the following names of these Dhyani Buddhas with their Bodisatwas and three incarnations *i. e.* Human Buddhas.

The Dhyani Buddhas :—

1. Verochana.
2. Akshobya.
3. Ratna Sambhava.
4. Amitabha.
5. Amogasidha.

Their Bodhisatwas :—

1. Samanta Vadra.
2. Vajrapani.
3. Ratnapani.
4. Padmapani (Avalokiteswar.)
5. Viswapani.

Their human Buddhas.

1. Kraku chanda.
2. Kanaha Muni.
3. Kasyapa.
4. Goutama.
5. Maitriya (to be born).

The Northern Buddhists worship all these Buddhas as so many gods. They have their temples and dagobas all over the Northern Buddhist countries.†

---

* Trinity or Triad is a belief of the Hindus from the time of the Vedas. (See Sir M. William's Brahmanism and Hinduism).

† "As the Dhyani and Tantra systems grew, the idols of the Dhyani Trinities and the Tantra gods and goddesses took their place in the monastaries and the temples of the Buddhists, and their figures with many eyes and heads and hands are painted in the books and on the

ADI BUDDHA.

They also accepted the Hindu *Infinite One* and called Him *Adi-Buddha,* a subject the great Master always avoided discussing, but never prevented his lay-followers from believing.

TANTRIK SYSTEM.

This system has always been a part of Hinduism from the time of the Vedas, though in later days its rituals and rites have been made mystic and ununderstandable. It is the worship of the Great Force of Nature,—the Wife of the Creator. In Hinduism it is worshipping Durga, Kali, or Tara, the wife of Siva. It has been bodily taken from Hinduism into the Buddhism of all the countries of the northern Asia.*

Rhys Davids remarks:—"The founder of this system seems to have been *Asanga,* an influential monk of Peshwar in the Punjab who lived and wrote the first Text Book of the creed,—the *Yogachara Dharma Sastra,*—about the sixth century of our era. Hiouen Thsang who travelled in the first half of the seventh century found the monastery where Asanga had lived and says that he had lived 1000 years after the Buddha. He managed with great dexterity to reconcile the two opposing systems by placing a number of Saiva gods, both male and female, in the inferior heavens of the prevalent Buddhism, representing them as worshippers and supporters of the Buddha and Avolokiteshwara. He thus made it possible for the half converted and rude tribes to remain Buddhists while they brought offerings to their more congenial shrines, and while their practical belief had no relation at all to the Truths or the Noble Eight Fold Paths. They busied

walls and put up in the sides of roads." See Rhy Davids' Buddhism, page 209.

* In Tibet, Mongolia and Manchuria, she is worshipped in the Hindu names of Tara, Vairavi etc. In China she is worshipped as *Kwan-Yin Kwan-noh,*—both meaning goddess of mercy.

themselves almost wholly with obtaining magic powers (sidhi) by means of magic phases (Dharanis) and magic (chakras.)*

ESOTERIC BUDDHISM.

It is nothing but the Yoga System of Hinduism.† All over the northern Buddhist countries, it forms the most essential part of Buddhism. The Yoga of the Brahmans and the yoga of the Buddhists are almost identical.‡

—:o:—

CHAPTER V.

RITUALISTIC BUDDHISM.

FOR the monks of his *Sangha*, Buddha prescribed little or no rituals. For them he discarded all Vedic Rituals and Sacrifices ;—for them he prescribed only self-culture, virtuous

* Buddhism p. 208. The principle of Tantricism is not so bad as represented and generally believed by the European scholars. This is not the place to discuss this important matter, but Tantric Occultism is a subject which requires a careful study to pass an opinion upon. [See Introduction of M. N. Dutt's English Translation of Mahanirvana Tantram.]

† See Raj Yoga by Swami Vivekanand.

‡ Sir M. Williams writes:—"The subject of mystical Buddhism ought not to be brushed aside as unworthy of consideration. It furnishes, in my opinion, a highly interesting topic of enquiry, especially in its bearing on the "neo-Buddhism" and Theosophy of the present day. At all events it is clear from what we have advanced in the present lecture that the practices connected with spiritualism, mesmerism, animal magnetism, telepathy, clairvoyance, thought-reading &c have their counterparts in the Yoga System prevalent in India more than 2000 years ago, and in the practices of mystical Buddhism prevalent in Tibet and the adjacent countries for many centuries.

and good conduct, and meditation. There were no prayers, no worship, no Pujah of any sort,—they were to depend upon themselves, and upon their own exertion for final achievement of Nirvana.

But to become a Bhikshu, we have seen, a candidate had to utter a formula, which ran as follows :—

"I take Refuge in Buddha
I take Refuge in Dharma
I take Refuge in Sangha."

It meant that a Buddhist monk was bound to believe in a Buddha,—a great Enlightened One,—he was to follow strictly the dictates of Dharma—all moralities and virtuous and good acts and he was also to become body and soul a part and parcel of the Sangha.

These were all the rituals and rites of the great Buddhist Sangha when Buddha founded it, but as soon as he was dead, he was canonised and deified ; his remains were buried in ten different Stupas which became the pilgrimages to his devoted followers and places of worship for his layity. He asked his followers to put faith in a Buddha ;—virtually Buddha was the God of the Buddhists. And his followers, after his death, made him a true God. Buddha ordered them to do it when he enjoined his disciples to say at the time of their Ordination "I take refuge in the Buddha."

The number of his Stupas increased from ten to *lacs* at the time of Asoka, and thus the Buddhist places of worship and pilgrimages became innumerable. Along with Buddha the Buddhists, or specially those of the Northern School, went on worshipping the Hindu gods and goddesses which Buddha, when living, never prevented his lay-followers to worship. Thousands and thousands of Buddha's figures made in stone, wood or clay were worshipped and adored all over India,—nay all over Asia.

Next came the Images of the Buddhas who proceeded Goutama Buddha, specially Kasyapa, Kanaha Muni and

Karaka-Cchanda. Then followed the images of the five Dhyani Buddhas. The images of Maitra Buddha who was to be born became the most desired object of worship in all the Buddhist countries.*

Then were introduced the images of the Buddhist Triad mamely, Manju Sri, Avolekiteswar, and Vajrapani. "In general Manju Sri is represented in a sedent attitude with his left hand holding a lotus and his right hand holding a sword of wisdom with a shinning blade to dissipate the darkness of ignorance."†

Avoloketeswar had eleven heads and one thousand hands and one thousand eyes. His female counterpart is represented as a woman (called Kwan-yin in China and Kwon-non in Japan) with a thousand arms and thousand eyes.

The image of Vajrapani is represented as holding a thunderbolt in one hand. With regard to the image of Tara or Sakti, she is represented as a green sedent figure, with her right hand on her knee, her left holding a lotus. Besides these, there are innumerable images of smaller gods and goddesses now worshipped by the Buddhists of Tibet, Mongolia, China, Japan, &c.

The third member of Buddha's great religion—Sangha,—also soon became personified and deified. Its images were made and worshipped;—besides it grew to be a gigantic Institution with "its shaven priests, its bells, and rosaries, its images and holy water, and gorgeous dresses, its service with double choirs and processions, and creeds and mystic rites

* Fa-Hien records that he saw in Northern India a wooden image of Maitrya Bodhisattwa which on fast days emitted a brilliant light (See Legge, p. 23) Hiouen Thsang also describes this image of Maitrya Buddha. (See Beal, I. 134). "In the present day the images of Maitrya often represent him with both hands raised, the fingers forming the lotus shaped Mudra, the body yellow or gilded" and the hair short and curly. Sir M. W.'s Buddhism, p. 486.

† See Sir M. William's Buddhism p. 486.

and incense, in which the laity are spectators only,—its abbots and monks and nuns of many grades, its worship of the double virgins, and of the saints and angels; its fasts confessions and purgatory, its images and idols and its pictures, its huge monasteries and its gorgeous Cathedrals, its powerful heirarchy, its Cardinals, its Pope.'' This is now known by the name of Lamaism.

The following quotations from various sources would give a clear idea of Lamaism in all the Buddhist countries. Sarat Chander Dass in his "Narratives" thus describes the discovery of the present Dalai Lama.

"After the death of an incarnate Lama, his soul is said ordinarily to remain in the spirtiual world for a space of at least forty nine days. In 1875, one year after the demise of the late Dalai Lama,—Thinle-Gya-tsho—the Regency and the College of Cardinals at Lassa consulted the celebrated oracle of Wachung bhoskyong about the re-appearance of the Dalai. The oracle declared that the grand Lama could only be discovered by a monk of the purest morals. Accordingly the Shar-tse-khanpo of the Golden monastery, who was well-known for his virtuous character and his profound knowledge of the sacred books, proceeded to Chhoikhor Gya where he sat in profound meditation for full seven days. On the night of the last day, he saw a vision in which a voice from heaven directed him to go and see a miraculous sight in the Ya-tsho lake of Chhoikhor Gya. Awakening from his sleep, the Khampo went to the lake, where in the crystal-like water, he saw the incarnate grand Lama sitting on the lap of his mother and caressed by his father. The house with its furniture was also

---

* See Rhys David's Buddhism p. 250. He remarks "these bear a strong resemblance to Romanism." We could have shown if space permitted us that Christianity as it was originally was but a child of Buddhism.

visible. All on a sudden this image-like appearance disappeared, and he heard the neighing of a horse. So much of his dream being fulfilled, he proceeded on the horse to the province of Kongpo; and on the way, he happened to call at the house of a rich and respectable family of the district of Tag-po. He recognised the house, the family and the child he had seen in the lake and at once declared that the real end of his journey was obtained. On his report the Government officials and the College of Cardinals headed by the Regent visited Tag-po and escorted the infant and its parents in great pomp to the palace of Rigyal near Lassa. The princely child was only one year old when he was discovered. He is now ten and bears the name of Nag-Wang—Lo-Ssang-Thub-dan-Gya-tsho. (The Lord of Speech and the powerful Ocean of Wisdom).

M. Huc thus speaks of the Mongolian mode of election of the Grand Lama.* :—

"The election and enthroning of the living Buddhas is extremely curious. When a Grand Lama is "gone away," *i.e.*, is dead, the event is by no means made a matter of mourning in the convent. There are no tears or regrets, for every one knows that the living Buddha will soon re-appear. The apparent death is only the commencement of a new existence, a new link added to a boundless and uninterrupted chain of successive lives. When the saint is in Chrysalis state, his disciples are in the greatest anxiety, and the grand point is to discover the place where their Master has returned to life. If a rain-bow appears, they consider it as a sign sent to them from their grand Lama to assist them in their searches.

Every one then goes to prayers, and especially the convent which has been widowed of its Buddha is incessant in its fastings and orisons, and a troop of chosen Lamas set out to consult the *Churchen* or the diviner of hidden things. They relate to him the time, the place, and circumstances under which the rainbow has appeared, and he then, after reciting some prayers, opens his book of divination and at length pronounces his oracle, while the Tartars who have come to consult him, listen on their knees with the most profound devotion.

"Your grand Lama, "says he," has returned to life in Tibet at such a place—in such a family ; and when the poor Mongols have heard the oracle, they return full of joy to their convent to announce the happy news. Sometimes the living Buddha announces himself at an age when other infants cannot articulate a word ; but whether his place of abode be found by means of the rainbow or by his spontaneous revelation, it is always at a considerable distance and in a country difficult of access. A grand procession is then made, headed by the king or the greatest man in the country to fetch the young living Buddha. The Mongols often go through incredit-able fatigue and hardships, traverse frightful deserts, and sometimes after being plundered by robbers, stripped of every thing and compelled to return, set out again with undiminished courage. When the living Buddha is found, however, he is not saluted as the Grand Lama without examination. Doubt-less the simple Mongols are in this matter often the dupes of those who have an interest in making a Grand Lama of the baby. The tittle of living Buddha having been confirmed, he is conducted in triumph to the monastery of which he is to become the Grand Lama, and as he passes along, the Tartars come in great troops and prostrate themselves before him. As soon as he arrives at the convent, he is placed on the altar, and every Tartar from the highest to the lowest in the land bows down before the child."

The following sketch of the high service in Lassa Cathe-dral is given by M. Koppen. It will show the reader the present stage of Lamaism.

"The entrance to the chief Temple of the holy city is through a large hall where holy water and rosaries are sold and in which stand four statues of archangels. The walls are covered with rude paintings of scenes from the legends of Buddha, and its roof is supported by six massive pillars covered with beautiful carving, spoilt by gorgeous paint and gilding. The church itself is a long nave divided by rows of pillars from two aisles and by silver screens of open trilis works from two chancels. Into the aisle on each side open fourteen chapels. At the end is the holy place, containing fifteen jewelled tablets, with mystic symbols of Sangsara and the other creations of Buddhist metaphysics; and in the furthest niche is a magnificent golden statue of the now diefied Goutama Buddha. On the left is the throne of the Dalai Lama; in the right that of the Pantshen Lama, and in order on either side, gradually decreasing in hight and splendour, the seats of Chutuktus, the abbots and the eighteen orders of inferior clergy. In front of the idol is the higher altar or table of offerings, raised by several stages above the floor; in the upper levels being images of gold, silver, and clay; on the lawn the bell and lamps and other vessels used in the holy service. At the sound of the horn or trumpet, the clergy assemble in the entrance hall wearing the cloak and cap; and at its third blast the procession, with the living Buddha at its head, marches down the aisle. When he is seated on his throne, each Lama bows three times before him, and then seats himself cross-begged on the divans according to rank. A bell is then rung and all murmur the Three Refuges, the Ten Precepts and other formulas. After silence is restored, the bell sounds again, and the priests now sing in choir larger pieces from the sacred books. It it be a fast day, the highest point of the service is reached in the *Tuisob* or prayer for sanctification when the offerings are blest. A bell is rung, and all the monks burst out into a hymn of prayer for the presence of the spirit of all the Buddhas. One of them raises aloft over his head a looking-glass, the idea of which seems to be to catch the image of the spirit as it comes; a second raises aloft a jug; a third a mystic symbol of the world a fourth a cup and other other sacred vessels or mystic symbols. Meanwhile the voices of the singers and the sound of the bells and drums and trumpets grow louder and louder, and the church is filled with incense from the sacred urns. The monk with the jug pours several times water mixed with sugar and saffron over the mirror which another monk wipes each time with a napkin of silk. The water flows over the mirror into the symbol of the world and is caught in the cup beneath. Thence the only mixture is poured on to another jug and a drop or two is allowed to trickle into the hands of each of the worshipping monks who marks the crown of his shaven head, his forehead, and his breast with the sacred liquid. He then reverentially swallows the remaining drops, and in so doing, believes himself to be mystically swallowing part of the Divine Being, whose image has been caught in the mirror over which the water has past."*

The ceremonial observances are not confined only amongst the Buddhists of the Northern School. They are now more or less prevalent in Burma and Ceylon; the Buddhists of the Southern School also have adopted much of the Mahayana system. We shall, therefore, to give an idea of the ceremonials prevalent amongst the Southern Buddhists, quote two passages from Sir Williams' work describing the ordination of monks in Burmah and Ceylon.

"On the day appointed for the induction ceremony, the young neophyte dresses in his gayest clothes, and mounted on a pony, passes at a foot's space through the town or village. A band of music goes before him, and all his friends dressed in their best garments of yellow in a crowd, the young men dancing and singing, the girls smiling and laughing. Thus he proceeds in procession to the houses of his relations, to bid them farewell. Of course, the introductory observance

* See Sir M. William's Buddhism p. 306. It is a summary of the description given in the *Burman* by Shway Yoe, nè Scott.

is intended as a kind of dramatic imitation of Goutama Buddha's celebrated abandonment of his own family and worldly associates.

The monks, seated in a row, carefully hold up their fan-like screens to shut out the female portion of the assemblage from their view. Portions of a Vinaya are then recited, after which the would-be novice is made to throw off all his fine clothes and bind a piece of white cloth round his loins. Then his hair is cut off close and his head is carefully shaved and washed. Next he is taken to a bath and after immersion in pure water is brought once more,—partially clothed, before the assembled monks. Prostrating himself three times before them, he raises his hand in reverence, and using the regular Pali form of words, asks to be admitted to the holy brotherhood. Upon that, the head of the monastery presents him with the yellow monastic garments. They are duly put on, and the mendicant's bowl is hung round his neck. The ceremony concludes by the funeral announcement of his having become a member of the monastery.

The present ceremony in Ceylon is of a simple form. It differs from the ancient form."*

—:o:—

CHAPTER VI.

SPREAD OF NORTHERN BUDDHISM.

We have said that one hundred years after Buddha's death, the Northern Buddhism became more powerful and influential than the Southern Buddhism. Their Council was called the Great Council, their doctrines were called Mahayana or Great Path, whereas the doctrines of the Southern

* See Hardy's Eastern Monarchism p. 23

Buddhists were called Hina-yana or Lower Path. Except in Magadha and its eastern dependencies,—the religion of the Hina-yana had no place in India. The religion of the Maha-yana spread all over India as far west as modern Afganistan. The reason is not far to seek. The religion of Maha-yana was nothing else, but the religion then prevalent in India, *i.e.*, Brahmanical Hinduism,—with some changes and alterations. It was but Hinduism reformed or expanded.

In the beginning of the Christian Era, it spread beyond the borders of India, for at that time a great king rose in the Northern India as Asoka was in the Eastern India; and this king was a zealous Buddhist. He sent missionaries to China, Mongolia and Tibet and did much for the propagation of the religion of the great Prophet. This king was the celebrated Kanishka of Kashmir.

The grand-father of Kaniska was Haviska. He was the king of Kabul, and when driven out from there, he founded a new kingdom in Kashmir. He was a Buddhist* and founded a monastery at Mathura.† He was succeeded by Haska who also built a Vihara.‡

"Kaniska's dominion extended from Kabul to the Hindukush and Bolor mountains, over Yarkhand and Khokan; throughout Kashmir, Ladhaka, and the Central Himalayas, down over the plains of the Upper Ganges and Jamuna as far as Agra, over Rajputana, Guzrat and Sindh, and thus the whole of the Punjab,—a magnificient empire equalled in extent from the time of Asoka to that of the Mogul."§

---

* It is clear from the coins of Haviska and Kaniska that Buddhism became the state religion of the north western parts of India at about the commencement of our Era:—Rhys David's Buddhism, page 238.

† See Cunningham's Archæological Reports, Vol. I., page 238 and also Dawson's "Ancient Inscriptions from Mathura, J. R. A. S. New Series Vol. V. page 182.

‡ Rhys David says that they were also fire-worshippers. See Buddhism page 238.

§ See Rhys David's Buddhism pages 238—239.

At the advice of his tutor, named Parsvika, king Kaniska held a Council of 500 monks under the presidency of Vasubandhu.* These monks drew up three great commentaries namely (1) *Upadesa* on the Sutra Pitaka, (2) *Vinya Vivasha Shastra* on the Vinaya, and (3) *Abhidharma Vivasha Shastra* on the Abhidharma Ritaka. These three works Kaniska said to have had engraven on copper plates and sealed up in a stone box over which he built a dogoba.†

Buddhism in Tibet.

Nya Khri Tsanpo was the first king of Tibet.‡ He was succeeded by several kings till at last came Srong Tsan Gampo who was born in 617. In the year 632, he began the work of civilising his subjects. With this intention he sent his minister Thumi Sambhota to India to learn Buddhist sacred books. This great man designed the Tibetan alphabet called Laucha on the model of the Indian letters then in use.

The first Tibetan author was this great minister Thumi Sumbhota. He composed a grammer and many other works. An important work that he translated was a Tantra work named Mani Kambum. This book describes the introduction of Buddhism into Tibet as well as the origin of the well-known six syllabled prayer of Tibet, namely *Om Mani Padma Hum*. This book contains 100,000 precepts. The teaching of Thumi Sumbhota was of an orthodox character; he was the founder of the strict school of Tibetan Buddhism

---

* This council is not mentioned in any of the books of Southern Buddhists as Asoka's council is also not mentioned by the Northern Buddhists. It is mentioned in the Hionen Thsang's Travels. See Julien, pages 95—98, Cosma, Asiatic Researches XX. pages 41—297.

† This is what is told by Hiouen Thsang in his travels. See Julien's Translation.

‡ This portion is a summary of Tibetan history as given by M. William in his Buddhism from Koeppen's great work.

called Kadampa which finally diveloped into the yellow robed sect as distinct from the red robed sect.

After the death of Thumi Sumbhota, the propagation of Buddhism in Tibet was carried on by two princesses—the two queens of king Srong Tsan Gampo, named Dolkar and Doljang*

After the death of king Srong-Tsan-Gampo, Buddhism declined in Tibet. One of his successors named Khri-Srong-De-Tsan who reigned from 740—786 tried to restore it. For this purpose he brought from India a large number of religious teachers. First came Santa Rakshita with twelve companions from Bengal. Then came the celebrated Padmasamvava from the lands of Udyana.† It was under his direction the great monastery of *Samye* was built. He was remarkable for his great learning. He it was who first furthered the translation of the whole of the Buddhist Cannon into Tebetan.‡ He was the founder of the Red Sect

---

* "The first two Lama Monasteries in Tibet called *La-brang* and *Ra-mo-che*, founded about A.D., 650, were erected at Lhassa by them or in their honour and each monastery contained a renowned wonder-working image which each princess had brought with her."

The great monastery *La-brang* is in the very centre of Lhassa and is regarded as the centre of the whole country. All the main roads of Tibet converge towards it. Doubtless the area of the monastery has been enlarged by occasional additions in the course of one thousand years, but not since it was partly rebuilt and restored in the 17th century. Its magnificient temple, Cho-Khang, is of the St. Peter's Lamaism. The immense number of monks inhabiting this monastery is proved by the fact that a huge cauldron is shown which holds more than 1,200 gallons of tea for the Lamas who perform the daily services." See Sir M. William's Buddhism pages 271 & 441.

† Dardistan.

‡ The Tibetan Canon commonly called Kanjur consisted of at least 108 vols. The present Tanjur of Tibet consists of 225 folio vols. of translations, commentaries and treatises, embracing works on all subjects, such as grammar, logic, rhetoric, poetry, medicine, astrology, alchemy, magic, &c.

in Tibet. A sect called *Urgyenpa*, a sect called *Brugpa or Dugpa*, and a sect called *Sankyapa* all belonged to the red sect and follow the doctrines of Padmasamvava. They are found in large numbers in Nepal, Bhutan, Sikim, Tibet and Ladak.

After the death of this king, Buddhism was in a declining state for many centuries, but in the second half of the 11th century the kings again tried to give it life and strength. Many learned men were brought from India, of whom Atisha was the most celebrated. This monk was a supporter of the stricter rules of Thumi Sumbhota, and his well-known Tibetan pupil named Brom Tom was also a great upholder of the yellew sect. Three great monasteries were built under them, namely (1) Raseng, (2) Sakya and (3) Brikheng. Raseng monastery monks belonged to the yellow sect, whereas those of the Brikheng were of the red sect. A great rivalry was bred between these two monasteries and each tried to claim supremacy over the other, till at last the Chinese Emperor declared the Red Sect to possess the highest authority.

Buddhism in Mongolia.

Mongolia received much of Buddhism from Tibet, and Tibet received much from Mongolia. Both the countries received Tantricism mixed with Buddhism from India which was known by the name of Samanism or Sramanism. Sir M. William writes :—" It is well-known that the great Mongolia conqueror Jenghiz Khan conquered Tibet at about A. D. 1206. Before that period Mongolia had come in contact with various religious cults, for example with Zoroastrism, Buddhism and Islamism. They had even had some experience of Christianity, for Nestorian Missions existed in Central Asia in the 6th and 7th centuries of our era, and penetrated into China in the seventh century. All these religions strove to convert the Mongolians, who soon became an important nation through the conquest of Jenghiz Khan. That conqueror however had a very simple religion of his own. He believed in one God in heaven and one king on earth; that is, he believed that God had given him the dominion of the whole world and he set himself to conquer the world. Yet he tolerated all religions. "As the hand," he said, "has many fingers, so there are many ways to show men how they may reach heaven."*

Khublai,† the greatest of all the descendants of Jenghiz was the first to elevate his people above a mere life of rapine and plunder, and it struck him that the best method of civilising them would be by adopting and promoting Buddhism which the greater number of the races subject to him already possessed. Khublai first appointed Phaspa of of the Sakya monastery as the Head of the Buddhist herearchy all over his Empire. It was Rhaspa Lama who invented the Mongolian Alphabet. He then undertook a new revision of the Buddhist Sacred Books comparing the Tibetan Sacred Texts (Kanjur) with the Chinese. Twenty nine learned men, versed in the Tibetan, Ugrian, Chinese, and Sanskrit languages were occupied with the task of collation, and a few years later the first Mongolian translation of the Sacred Texts was begun by the Sakya Lama named, Choskyi Odser.

The greatest name amongst the Mongolian Buddhist monks is that of Tsong Khapa. Sir M. William thus speaks of him:—"Tsong Khapa, whose name is as much celebrated in Mongolia and Tibet and among the Kalmuk Tartars as that of the founder of Buddhism, is said to have been born in the year 1355 or 1357 of our era, in the land of Amdo where the celebrated monastery of Kunbum was situated north of Tibet on the borders of China.

In process of time, Tson Khapa set out on a journey from Amdo to Tibet, his object being to acquire the knowledge of

* See Buddhism, pages 274—275.

† Khublai reigned from 1259—1294 A.D.

the doctrine from the original sources. He is said to have studied the Law of Buddha at Sakya, Bhrikheng and Lassa. It was in this way that he became impressed with the necessity of purifying and reforming the Discipline of Tibetan Buddhism, which the red sect had corrupted by allowing the marriage of monks and by laxity in other matters. Innumerable pupils gathered round him, all of whom adopted as their distinguishing mark, the orthodox yellow garments of primitive Buddhism.

Tsong Khapa soon acquired vast influence, and in the year 1409 was able to build on a hill about 30 miles from Lassa, the celebrated monastery called Galdan of the Yellow School. Of this Tsong Khapa was the first Abbot. His followers however rapidly became too numerous to be comprehended within so limited an area. Hence there arose in the immediate neighbourhood of Lhassa two other great monasteries namely *Brepung* and *Sera*; these monastries once held 30000 monks of the yellow sect, but now have only 16500."*

Buddhism in China, Japan Koria &c.

Buddhism had long before this penetrated into China,† along the fixed route from India to that country, round the north-west corner of the Himalayas and across Eastern Turkistan. Already in the second year B. C. an embassy, perhaps sent by Haviska, took Buddhist books to the then emperor of China A-ili and the Emperor Ming-Ti (62 A. D.) guided by a dream is said to have sent men to Tartary and Central India and brought Buddhist books to China. From this time Buddhism rapidly spread there. Monks from Central and North Western India frequently travelled to China, and the Chinese themselves made many journeys to the older Buddhist countries to collect the sacred writings

* See Sir M. William's Buddhism p.p. 277-278.

† See Rhys David's Buddhism p.p. 241-242.

which they diligently translated into Chinese. In the fourth century, Buddhism became the state religion, and there have been and still are monks in China belonging to most of the different schools of later Norther Buddhism, though no new sect seems to have been formed.

Into Koria, Buddhism was introduced from China as early as 372 D. D. and thence into Japan in 552, in the 13th year of king Kin Mei Teno. The old religion of Japan was a worship of the powers of Nature, the latest development of which has been preserved in the work on Sin To, by a learned Japanese woman of the twelfth century; and in the 13th century a monk, named Sin Ran, who died in 1262, founded a new Buddhistic sect, which incorporates into its belief much of the old creed and the monks belonging to which wear the ordinary dress and marry. Many of them are thus allied to the noble and even to the royal family.

Kochin China and Ava, the Island of Formosa and Mangolia, probably received their Buddhism from China during the fourth and fifth centuries, and before that it had spread westwards and northwards from Kabul and Yarhkhand to Balk, Bokhara, the Balkash or Deugor Lake, and into China again by the way of Junguria and Kobdo.

THE END.